LAS VEGAS
Weddings

SUSAN MARG

S Las Vegas BLVD 800

STOP

LAS VEGAS
Weddings

A Brief History,
Celebrity Gossip,
Everything Elvis,
and the
Complete Chapel Guide

itbooks

AN IMPRINT OF HARPERCOLLINS PUBLISHERS

FIRST EDITION

Design by Shubhani Sarkar

Printed on acid free paper

Library of Congress Cataloging-in-Publication Data
Marg, Susan.
    Las Vegas weddings : a brief history, celebrity gossip, everything Elvis, and the complete chapel guide / by Susan Marg.— 1st ed.
        p. cm.
    Includes bibliographical references.
    ISBN 0-06-072619-9 (pbk.: alk. paper)
        1. Weddings—Nevada—Las Vegas. I. Title.
GT2711.L37M37 2004
395.2'2—dc22

                                                    2004047283

19   WBC/LSC   10 9 8 7 6 5

For my parents, Joe and Elaine Marg,
for their love and support

"I remember when Las Vegas wasn't much then. Just a little place people came to get married."

"Hmmm. Still do I guess."

—Ann-Margret and Elvis Presley, in *Viva Las Vegas*, 1964

"Let's go."

"Where?"

"City Hall."

"Oh, for what?"

"Because you can't get married without a license, even in Las Vegas."

"Married?"

"Married."

—Warren Beatty and Elizabeth Taylor, in *The Only Game in Town*, 1970

"Ellen, I know what we can do. We can get remarried. Right now. There's a honeymoon slots tournament over at the Golden Nugget. And guess what? Newlyweds get in for free."

—Chevy Chase, in *Vegas Vacation*, 1997

Contents

Acknowledgments

I would first like to thank my husband, author James C. Simmons, for his daily positive reinforcement, as well as for sharing his insights and lending his experience to this undertaking. He never steered me wrong.

I would also like to thank the staff of the Nevada State Museum and Historical Society, particularly Frank Wright, for their friendly assistance whenever I visited; Richard Moreno of *Nevada* magazine, for providing information that helped get this book off the ground; and Ron DeCar of the Viva Las Vegas Wedding Chapel for his gracious hospitality. I am also indebted to the wedding chapel operators for taking the time to meet with me and relating their thoughts and feelings about the wedding business, as well as the couples who let me sit in on their ceremonies. I wish them the best.

Introduction

Kitschy, funky, depressing, romantic. Everyone has an opinion about Las Vegas weddings. With the exception of Las Vegas itself, and possibly Elvis, it is about the only part of pop culture that draws an immediate, visceral response. Sometimes the reaction comes from personal experience. "My [sister, parents, best friend, or fill in the blank] got married there." Other times it is based on images from the movies and television shows or from news coverage of the rich and famous who married in Las Vegas. But whether the perception is good, bad, or just plain ugly, Las Vegas weddings are not only part of pop culture, they are popular, too, and growing more so all the time.

The number of visitors to Las Vegas has increased fivefold since 1970, to 36 million, and the number of marriage licenses issued by Clark County has tripled. Since the millennium, more than 120,000 couples each year have said their vows in what used to be known for good reason as Sin City, and an estimated additional 40,000 to 50,000 couples have had renewal-of-vows ceremonies. That means about 5 percent of all weddings performed in the United States in a given year take place in a county that accounts for less than 0.5 percent of the population of the country. With Las Vegas weddings becoming more formal and often attended by upwards of fifty guests, the industry contributes approximately $1 billion to the town's $30 billion tourist economy, the remainder coming from gaming, entertainment, lodging, and dining.

All types of people for all sorts of reasons on a wide range of budgets get married in Las Vegas. The many venues for wedding services, over fifty by one count, make it possible to satisfy just about everyone. The freestanding, independent chapels north of the Strip on Las Vegas Boulevard live up to their anything-goes attitude for the happy-go-lucky. The in-hotel chapels of the luxury resorts deliver on romance for the lucky in love. For something completely different, ceremonies in a helicopter or on horseback at Red Rock Canyon can be arranged. A growing trend is that of same-sex couples partaking in commitment ceremonies. Another trend, whereby an Elvis impersonator officiates, has been around for a while. Diversity is part and parcel of the wedding scene of Las Vegas today.

The history of Las Vegas weddings is no less varied or any less entertaining, particularly as it is intertwined with the history of Las Vegas itself. Movie stars and rock 'n' roll stars, gangsters and gamblers, and entrepreneurs and industrialists are part of the story. The first wedding on record was in 1909, four years after the founding of the dusty frontier town. The wedding industry got its first boost in 1912, when California enacted the so-called gin law, developed to keep people from marrying drunk. Young couples in love who could not wait the required three days from getting their marriage license to saying their vows went across the state border instead. In 1933 a resourceful minister turned his home into a twenty-four-hour-a-day wedding chapel "as a convenience to local and out-of-town brides and grooms." Yet, ironically, it took Clark Gable's 1939 divorce to make Las Vegas a household name across the country.

Through the decades celebrity weddings have propelled Las Vegas's popularity as a marriage mecca. Each and every one of them tells a tale about eternal love or marriage disaster, dashed hopes or dreams come true. The parade of stars across the desert began in 1930 with the wedding of William Boyd, better known to fans of early Westerns as Hopalong Cassidy. For his fourth, but not his last, marriage, he took a day off work, chartered a plane for the wedding party, and exchanged vows in a room in the National Hotel. More recently the quickie wedding and fifty-five-hour marriage of pop princess Britney Spears and a childhood sweetheart garnered headlines and captured the public's attention, continuing to provide fodder for fan magazines and television talk shows long after it was over.

Las Vegas weddings are a phenomenon not quite like any other. The industry attracts cheers and jeers, but it touches a couple of hundred thousand people annually on the most important day of their lives. Let's go the chapel now and see what all the excitement's about. Who knows, maybe even Elvis will be there!

1

ONCE UPON A TIME

Wee Kirk o' the Heather has been
providing one-stop wedding services
at the humble house turned chapel
since 1940.

NEW SUPER SERVICE TO "Tie the Knot" was the headline of a small inside article of the *Las Vegas Evening Review-Journal* on September 29, 1933. In an interview for the story, J. D. Foster, the man behind the idea, was asked why he decided to undertake such an enterprise. He responded, "So many out of town couples come into Las Vegas to be married and have no idea where to go to have the ceremony performed or who to get to tie the knot. So, the wedding chapel was begun here as a convenience to local and out of town brides and grooms." Pressed for additional details, the reverend added, "In fact, we [will] never close." And with these immortal words, the Las Vegas wedding industry was born.

The Wedding Chapel was located in the reverend's home at 513 South Fifth Street, the street which would eventually be renamed Las Vegas Boulevard and would link the casino hotels on what would be called "the Strip" with downtown. For less than $5, a couple could be married in pleasant surroundings and soon be on their way as husband and wife. The chapel would take care of all responsibilities associated with the nuptials, including supplying a corsage for the bride, if desired, and witnesses of the service. In a two-inch-square ad for the Wedding Chapel that ran a few days later in the same paper, it was noted, "We arrange all the details."

Seventy years later, Las Vegas wedding chapels, many bigger and better than ever, others merely made up to cover the aging spots, are doing a booming business. They are located up and down Las Vegas Boulevard South, from Wee Kirk o' the Heather at the corner of Bridger Street, near the courthouse and a few blocks from Fremont Street, to the Little Church of the West, now located past Mandalay Bay, the southernmost casino on the Strip. The most noticeable chapels are the freestanding and independent ones, proclaiming their presence with neon signs.

Just like the first wedding chapel, they are situated in homes as much as half a century old, to which have been added a picturesque steeple and, possibly, a white picket fence. More chapels are hidden away in the magnificent resort casinos built in the last years of the twentieth century for a billion dollars, give or take a couple hundred thousand.

The Wedding Chapel at Bellagio, in the resort-casino of the same name, places a premium on comfort and luxury. In its brochure, the chapel promises surroundings "as beautiful as the love you share" in an "atmosphere of elegance and splendor." Its crème-de-la-crème wedding package leaves no need unattended, no craving unsatisfied, no dream unrealized. The cost is a steep $15,000, and the many extras include limousine service from McCarran International Airport; tandem massage for bride and groom in Spa Bellagio; hairstyling, makeup consultation, manicure, and pedicure for the bride in Salon Bellagio; one penthouse suite for two nights, with breakfast in bed; dinner in the hotel's Picasso Restaurant; and two tickets for the resort's most popular show. What more could a girl want on her big day?

Both Las Vegas and its famous, or make that infamous, wedding industry have come a long way, baby. Once known as Sin City, its claim to the title of "Marriage Capital of the World" has merit. More than 120,000 marriages and about another 50,000 renewals, commitment ceremonies, and other professions of "till death do us part" take place in Las Vegas each year; second-place Reno, with 25,000 marriages, and third-place Hawaii, with 10,000 marriages, are distant runners-up. The city has cleaned up its act, done away with the sleaze (or most of it), and now offers love and romance beneath the twinkling lights. A dusty frontier town no more, Las Vegas is one of the world's premier resort destinations, with nine of the ten largest hotels anywhere looming over the boulevard, and something for just about everyone strolling along the Strip.

CHAPTER 1

From Cow Town to Mobster Central

IN THE BEGINNING

*L*ucky at love, unlucky at cards" goes the saying, and the history of the Las Vegas wedding industry is inextricably linked to the history of Las Vegas itself. The mob has molded it, the movies have shaped it, and celebrities who have played on its stage have glamorized it until its past is mired in myth. Like the stories in the Bible, the history of Las Vegas takes place in the desert. Chronicles of fire and floods, tales of good battling temptation, and accounts of weakness giving in to the pleasures of vice have been told and retold, the town's notoriety for rowdy bars and bawdy broads going back to its beginnings.

Las Vegas is the site of life-sustaining artesian springs. When in 1826 Spanish-speaking traders came across the unexpected oasis the springs produced, they named the area "the meadows." About seventy-five years later, the San Pedro Railroad decided the watering hole was a logical railroad stop, given that it was the midpoint between Salt Lake City and Los Angeles. When the last tie in the track was put down, the railroad auctioned off the parcels of land around the station. Hyped by publicity and bolstered by inexpensive train tickets to bring in speculators, the properties sold quickly, some going for as much as $1,750. This was May 15, 1905, a day the temperature reached 110 degrees in the shade, if there was any shade, and the day that Las Vegas was officially founded.

That same year the town's first newspaper, first bank, and

even its first hotel, the Hotel Las Vegas, a thirty-room building with a canvas roof, opened. The tent town of saloons, stores, and boardinghouses for railroad construction workers, miners, and cowboys was slowly being replaced with somewhat more permanent fixtures, ones with at least a wooden façade. The Las Vegas Ranch also opened. Constructed on the site of the first working ranch in the area, it was fashioned as a retreat, with a swimming pool and billiard hall, and was a forerunner of things to come. Las Vegas also experienced its first fire, one of unknown and, therefore, suspicious origins. It started in Chop House Bill's kitchen and quickly spread through five nearby buildings, destroying everything in its path.

This drinking establishment circa 1905 clearly demonstrates that Las Vegas has always had an "anything goes" attitude.

Not everyone getting off the train was impressed with Las Vegas, and many chose to turn around or head on rather than stay and deal with the dust and wind. A flood in 1906 washed out part of the railroad, discouraging others from staying, although the line was repaired. Still, another hotel, the Nevada, was soon ready for business, followed by the MacDonald Hotel on Fifth Street shortly after.

In keeping with a boisterous frontier town, a rough-and-tumble red-light district grew up where whiskey cost a dime a shot and burros bellying up to the bar did not bother anyone. The parcel of land, known as Block 16, was bounded by First and Second streets, and Ogden and Stewart avenues, immediately north of Fremont. It was the only place where liquor could legally be sold, except for hotels and restaurants, because of an encumbrance the railroad had included in its deeds. Needless to say, bordellos and gambling clubs followed the saloons, and the area was a favorite of anyone with a thirst to quench or an itch to scratch. Predating Nevada's reputation for an independent, devil-may-care attitude, the patrons of the Arizona Club and other concerns of Block 16 were quick to ignore the 1910 state law outlawing gambling, passed as part of a national reform movement, and the later 1919 Prohibition Enforcement Act banning alcohol.

In 1907 Fremont Street got electric lights, and the town continued to grow. When Clark County was founded July 1, 1909, the city of Las Vegas became the county seat. With as few as 19 residents in 1900, Las Vegas was home to 1,500 people when it was incorporated as the first city in Nevada in 1911. By the time electricity was available twenty-four hours a day in 1915, its population had grown to over 3,000 people.

About this time neighboring California first gave young couples or those young at heart and madly in love a reason for crossing the desert, frequently late at night, usually with no forethought and little planning. Wanting to protect its citizens from themselves, the state decreed a three-day waiting period between receiving a marriage license and saying the marriage vows. Referred to as the 1912 "gin law," it was enacted to keep people waking up with a hangover from adding to their misery by learning that they had gotten married while drunk. Without any effort at all, Vegas's incursion into the wedding business had begun, as those too impatient or immature to wait found their way to the other side of the Mojave.

LAS VEGAS, BE DAMMED

The fortunes of Las Vegas were not easily made, however, and the next decade was a difficult one for the town. In 1917 the Las Vegas and Tonopah Railroad went broke, and the San Pedro, Los Angeles and Salt Lake line was sold to the Union Pacific Railroad, throwing into jeopardy not only jobs, but the entire commercial viability of the area. Five years later, when the railroad moved its repair shop out of Las Vegas in retribution for local workers' participation in a strike, things looked dire, indeed. The boom times for the mining towns that Las Vegas serviced were over. Rhyolite, Goldfield, and Bullfrog had become ghost towns by the end of World War I. Las Vegas, too, could have become a ghost town. "Without air conditioning Las Vegas is almost uninhabitable in the summertime," historian Hal Rothman has observed. "And there were relatively few people here and relatively little reason for anyone else to come here."

There was some progress. In 1925 Fremont Street, as part of the state highway, was paved from Main Street to Fifth Street, although only down the middle. "You parked on each side of the pavement," John F. Cahlan, one of the town's first newspapermen, recalled in later years. In 1926, Western Air Express, which would play a role in spiriting newlyweds to and from their elopements, began commercial flight service to Las Vegas. Yet, salvation did not arrive until 1928, when Congress passed the Boulder Canyon Project Act. The $175 million budget to build what became known as Hoover Dam, thirty miles southeast of Las Vegas along the Colorado River, was like federal manna from heaven. As historians Barbara Land and Myrick Land commented in their book *A Short History of Las Vegas*, "Grubby little Las Vegas was about to become the center of worldwide attention."

The townspeople knew it, too. "It's a miracle," they cried, and then they partied like there was no tomorrow, bootleg liquor flowing as if it were legal. Soon the town was overflowing with the Great Depression's unemployed from across the nation. They had come by any means they had at their disposal, some by car or railroad boxcar, others on horseback or even by foot. They were seeking the jobs that a construction project being called the eighth wonder of the world would bring, and the population of Las Vegas increased to 5,165 in 1930 and exploded to 7,500 shortly thereafter.

The dam builders were eventually located in Boulder City, a town the government built under federal jurisdiction to keep everyone on the straight and narrow. Still, the workers were free to come and go as they liked. They knew where the action was and how to find Block 16. With gambling profits, Las Vegas began to modernize. Even before an ounce of concrete for the dam had been poured, streets were paved (presumably from curb to curb), new businesses opened, and the first celebrity wedding took place.

Movies of this era frequently centered on a good-looking hero, pure of heart, triumphing over trouble, prevailing over adversity. William Boyd fit the bill perfectly. While he hadn't yet been cast as Hopalong Cassidy (that wouldn't come until 1935), he had easily made the transition from dramatic leading man of silent film to the he-man of comedies and melodramas of the talking movies. He was a star, and when he arrived in Las Vegas on December 18, 1930, he received star treatment.

Boyd, 35, was in Las Vegas to get married, having taken the day off from his studio in Los Angeles, where he was making a picture. His bride, Dorothy Sebastian, a vivacious 24-year-old blond beauty, was also in the movies. They had met earlier in the year on the set of *Officer O'Brien*. It was his fourth marriage, her second. In true tabloid style, the *Las Vegas Evening Review-Journal* enthusiastically reported on the joyful occasion, supplying lots of delicious details.

The couple arrived by chartered plane shortly after 11:00 p.m. Thursday night and checked into the National Hotel. The ceremony, initially scheduled for 10:00 the next morning, was inexplicably postponed until 11:30 a.m. As a courtesy, the county clerk came to them, armed with his "big marriage license book," rather than having the couple go to the courthouse a short walk away. F. George Walker, best man and executive of Radiotone Pictures, paid the $2 fee for the license, saying, "Here it is. This big bozo," referring to Boyd, "paid for mine in Phoenix, now I'll get even with him." With the account settled and the required documents signed, it was time to begin.

The nuptials took place in front of Judge William E. Orr in

one of the small hotel rooms. Space was tight, and the judge and the betrothed were positioned between the two beds in the room, while the wedding party of eight stood wherever they could. The ceremony was proceeding smoothly until it was the bride's turn to say, "I, Dorothy, take you, William, to be my lawfully wedded husband." Breaking down in tears, she could not get the words out of her mouth. Finally composing herself, she took her vows, and the service was concluded.

Of course, weddings are not over until they are sealed with a kiss. Walker, in his duties as best man, held the bride and groom's heads together until he was satisfied that all requirements were met. Then Boyd, "in true lover style, grasped his new wife in his arms and tenderly sought to dry her tears." The bride, now fully recovered, "rushed over to the judge, threw her arms around his neck, and bestowed on the judicial lips, one of the her best movie kisses."

The party returned to Los Angeles shortly after noon, having spent just over twenty-four hours in town. The newly titled Mrs. Boyd wore a black traveling dress with a heavy fur coat thrown over her shoulders, tan stockings, and brown shoes. Not changing after the ceremony, Mr. Boyd had on a gray business suit. The marriage, by the way, lasted six years. Both remarried.

And that is how it was done back then. Ring any bells?

WHAT DEPRESSION?

"Rip-roaring, no-holds-barred pursuit of pleasure was Las Vegas's stock in trade," Joseph E. Steven wrote in *Hoover Dam: An American Adventure*. "And, all that separated it from the frontier towns of the nineteenth century were the automobiles parked in front of the battered hitching posts and the flicker of neon tubes where wooden signboards had once creaked in the wind."

In 1931, however, Las Vegas was beginning to change.

Construction of the dam got under way in March, and investors were willing to gamble on the growth it would bring to the town. Older, flimsy frame structures gave way to better-built edifices. Houses were subdivided into apartments for a growing population, while office space and warehouses were created for new businesses. The city commission, too, was prepared to go the distance, authorizing bonds to improve the streets with sidewalks, gutters, curbs, and streetlights, expand the sewer systems into the newer neighborhoods, and beef up the police department. Federal money also made a difference. A federal building and a post office went up, while New Deal funding went into projects that not only improved the quality of life, but provided recreation as well. These included a new and larger high school, a convention center, and a public golf course, the latter two adding to Las Vegas's early appeal as a holiday destination.

Also in March, Nevada governor Fred Palzar signed two pieces of legislation that would cement the Silver State's maverick reputation in the national imagination and lay a distinct path to the future, one paved with gold and other riches. The first law made gambling legal once again, and everyone knows where that led—to a virtual monopoly on gaming until it was legalized in Atlantic City in 1978. Even in 2000, with additional competition from lotteries and Indian casinos across the country, Las Vegas's revenues from gambling alone were almost $9 billion. The governor had figured, rightly it turned out, that there is a lot of money to be made from gambling and that people will gamble whether or not it is legal. He felt it was only right that the state should get its cut.

The second law reduced the state's residency requirement for a divorce to six weeks, shocking the nation with its apparent lack of respect for the institution of marriage. Going back (and not that far back, either) to its frontier days, Nevada had always had a liberal attitude toward marriage and divorce. For marriage, it placed almost no restrictions on two people being united in wedding bliss. For divorce, its straightforward approach made it as easy as possible for miners to ditch their wives back east and pacify with a wedding ring their newly acquired common-law wives in the camps. The initial six-month residency requirement was reduced to three months in 1927, when Mexico and France, hoping to attract future divorcées, were considering doing the same. The six-week law came about because Idaho and Arkansas, a little too close to home for comfort, enacted a three-month residency. Nevada, never concerned about public opinion except when it was in its interest, wanted to keep its edge.

Reno, the largest town in the state, benefited from the relaxed law almost immediately. It had already earned a reputation as a hospitable location for spouses wanting to shed their spouses. These were usually wealthy women with time and money on their hands. They made the locale fashionable by touting to their friends back home the horseback riding on dude ranches with cute cowboys. The 1906 divorce of Mrs. William Ellis Corey, wife of the president of U.S. Steel, and the 1919 divorce of actress Mary Pickford, who then was free to marry Douglas Fairbanks, further enhanced its image.

Las Vegas, on the other hand, had some catching up to do. It was neither a household name nor a tourist attraction, and its small casinos with their frontier-saloon atmosphere were less appealing than the grander ones up north. Still, with the opening of the Meadows Club, a sophisticated establishment for dining, dancing, and, of course, gambling, followed in 1932 by the Apache Hotel, the town's first luxury hotel with an elevator and a three-hundred-person banquet hall, the town began to come into its own. Other downtown hotels, like the Nevada, added rooms and floors to accommodate the anticipated influx of tourists. The repeal of Prohibition in 1933 was a boon all around, as gambling and drinking go together like love and marriage.

Even before it was completed in 1935, two years ahead of schedule, Hoover Dam was a big draw, giving historic import to the phrase "If you build it, they will come." Almost 100,000 visited the site in 1932, 132,000 in 1933, and 265,000 in 1934. "The dam is to Americans what Chartres Cathedral was to Europeans, what the Temple at Karnak was to ancient Egyptians," Richard G. Lillard wrote in his 1942 book *Desert Challenge*. "The clean, functional lines, the colossal beauty, and impersonal mass and strength of the dam itself are as symbolic as real." About 75 percent of those visiting the dam also visited Las Vegas. Las Vegas, with its own diversions and attractions, had, in turn, 100,000 visitors in 1932, 230,000 in 1933, and 300,000 in 1934.

When the dam builders pulled out of the area in 1936 and New Deal spending eased in 1937, the Las Vegas economy faltered. While the divorce business brought in some revenues, it was not enough to keep things on the right track. The chamber of commerce began to focus even more intently on tourism, convinced that it was the key to the town's continuing good fortune. Covering all points of interest, they adopted the slogan "The Last Frontier, a Desert Oasis, and the Gateway to Boulder Dam" as their rallying cry.

A TALE OF TWO CITIES

Before 1960 Southern Californians constituted up to 75 percent of all visitors to Las Vegas. Angelenos were quick to discover that the town was within easy driving distance for a weekend visit, and flying was even faster and not that expensive. In a 1935 advertisement for Western Air Express, a round-trip ticket between Los Angeles and Las Vegas was touted at $25. Potential customers were reminded that there were no meals to buy and no overnight costs for the short flight. San Diego and Salt Lake City were the southern and northern points, respectively, on the route.

Western Air Express also participated in publicity events, promoting itself as a "honeymoon express" and Las Vegas as the "Niagara Falls of the West." For a story in *Life* magazine, the airline flew a Los Angeles couple and their witnesses to Las

In the thirties the Apache Hotel and Casino downtown was the place to see and be seen.

Vegas. At the airport they were issued a marriage license by the county clerk and married on the spot. The newlyweds were then photographed at all the scenic hot spots, from the Apache Hotel downtown to a luxury boat docked at Boulder Lake, before being returned to the coast.

Las Vegas was a natural destination as a honeymoon spot, especially as more and more out-of-towners chose to get hitched there. In 1935, 2,122 marriages were performed, almost doubling the number in three years. There were only a quarter as many divorces, on the other hand, and they were essentially flat over the same time period. As the number of marriages in town continued to increase, the *Las Vegas Evening Review-Journal* diligently announced the results. Looking at the final figures for 1935 and observing that New York granted 10,037 licenses, the paper made the following comment: "Las Vegas, with a population of a few thousand and New York with millions, the percentage of weddings is far greater here than in the eastern city and reveals interesting facts on the attraction of Las Vegas." While not an unbiased position, it was an accurate one.

William Boyd and his beautiful bride were not the only Hollywood stars who had their nuptials in Las Vegas in its nascent years, a fact appreciated by a movie fan working in the county clerk's office. Clippings of celebrities' weddings, including those of John Gilbert to Ina Claire and Clara Bow to Rex Bell, were posted on a bulletin board behind the marriage license desk, an early form of advertising for the budding business. Although a few wedding chapels had opened, most of the weddings were performed by a justice of the peace, either at the county clerk's office when time was short, or in a hotel room if the newlyweds wanted something a little more elaborate.

Some of the celebrities, like Fred MacMurray and Lillian Lamont, both 27, were getting married for the first time. The couple had planned their trip, taking a Western Air Express flight the night before the ceremony, and they had brought his mother as witness. Perhaps it was a good omen that the nuptials fell on his parents' wedding anniversary; the marriage lasted until Lillian's death in 1953.

It was the first time, too, for Martha Raye, 20, a burgeoning young comedienne sometimes described as a female Joe E. Brown; she and boyfriend Hamilton Westmore, 21, a movie makeup man, eloped after a soiree at a Los Angeles nightclub. After driving through the night, the couple took their vows at an eleven o'clock Sunday morning ceremony. The bride was still in her party clothes, a blue chiffon evening gown with black velvet wrap. The groom was dressed in a tuxedo. Before returning to Hollywood, the now married couple went to Boulder Dam, just like the thousands of tourists that had come before them. Unlike the MacMurrays, Martha and Hamilton were soon divorced. She next married David Rose, the composer and musician, who went on to become Judy Garland's first husband in another Las Vegas wedding.

Behind every wedding there is a story, but not every star wants the story told. The first time Lew Ayres was in Vegas, when he was 22, the good-looking star of *All Quiet on the Western Front* denied that he was the actor, although it was his name on the marriage license. As the *Las Vegas Evening Review-Journal* relayed the story, "The dead image of the famous Ayres" eventually admitted "he was good friends with Ayres." It turned out not to matter, since he could not find a justice of the peace who was available to conduct the service, and the couple returned to Los Angeles without saying "I do." A few months later, he returned with another woman, actress Lola Lane, and went through with the proceedings. The marriage did not last, and Ayres gave up on Vegas. Three years later, however, Lola Lane was back in town to try again.

Others, too, immediately identifiable from the characters they had brought to life on the silver screen, denied they were themselves. Bela Lugosi, also known as Count Dracula, was one. Now, who wouldn't recognize Bela Lugosi in 1933, when horror movies were most in vogue? Johnny Weissmuller, the best-known Tarzan, was another. Various reasons for the charades can be hypothesized, but sometimes it was as simple as wanting some privacy.

Bob Burns, a well-known actor and radio star of the time, explained his behavior to newsmen after his Vegas elopement: "I don't mind crowds as a general rule, for they're part of our business. But on a man's wedding day, it's different. I wanted a quiet ceremony and a quiet time before and after. That's why I hid out on the boys." To get his privacy, Burns spent nine hours dodging reporters before he and his intended left for Vegas. He took a back road to the Burbank airport, found cover in a locker room, and boarded the plane while it was still in the hangar. While he escaped Los Angeles undetected, the effort was only partially successful. Louella Parsons, gossip columnist supreme, had broken the story of his wedding plans, and an enterprising reporter greeted Burns and his fiancée upon their arrival in Las Vegas.

RIA DOES VEGAS

The gods of good fortune, if not good weather, were smiling on Las Vegas one dreary, rainy day in mid-January 1939 when Mrs. Ria Gable drove into town. The soon-to-be ex-wife of actor Clark Gable had chosen Las Vegas as her place of residence while awaiting her Nevada divorce. The timing could not have been better, because the town needed national exposure, and it needed it badly. A large source of its revenues had dried up when Hoover Dam was completed and most of the dam workers had left the area. The tourists, too, were no longer turning out in the numbers necessary for the town to maintain the lifestyle to which it had become accustomed. Reno, better known, was doing better.

It was a publicist's dream come true. Clark Gable was at the height of his popularity, the number one movie box-office star. Here was a larger-than-life man who could change the state of the underwear industry by what he was wearing underneath his shirt. He was greeted by mobs of swooning women at his public appearances, having achieved superstar status before there were superstars. He was currently filming *Gone With the Wind*, cast as Rhett Butler, because his adoring public had insisted upon it. Imagine what he could do for Las Vegas, the city's publicists fantasized, even if it was only by association.

For two years Clark had beseeched Ria for a divorce, but she loved him, and with all her money, she thought she could keep him. Yet forces were against her. Clark was in love with Carole Lombard, a very sassy, very blond, young actress who could create her own buzz. The couple, however, were under pressure for their living arrangements, having been outed in *Photoplay* magazine as one of "Hollywood's Unmarried

Husbands and Wives." The studio was concerned that negative publicity, on a morals issue, no less, would affect their movie. Fans, in turn, just wanted the Hollywood sweethearts to be happy. Ria, seemingly responsible for the peace of mind of millions, finally agreed to file for divorce.

Ria planned for a quiet retreat while serving her residency time. "I have a lot of reading I have wanted to do for a long time," she told reporters. "And I expect to spend some of my time catching up. I also will knit, do some needlework and take short walks." That was before the publicists put their plans into play. They made sure that Las Vegas's most famous resident was entertained according to her stature, and then some. Not only was she taken dining and dancing, but she also dealt blackjack and spun the roulette wheel at the Apache Hotel. For daytime excursions, she went fishing and horseback riding, always in the most scenic settings. And whatever Ria did, wherever Ria went, a writer and a photographer were sure to follow. Sure enough, the stories that were generated made newspapers from coast to coast. While Ria enjoyed the attention, Vegas garnered the publicity and a certain cachet.

The trial itself was short and sweet. It lasted barely five minutes. Clark did not show up, but instead sent a document which stated his agreement to the proceedings. A few weeks later, he took a day off from filming and drove with Carole to Kingman, Arizona, where they married in the house of a Protestant minister. Las Vegas had become too well-known, too hip, for their liking. And there was way too much press there for their comfort.

Events across the border continued to have an impact on Las Vegas. A few months after *Gable v. Gable* was resolved, California once more tightened its marriage regulations and once again gave the Las Vegas wedding industry a booster shot in the arm, ensuring its health for many years to come. The new law, designed to prevent the spread of venereal disease, required a blood test before the issuance of a license. It was enough of a nuisance that the *Las Vegas Evening Review-Journal* reported that officials in Los Angeles expected "at least three quarters of the normal marriage license business will be diverted from California each day, and therefore, Las Vegas is expecting a great boom." It was a great boom, too. On October 9, three weeks after the law went into effect, the newspaper stated, "California's engaged couples continue to pour across the state line to southern Nevada to avoid compliance."

The demand for marriage licenses maintained its record-breaking pace, putting a strain on the offices of the county clerks in both Washoe County, where Reno is located, and Clark County, where Las Vegas is located. In attempting to deal with the workload, the Washoe County clerk announced that his office would no longer accept marriage-license calls at night or during holidays. Clark County clerk Lloyd S. Payne reacted differently, even though his office issued more than six hundred licenses in October and almost seven hundred in November. He told the *Las Vegas Evening Review-Journal*, "We feel that we are performing a community service, and as long as the merchants of Clark County are satisfied we will continue to issue marriage licenses out of regular offices hours." In so doing, Payne personally helped along the Las Vegas wedding industry. Two years later, business was such that he hired two extra deputies whose exclusive assignment was to be "on call" after hours, providing round-the-clock service.

Still, Mr. Payne, a hardworking, well-meaning county employee, did not do as much for Las Vegas over a lifetime of civic service as Mrs. Ria Gable inadvertently did in six short weeks. That's star power.

WESTWARD HO!

When Tom Hull selected the site for the El Rancho Vegas in 1940, he might have been singing, "Give me land, lots of land under starry skies above, don't fence me in." He was the first businessman to put lodging and a casino at the southern edge of

Las Vegas past the city limits, where there were some lizards and snakes playing hide-and-seek among the creosote bushes, but little else. It was an astute decision, as he did not need to secure a gambling license from city officials or pay city taxes on his gambling revenues. The resort was also the first oasis on Route 91 that drivers came upon after the seven-hour trip from Los Angeles. To underscore that point, he placed a huge swimming pool right by the highway rather than hidden on a private patio. "It was a stroke of showmanship," a writer for the *Saturday Evening Post* observed. "No traveler can miss the pool, few can resist it."

In keeping with its setting, the El Rancho had a Western motif. Hacienda-style cottages surrounded the low-rise main building, in which a rustic casino, a nightclub, a restaurant, and shops were housed. The layout kept guests on the premises rather than having them wander off to lose their money elsewhere; and resorts up and down the Strip copied it for generations. Air-conditioning, an unknown luxury just about everywhere else, kept guests cool while an assortment of activities kept them occupied. While gambling was the preferred evening diversion, guests could sightsee or swim by day. And, of course, there was always horseback riding!

Las Vegas prided itself on being "the Last Frontier" and celebrated its past with Helldorado Days, an annual festival honoring its pioneer heritage. Rodeos, folk singing, square dancing, and parades made up the festivities. For the occasion, townspeople and visitors alike dressed as cowpokes in Levi's jeans or fringed leather skirts and wore fashionable accessories such as boots, bandannas, and five-gallon hats. Hitching posts, watering troughs, and other antiques of bygone times decorated the streets. And the next resort to be built two years later carried through with this theme.

A mile farther south on Highway 91, the Last Frontier Hotel tried to outdo the El Rancho in being all things Western. Everything was larger, more elaborate.

The Hitching Post Wedding Chapel added neon in its second decade but kept its folksy atmosphere.

Cow horns hung on the wall over the beds in every guest-room. Large stuffed animals decorated the trophy room in the main building. Lighting fixtures shaped liked wagon wheels hung in the bar. As a customer service, a horse-drawn stage-coach collected guests arriving at the train station or airport. The romantically inclined could arrange a marriage ceremony at the Little Church of the West, a chapel on the grounds of the resort.

The chapel described itself in its early advertisements as a "modern replica of the little pioneer churches." Those who vis-ited found it charming. "Hav[ing] some one take yuh in that there little church is a treat . . . to say nothin' of getting married in it," the *Las Vegas Evening Review-Journal*'s Doc wrote in his column "Loco Weed" in 1943. "It's sorta peaceful and quiet, yuh can set down in them there pews and get a little closer to the Big Range Boss." For weddings, white drapery and trailing ferns covered the altar, and a lit candelabra stood nearby.

The Hitching Post was another chapel, again with the West-ern name, serving the many marriage-minded couples who came to Las Vegas in the early 1940s. The owners of the chapel, the Stewarts, were Hollywood expatriates. Halley Stewart had written lyrics for film musicals. Mildred Stewart was a profes-sional singer. After their family and friends gave them rave reviews for their own Vegas wedding, they decided to go into business for themselves, bringing a touch of the picturesque to the wedding industry. "We felt there was a demand for pleas-ant, colorful weddings among people who, perhaps, couldn't afford the usual expense," Halley Stewart said in an inter-view at the time, "or, who disliked the formality of a home-town marriage." The weddings at the Hitching Post were so well received that repeat customers proved common. Many couples returned to renew their vows, sometimes as often as once a year.

About this time Las Vegas began to leave Reno in the dust, statistically speaking, issuing more marriage licenses and grant-ing more divorce decrees than its upstate rival. Its population was growing at a faster rate, too. One of the reasons for Las Vegas's emergence as a marriage mecca was the speed with which a couple could tie the knot. Airlines targeted "couples who can't wait another minute" with the slogan "Only one and three-quarter hours to Paradise," and promised couples that they could be married in "less than an hour after you arrive, day or night." Another reason was novelty. Services that lasted less than three minutes with no muss or fuss were considered to be modern and different. Going to a jeweler's for a wedding ring or a bakery for a cake at 3:00 a.m. only added to the novelty. A third reason was cost. A $12 ceremony included the license, the parson, music, and "a nice homelike atmosphere," the latter being a benefit at that time and place. Pictures, an extra song, and, perhaps, a corsage of gardenias brought the cost of an average wedding to $20. Now, that was a great deal!

There were so many chapels along Route 91 in 1941 that a writer for *Collier's* quipped that the road should be renamed "the Honeymoon Highway." However, Guy McAfee, a former vice cop from Los Angeles who had moved his gambling operations to Vegas and made them legal, had bestowed another nickname. Traveling back and forth between the Golden Nugget, his downtown operation, and the Pair-O-Dice Club on Route 91, he decided in a nostalgic moment to call the desolate stretch of road "the Strip," after Los Angeles's Sunset Strip. And it has been "the Strip" ever since.

A GOOD DEFENSE MAKES A STRONG OFFENSE

"Bursting, hot, dirty, thirsty, noisy, flush, and happy" was the way one writer described Las Vegas in the October 1942 *Saturday Evening Post*. And it all came about because the federal government was gearing up for the war effort.

The advantage of locating a magnesium plant near the Hoover Dam, a source of hydroelectric power, was obvious, but at first the impact on nearby Las Vegas was less so. Magnesium, it turned out, was a vital metal in the manufacture of aircraft. The Basic Magnesium Company plant cost $150 million, about three times as much as the Hoover Dam, and required more than twelve thousand construction workers, more than twice as many as had labored on the dam. When several thousand workers then stayed in the area to operate the facility, the contribution of the facility to the economic well-being of the region became clear.

The newly opened Nellis Air Force Base also contributed to Las Vegas's happy days. The government selected the site, as it did many military installations in the Southwest, for its climate, which offered perfect flying conditions year-round. The pilots-, gunners-, and bombardiers-in-training all found their way to Vegas in their time off. With the influx of people and money and more people, the transition from small town to modern city had begun.

Although the town flourished during the war years, the wedding industry languished. From over twenty thousand marriage licenses issued in 1942, the number fell to fewer than nine thousand in 1943. It was not until 1946 that the issuance of licenses surpassed the prewar level. Gas rationing had made it difficult for couples to travel the three hundred miles from the West Coast, but there were those who found a way. Many of these were soldiers with three-day leaves and girlfriends on their arms. Movie actress Linda Darnell eloped with cameraman, now army sergeant, Pev Marley. A couple of friends accompanied them. When singer Dinah Shore tied the knot with cowboy actor, now corporal, George Montgomery, a car caravan escorted them across the desert. Pinup Betty Grable and big-band leader Harry James traveled by train to get married in Las Vegas. She came from Los Angeles, he from New York.

Despite the war, the Little Church of the West put on its best face for its inaugural wedding on May 22, 1943. Captain George N. Calvert of the Fourth Armored Division and Helen Gates of Hollywood were the lucky couple who benefited from the chapel's largesse. Because of travel restrictions, they had planned a small ceremony; only the best man, a maid of honor, and the mother of the bride had accompanied them. However, the Last Frontier Hotel, acting as host, rounded up a hundred guests, dressed them in Western and pioneer costumes, and asked movie actor Roy Rogers and radio star Chester Lauck to be ushers. The chapel was beautifully decorated with candelabra and tall baskets of white gladioli. Mendelssohn's "Wedding March" played as the bridal couple walked down the aisle. Afterward a celebratory dinner was held in the Ramona Room of the hotel. The wedding proved to be quite an affair.

THE BUG AND THE FLAMINGO

Any history of Las Vegas is incomplete without the story of Benjamin Siegel. He was called "Bugsy," but never to his face, because he hated the nickname. He thought it made him sound crazy—dangerous, too, but mostly crazy. He was credited with founding Las Vegas. Some even believed he was mayor. Neither was true. He wanted a career in the movies, but had to settle for creating the Las Vegas of the movies. Not that he lived to see his dream come true. His mobster buddies at Murder, Inc., blew him away, one of the nine shots going through one of his beautiful blue peepers, so those in the know knew it was personal. And none of his Hollywood friends could do a thing about it.

The Flamingo, the casino in the desert named after his girlfriend Virginia Hill's long, birdlike legs, was Bugsy's vision, creation, and extravagance. We do not know whether he was murdered for overspending on its construction or for claiming some of the investors' monies as his own. It doesn't matter. When the Flamingo opened ceremoniously on December 26, 1946, and then reopened in March 1947 after the hotel was completed, every penny that had gone into the place had been well spent. It was "undeniably the most glamorous hotel

Dressed more modestly than
entertainers nowadays, the showgirls
at the Last Frontier in the forties
display their ample charms with
a smile.

in Las Vegas," enthused Eugene P. Moehring in his book *Resort City in the Sunbelt*.

Bugsy had displaced the atmosphere of the cowboy casinos found down the road and replaced it with an ambience of sophisticated luxury throughout the resort. In the richly appointed rooms every comfort was within easy reach. In the casino only the finest materials, such as plush carpet, imported marble, and rare woods, covered the floor, walls, and ceiling. On the grounds an exotic garden with Oriental date palms and rare Spanish cork trees was planted. On opening night and every night thereafter, first-class entertainers, such as Jimmy Durante, Xavier Cugat, and Rose Marie, performed in the showroom. The scent of sex was in the air, too. The male dealers and croupiers were impeccably clad in tuxedos, while the cigarette girls, cocktail waitresses, and showgirls were barely clad at all. Everything was done to entice the big spender, the hotshot, and the world-renowned personality. And enticed they were. Bugsy Siegel had changed Las Vegas forever.

CHAPTER 2

The Golden Oldie Days

LET THE GOOD TIMES ROLL

*P*ostwar Vegas boomed. Legal gambling, no-curfew drinking, easy divorces, and quickie marriages appealed to those wanting to celebrate, and that was just about everyone. As described in a 1947 *Life* magazine article, the amenities were too good to pass up. Who wouldn't want to "stay at million-dollar hotels for as little as $4 a night, dance to the nation's finest orchestras and pay no cover charge, or watch top-billed floor-shows for nothing"? The average wedding now cost $65. Both the average Joe and his intended as well as the movie stars they so admired came to town to say, "I do."

With Las Vegas weddings now the fad of the country, new jargon entered the popular lexicon. "Let's go to Vegas" was commonly meant as a proposal, one to be realized posthaste. Meanwhile, the Las Vegas and Hollywood connection was so firmly established that when a movie star told reporters that he and his beloved were planning a quiet wedding, it was understood that the betrothed intended to elope to Vegas.

Then as now, the goings-on of the rich and famous were entertaining subject matter. Vegas weddings of celebrity couples were duly noted in the *Las Vegas Review-Journal* and then picked up across the country. Mickey Rooney grabbed headlines when he first married in Las Vegas at Wee Kirk o' the Heather in 1949. It was his third marriage, but not his last. He would return to Vegas to do it again. Zsa Zsa Gabor, better known at the time as the former Mrs. Conrad Hilton, made the front page when she married British actor George Sanders at the Little Church of the West that same year. It, too, was her third time. She, too, would return to Las Vegas to marry. Three years after his divorce from Judy Garland, musician David Rose returned for his second Vegas wedding, his third trip down the aisle. Although neither a star nor a socialite, he was a name, and his nuptials were described in detail on page 4 of the local newspaper. His bride was a 21-year-old model from New York. They took their vows in a bungalow at the Hotel El Rancho Vegas. The wedding party included his mother.

Not everyone found the comings and goings of matinee idols and idle matrons amusing, believing instead that the loose morals of movie stars and anyone even remotely associated with them were leading the public astray. In 1947 Catholic, Protestant, and Jewish religious leaders, led by the Right Reverend Monsignor Fulton J. Sheen, banded together to decry the high Hollywood divorce rate and the "flaunting of promiscuous behavior." A spokesperson for RKO, still one of the influential movie studios, addressed the criticism. "When you've got genius on your hands, anything can happen. You can't force or expect them to follow normal lives." Well, that might be true, but bad behavior wasn't the sole prerogative of the cinematic elite. Las Vegas district judge A. S. Henderson was also mortified at modern conduct, but he blamed the ills of the nation on ordinary couples like the Hunts.

As reported in the *Las Vegas Review-Journal*, Mrs. Hunt took off with Mr. Hunt's $300 following a postmarital disagreement. While the situation was indeed unfortunate, the groom's misery was compounded because he had no way of getting in touch with the bride. "He didn't know where she lived. He didn't know her first name because he always called her 'Honey.' He married her, according to news releases, right here in Las Vegas four minutes after he met her," the judge exhorted. "With courtships like that, how can you expect marriages to be permanent?" Well, you probably can't, but the term "quickie" when applied to a Vegas wedding came to take

on new meaning. Referring not only to the length of the ceremony, but to the length of the courtship as well, another Las
Vegas wedding myth was born.

A WALK ON THE WILD SIDE

In the fifties America's relationship with Las Vegas became an illicit
love affair. Southern California's car culture, whereby driving
several hundred miles made for a nice weekend excursion,
fostered the fling. The excitement of gambling and the titilla-
tion of partaking in what would be considered vices anywhere
else made the danger of the liaison's being discovered worthwhile. In 1950 the city attracted as many as 11 million visitors,
who parted with $50 million gambling. Ten years later that
had grown to $300 million. "Vegas was like another planet,"
comedian Alan King reminisced about those days, "and all of
a sudden all the things that were illegal all over the country
became not only acceptable—it was what drove this town."

Gangsters, of course, were the ones who made it all possible. They brought the money that fueled the city's growth and
built the glitter palaces where gambling reigned. Rather than
scaring people off, the presence of the mob only increased the
city's attraction, contributing to the feeling of sophisticated
danger without any real risk. Bob Stupak, former chairman of
the board of the Stratosphere Tower Corporation, believes that
gangsters back then were a tourist attraction. "When you came
here, you know, you thought every time you saw a guy with a
violin case, there was a tommy gun in there," he noted. "And
there was a hood behind every tree just looking out." There
was certainly never any reason for the average visitor out for
a good time to be fearful for his or her safety. As actress and
hotel owner Debbie Reynolds pointed out, "No one got killed
that wasn't supposed to." That was Bugsy Siegel's perspective, too. He once proclaimed, presumably to reassure some
of his guests, "We only kill each other."

David Thomson points out in his book *In Nevada*, "Las

Vegas traded on being a dangerous place." However, it was in the Mafia's best interest to keep the streets of Las Vegas clean and crime free. Spilled blood would only scare off the customers. Bugsy's assassination a few years earlier had created shock waves, but it had taken place in Beverly Hills, not Las Vegas. Some say if he had not left town, he would not have been murdered. Also, organized crime, while staying organized, wanted to blend in, to become legitimate, or at least appear legitimate. Maintaining a low profile was one of the best ways of taking care of business, the business of laundering money from illegal operations in Chicago, Cleveland, and anywhere else there was a wiseguy. And the only way to skim money off the top, another profitable venture, was to be in business—the casino business.

LET ME ENTERTAIN YOU

There were a lot of hotel rooms to fill up and always more being built. The new resorts, most of which were mob controlled, were modern and luxurious, each offering something a little bit different from the ones that came before.

The Desert Inn opened in 1950. For over a decade it was considered the crown jewel of the Strip, "one of the classiest joints in town," to quote one admirer. Set among richly landscaped grounds, its pastel walls sparkled in the sunshine, calling to mind Miami, Havana, and other exotic locales. The Sahara was an immediate success when it opened in 1952. Its trademark camel caravan, aligned in front of the hotel, reflected its African motif. A few weeks later, the Sands opened. It heralded its presence with a sixty-foot-tall neon sign that promised "A Place in the Sun." With its cosmopolitan atmosphere and round-the-clock amenities, it, too, prospered from the start. In 1955, the Riviera became the first high-rise on the Strip. The Dunes, displaying an *Arabian Nights* theme, opened that same year. In 1957, the Tropicana earned the appellation of "Tiffany's of the Strip." Its lobby was extravagantly paneled

in mahogany and lit by Czechoslovak crystal chandeliers. In 1958 the Stardust opened with more than one thousand hotel rooms. It was the largest resort in the world.

Just like today, slot machines in the fifties were fun, addictive moneymakers—for the casino.

The great Las Vegas hotels satisfied America's need to indulge itself, while making the city a premier resort destination. However, it was the entertainment in the theaters, lounges, and clubs in the great hotels that made the fifties the city's golden age. At one time or another the brightest and most glamorous superstars of the day made an appearance in Vegas, either to see or to be seen. The most popular crooners made music, the funniest comedians cracked jokes, and the longest-legged dancers kicked up their heels on stages up and down the Strip. When the performers weren't entertaining, they were in the audience, being entertained.

Naturally, many celebrities made their way down the aisle when they were in town. Celebrities could get married in Vegas as easily as anyone else, and being a celebrity meant getting the royal treatment, and some publicity as well. Beldon Katleman, the owner of the El Rancho Vegas, hosted many weddings, either at his home or in one of the bungalows at his resort, for his show business friends. When Steve Lawrence and Eydie Gorme married, Eydie was appearing at his resort. Subsequently they performed together as a husband-and-wife team. Their union and their careers lasted to the end of the century and then some. Paul Newman and Joanne Woodward were also newlyweds who enjoyed the El Rancho hospitality (and whose union and careers lasted forever), as was David Janssen, starring as television detective Richard Diamond at the time, when he married interior decorator Ellie Graham.

The Little Church of the West at the Last Frontier Hotel, likewise, continued to be a popular place for celebrity nuptials. Handsome Fernando Lamas and the lovely Arlene Dahl were married in the chapel, as was Sally Rand, the internationally renowned fan dancer. In between shows at the resort's Silver Slipper, Sally slipped into a simple frock for the 12:15 a.m. ceremony and then changed back into her fan costume for her act. In 1952 Betty Hutton, the versatile nightclub performer and screen star, said "I do" at the chapel and stayed at the resort for a short honeymoon. Returning in 1955 to try again with someone else, Betty moved uptown to the swank Desert Inn. The surroundings did not have any more of an impact on the longevity of this marriage, either, and she took another husband in another Las Vegas ceremony in 1960.

Private suites in the newer hotels were popular among the jet set. American beauty Rita Hayworth and singer Dick Haymes took their vows at the Sands Hotel, while actor Kirk Douglas and Anne Buydens preferred the Sahara Hotel. Comedian Zeppo Marx married an ex–Riviera showgirl at the Riviera, and the couple took their honeymoon on the hotel yacht on Lake Mead. Movie actress Joan Crawford and soft drink magnate Alfred Steele booked a penthouse at the Flamingo, as did glamour girl Eva Gabor and her millionaire husband-to-be.

Eva, giddy after getting married less than twenty-four hours after the proposal, undoubtedly spoke for everyone in a similar situation when she said, "This time is for real." Red Buttons, headlining at the Tropicana, gave her away.

LEARNING TO LOVE THE BOMB

More than one hundred nuclear weapons exploded in the air at the Nevada Test Site from 1951 to 1962. Then the testing moved underground. No one was supposed to get hurt, although thousands are now believed to have suffered from the radioactive fallout. At first the Atomic Energy Commission wanted to keep the goings-on at places named Yucca Flat and Camp Desert Rock secret. However, when a dozen or so scientists in white coats periodically checked into the Last Frontier Hotel and left wake-up calls for two in the morning, someone was bound to notice that something was up. There was also that strange-looking mushroom cloud that appeared on the horizon following a loud explosion. Yes, something was in the air.

Las Vegans learned to live with the bomb. They got up early when an explosion was expected, so they could later discuss the light, shock, and number of booms of the blast with their neighbors. Less than one hundred miles from the atomic tests, they believed they had a role in keeping America safe and were proud of their efforts. Then they got down to business. Would the explosions bounce the dice off the tables or cause the roulette balls to skip tracks? More important, would gamblers, the lifeblood of the city, stay away?

Of course not. To make certain, the city's press agents quickly developed ways to use the blasts to their advantage, generating headlines across the country. The chamber of commerce released publicity shots of the "Atomic Hairdo," designed by the beauty parlor at the Flamingo, and the winner of the "Miss Atomic Bomb" contest, sponsored by the Sands Hotel. Cocktail lounges advertised the best rooms with views of the blast and served "Atomic Cocktails," an out-of-this-world concoction of vodka, brandy, champagne, and sherry. Some casinos sponsored special early-morning picnics for those who wanted to be as close as possible to the spectacle. But the high rollers, on a winning streak or not, hardly flinched when most of the crowd with drinks in hand left the casino for a look.

Either completely enamored with the atomic explosions—there were many that found them frighteningly beautiful—or just opportunistic, Lili St. Cyr, the resident stripper at the El Rancho Vegas for much of the decade, was determined to use the test bombs as a backdrop for her wedding. Billed as "the most fabulous girl in the world," she regaled customers in one routine by swinging in a gilded birdcage, seductively dropping her lingerie on the awestruck audience below. In another act she emerged from a bubble bath, clothed only in some well-placed bubbles, and then coyly rinsed off in an onstage shower. She was the type of girl for whom only something as dramatic as a nuclear blast would suit the occasion, and she postponed her nuptials three times to ensure they coincided with a blast.

Lili was finally married in the early-morning hours of February 21, 1955. "By the time the flash had faded and the champagne glasses stopped jingling," Katharine Best and Katharine Hillyer recounted in "Fanciful Press Agentry" from their book *Las Vegas: Playtown U.S.A.*, the couple had exchanged vows and were cutting a mushroom-cloud-shaped cake." Apparently the gimmick, if that was what it was, worked. "Newspapers found this romanticized angle on nuclear fission irresistible," Best and Hillyer elaborated, "and captioned their photographs with the additional information that the 'couple are honeymooning near the atomic proving grounds.'" Near the atomic proving grounds meant that the couple never left the grounds of El Rancho Vegas.

The series of atomic tests called Operation Teapot ended a few months later, around the fiftieth anniversary of Las Vegas's founding. "Yesterday's device burst at 5 a.m. with a glaring golden light that faded rapidly to orange and then to pink," a reporter for the *Las Vegas Review-Journal* wrote. "The flash was followed by a fireball lasting three or four seconds. The usual mushroom cloud rose quickly to 37,000 feet and drifted away."

AND HE DANCED FOR THEM

Sammy Davis Jr.'s Las Vegas wedding to Loray White was one of the most celebrated in the last half century. However, it wasn't on Sammy's top ten personal best list, nor should it have been.

Sammy was a local hero of sorts, having performed in Vegas as a member of the Will Maston Trio since 1945. The public loved him there. He started with his father and uncle at the El Rancho Vegas for $500 a week and eventually became one of the most famous headliners on the Strip. Yet he did not get a hero's welcome when he came to town, except onstage. Not that he was treated differently than any other black entertainer. Harry Belafonte, Pearl Bailey, Lena Horne, Nat "King" Cole, Louis Armstrong, and Count Basie were always greeted with open arms when they arrived at the stage door of the casino showroom, but shown the exit as soon as their act was over. The strict segregation policy in place through the fifties earned Vegas the title of "Mississippi of the West."

Sammy railed against the hatred and hypocrisy, but there wasn't too much he could do about it. So he carried on with his life, just being himself. He worked on developing his immense talent, and without any work at all he made himself lots of friends, in and out of the business, black and white. And that's when he got in trouble with the other side, the side that was supposed to be his. For partying after hours with his friends, because he was barred from clubbing in Vegas, he garnered headlines in the black press. "Is Sammy Ashamed He's a Negro?" was one that really hurt. For dating Kim Novak, he received a pen and paper lashing that read in part, "Sammy Davis, Jr., once a pride to all Negroes, has become a never-ending source of embarrassment. . . . Look in the mirror,

41

Sammy. You're still one of us." He was so angry one night that he tried to solve his problems the old-fashioned way, by losing $39,000 at the blackjack table and drinking Jack Daniel's. Many drinks later he ran into Loray, an old girlfriend, and proposed.

Anything Sammy did created news. When Loray accepted, the engagement hit the papers before he had recovered from his hangover. Although he had time to claim it was all a misunderstanding, the good cheers and hearty congratulations he received, not to mention the positive publicity that came his way, were too good to pass up. So he and Loray negotiated a deal. She would receive a flat $10,000 for six months of marriage, no options. The contract was executed on January 11, 1958. That night, with Loray ringside, Sammy did only one show at the Sands. Then he got married. His friends, both black and white, laughed at his jokes, applauded his performance, and believed in him even though he had messed up. For that he knew he was truly blessed.

SWING, SWING, SWING

When Frank Sinatra and his friends and costars Dean Martin, Sammy Davis Jr., Peter Lawford, and Joey Bishop performed at the Copa Room at the Sands in between takes of the 1960 movie *Ocean's Eleven*, everything was kicked up another notch. The who's who of Hollywood—Spencer Tracy, Gary Cooper, Natalie Wood, and Robert Wagner—always turned out for Frank, and opening night for the Rat Pack was no different. Lucille Ball, Peter Lorre, Dinah Shore, and Zsa Zsa Gabor were some of the celebrities in the audience. Only now the music was louder, the jokes were funnier, and the carousing both on and off the stage went on all night. It wasn't just the Sands that was swinging, either. It was happening all over town, and it lasted almost a whole decade.

The big rooms were showrooms for the stars. In addition to Frank, Dean, and Sammy, many others, like Red Skelton,

Tony Bennett, and Ella Fitzgerald, packed them in. The usual formula required an orchestra and a supporting act, usually a relatively unknown comic backed up a celebrity voice or vice versa. The French girlie shows were popular, too. The Lido at the Stardust, the Folies at the Tropicana, and the Casino de Paris at the Dunes, extravaganzas all, featured bare-breasted women strutting their stuff, accompanied by a few acrobats, a couple of jugglers, or maybe a magician doing tricks.

The pay was better than good. The big names were paid big bucks, approximately twice what they would earn in a night-club anywhere else, while being put up in luxury for a few weeks. To the smaller acts in the all-night lounges, perform-ing in Vegas meant steady employment and the chance to be discovered. To the casinos, entertain-ment was a worthwhile money-losing venture. "The purpose of all the enter-tainment is, bluntly, to lure the people in," observed Dick Schaap in the De-

Frank Sinatra, Dean Martin, and Joey Bishop cavorted and caroused onstage at the Sands Hotel individually and collectively as part of the Rat Pack.

cember 1968 issue of *Holiday* magazine, "to get them into a position where they can sense, smell and eventually sample the heady wine of gambling."

Once drawn into the web it was difficult to extricate oneself, because the free drinks and food just kept coming. One couple from Long Beach, California, playing at the Horseshoe casino did not want to leave, despite having plans to get married. They were ahead at the slot machines, and as the *Las Vegas Review-Journal* noted, they were "having too much fun." It was July 1961, and Hank Kovell, the press agent for the downtown hotels, was at the top of his game. Sensing a news story with an opportunity for photos, he called Judge Myron Leavitt to perform the ceremony on the premises. The judge expected an underwater wedding along the lines of the recent floating crap game in the swimming pool at the Sands, so he was relieved to learn he could keep his clothes on. Wearing a traditional suit and tie, he officiated in front of the keno booth on the floor. Their eyes on the roulette ball, most of the players paid no attention.

BEAT THE CLOCK

On Thursday evening, August 26, 1965, 132 couples descended on Las Vegas for reasons that had nothing to do with fun and sun, entertainment, or other amusements. They were there to get married. They crowded the marriage license bureau, filled the corridor, and spilled outdoors. Two police units directed traffic and controlled the crowds. In about two hours the bureau clerk had issued all but 8 of the couples licenses, a particularly astounding record considering that the usual number of licenses issued on a weekday night was 10. In the same amount of time, the justice of the peace, James Brennan, completed 63 nuptials. "I could've married them en masse," he commented afterward, "but they're people, not cattle. People expect more when they get married." The chapels were busy, too, with waits of forty-five minutes or longer.

Most of the young couples had driven from Southern California, but some had flown from as far away as Newark, Pittsburgh, Chicago, and Denver. On average the grooms were 20 years old. Waiting their turn, they appeared nervous, silently smoking or pacing the floor. The brides, about two years younger than the husbands-to-be, were much more comfortable with the situation. They chatted happily, exchanging advice and helping each other primp. Parents accompanied some of the couples. They were there to provide moral support or to give their consent for an underage child, or both.

Earlier that day President Lyndon B. Johnson had signed an executive order and set off the mass pilgrimage. He proclaimed that men 19 to 25 years old who were married after midnight were subject to the draft on the same basis as single men. Just like that, the president had the additional manpower needed to fight the Vietnam War. "I am glad Jack is marrying Linda tonight," one mother at the Vegas courthouse told a reporter. "I would much rather have him married than off to Viet Nam."

Only in Las Vegas was there a chance of beating the clock.

AND THE BEAT GOES ON

The parade of stars continued to do the Las Vegas Wedding Bell March. The tune was familiar and the steps were uncomplicated. It was simply a matter of putting one foot after the other. Although no experience was necessary, it seemed to bolster the confidence of the parties involved.

Actress Janet Leigh is a case in point. One day after receiving her 1962 Mexican divorce, she married wealthy stockbroker Bob Brandt in a civil ceremony in the Presidential Suite at the Sands Hotel. For the "happy occasion," as she described it to reporters, she wore a pink dress with a pink ribbon in her hair. Janet was 34 years old, and she was beginning her fourth marriage. Her first had been annulled after one day because she had been only 14 years old. Her second was to a college

sweetheart, while her third, to actor Tony Curtis, made her one-half of a very famous Hollywood twosome for eleven years. However, Tony "no longer wanted to be married," she told a divorce court, so she struck out on her own and did very well for herself. "I guess you'd call him tall, dark, and handsome," Janet said of her new husband. "He surfs, he swims, he plays tennis. He even taught me to ride a motorcycle."

Pretty in pink, Janet Leigh looks pleased as punch with her fourth husband, Bob Brandt, following their nuptials.

In turn Tony Curtis took his next wife in Las Vegas in 1963 at the Riviera Hotel. In 1968 he married his third wife at the Sahara Hotel, and his fourth wife out of town. In 1993 he married his fifth wife at the MGM Grand. Tony apparently believes in marrying the one he's with.

Among the stars there were some first-timers, too, songbirds who became lovebirds, at least for a time. Shortly after appearing as Liberace's opening act in 1963, Barbra Streisand married Elliot Gould, while Elvis Presley waited until 1967 to profess publicly his love and devotion to Priscilla Beaulieu. Elvis had to borrow $15 to cover the cost of a weekend wedding license, by the way, because he never carried any cash. They took their vows in room 246 at the Aladdin. Ann-Margret and Roger Smith, one act that never closed, did the same thing a week later at the Riviera, where Ann-Margret was frequently a headliner. In 1968, well on his way to becoming the King of Las Vegas, Wayne Newton married Elaine Okamura. The newlyweds were feted at the Flamingo by owner Kirk Kerkorian.

Although none of these warblers had very auspicious Las Vegas debuts, they all became superstars. Their glitter and glamour went far beyond the city borders, but also occupied a specific place in the city's history. Barbra needed Liberace's assistance in warming up the audience because they did not take to her, but in 1969 she opened the International Hotel and Casino to a packed house. In 1993 she did the same for the MGM Grand. Elvis received a lukewarm reception at the Last Frontier in 1956, although "Hound Dog" was number one on the charts. He, too, returned to sellout crowds for month-long engagements over seven years until his early death in 1977. Ann-Margret and her college group the Suttle-tones had driven cross-country for a gig that did not pan out. By Christmas of that year, she was trading repartee with George Burns in his show at the Sahara. Her career had legs, and she danced her way up and down the Strip through the decades. Wayne started in a downtown lounge doing six shows a night before playing in the showrooms, and he's still around.

Sometimes the celebrities were local, or at least they were such a large part of the scene that they were thought of as locals. Louis Prima and Keely Smith, the duo credited with creating the lounge act and then transforming it into an art form, were such a pair. They turned the town on its ear with their particular combination of swing plus rock when they arrived in 1954. Night after night, sometimes all night, for seven years they filled the Casbar Lounge at the Sahara Hotel with hot sounds and happy crowds. Frank Sinatra and company were part of their following.

When the act was moved to the big room, Louis changed. He started acting like a star, and he took up drinking, smoking, and stepping out with other women. In retaliation, Keely had a short affair with Sinatra. The couple were unable to reconcile after the personal betrayals, and the old black magic disappeared. Then they both tried it again. Louis found another singing partner, Gia Maione, whom he married in 1962 on a show break in Lake Tahoe. Keely went solo for a time,

ONCE UPON A TIME

eventually remarrying to a recording company executive at the Chapel of the Bells on Las Vegas Boulevard in 1965. Although Keely had become enmeshed in the fabric of the town, the same could not be said about her manager-brother. The rites following her lounge show at the Sands were delayed over an hour because he could not find the chapel.

Geographical proximity, however, was not a prerequisite to getting married in Las Vegas. In 1966 international movie star Brigitte Bardot and wealthy German playboy Gunther Sachs endured a thirteen-hour flight from Paris to marry in a private ceremony at the home of a Las Vegas lawyer. "We had to be married here because in Europe it's not possible without all the photographers," Gunther told reporters when they caught up with the couple. "We came here to make it fast and good." Well, they made it fast and good, but they were still spotted by those crazy guys with cameras when visiting the Tropicana Hotel-Casino. The newlyweds, either shunning the publicity or creating it, led the paparazzi on a merry chase from the coffee shop through the casino to a cab outside. At 31, Brigitte was marrying for the third time. Her first husband, French film director Roger Vadim, had married the actress Jane Fonda in a Las Vegas ceremony the year before.

In the swinging sixties even hairstylists were stars, or at least could attract as much attention as if they were. In 1967 famed British hairdresser Vidal Sassoon married Beverly Adams, the actress who played Dean Martin's sexy secretary in the Matt Helm movies. As reported in the *Las Vegas Review-Journal*, the ceremony took place in a suite at the Sahara Hotel on the spur of the moment, as the couple's plans to marry in Santa Barbara had fallen through. The bride wore a pink sheath with a matching pink coat. "I didn't do her hair for the wedding," said Sassoon. "I cut it a few days ago and it's so short, all she has to do is go through it with a damp comb."

A few months later another hairstylist, Jon Peters, married actress Lesley Ann Warren.

When the sun was shining, the swimming pool was the place for swingers in the sixties.

Early in the day the couple encountered a two-and-a-half-hour delay getting their marriage license at the courthouse because they did not have the proper identification. Despite Lesley's success on Broadway and notable appearances in Disney films, she was not yet a recognizable figure, nor had Jon's celebrity status kicked in. He would have to hook up with Barbra Streisand and become a movie producer before that happened. Still, the couple dressed as somebodies, and they finally convinced the clerk of their identities. In the fashion of the times, the groom had on a far-out off-white, double-breasted English-style suit. The bride wore a tiered-lace mini-dress with six-inch-long lace earrings to match. The wedding was held in a suite at the Sahara Hotel where many other celebrity weddings had taken place. But where were the photographers when you needed them?

VENI, VIDI, VICI

Just like an orgy in the glory days of ancient Rome, the opening party for Caesars Palace on August 5, 1966, cost $1 million and lasted three days. Over 1,800 invited guests consumed two tons of filet mignon, devoured three hundred pounds of crabmeat, and quaffed fifty thousand glasses of champagne. Attractive minitoga-attired waitresses greeted the attendees. "Welcome to Caesars," they cooed. "I am your slave."

The public had never seen anything like Caesars. They loved it, just as the developer Jay Sarno had known they would. It was the first Strip resort to fully integrate its theme throughout the casino hotel complex. Italian cypresses lined the driveway, and Carrara marble lined the walkways. Romanesque fountains flowed freely, and Florentine statuary stood proudly wherever one looked. The coffee shop was named the Noshorium, combining the Yiddish word *nosh* for snack and the Latin word *orium* for deli. A nearby frieze depicted the Battle of the Etruscan Hills.

In the most flamboyant manner imaginable the resort

brought to life the fantasy that everyone is a Caesar, while on the imperial premises at least, and should be treated royally. The *Las Vegas Sun* proclaimed, "Caesars Palace established a new standard of elegance and luxury for the Nevada hotel industry and perhaps the world." When Frank Sinatra forsook the Sands to perform at the casino's eight-hundred-seat Circus Maximum Theater, the resort's status as the in place was secured. Unlike the Aladdin Casino, which had opened a few months earlier, it made money hand over fist from the moment of its inception.

Later that year multimillionaire recluse Howard Hughes came to Las Vegas and conquered all in his purview. With a check in his back pocket for $546,549,171 for his shares in Trans World Airlines, he arrived in town by train at 4:00 a.m. the Sunday after Thanksgiving and began a buying spree before Christmas. His first purchase was the Desert Inn. When asked to vacate the top two floors of the hotel so that high rollers could use the luxury suites, Hughes instead made the mob owners an offer they couldn't refuse. Soon after, he acquired the Silver Slipper because its brightly lit, revolving sign outside his bedroom window annoyed him when he wanted to sleep, as well as the Sands, the Frontier (formerly the Last Frontier), the Castaways, and the Landmark. Although he controlled almost 15 percent of the state's gambling revenues, Hughes did not make much money from his casino investments, an indication that the skimming originally done at the behest of the previous owners was still going on. Yet neither Hughes nor anyone in his closest circle of aides ever stepped foot on a casino floor to find out. Four years later, Hughes moved on to Paradise Island in the Bahamas, leaving just as quietly as he had arrived.

Hughes's stay had a decided impact on Las Vegas, especially in the realm of public relations. If a man of Hughes's stature was involved in gaming, surely the industry could not be as sleazy as had been thought. Perceptions of the town and its primary source of revenue began to improve, slowly taking on a greenish tint, the color of money. Hughes also had a reputation as an ingenious entrepreneur. "If gaming was good enough for Howard Hughes," Hal K. Rothman commented in his book *Devil's Bargains*, "it was certainly good enough for the Hilton, Holiday Inn, and Ramada corporations."

Under intense pressure from lobbyists led by Hughes himself, the state of Nevada enacted the 1969 Corporate Gaming Act and thereby changed the law that governed casino ownership. For the first time a publicly held company could acquire a gambling license without each and every stockholder undergoing a background check. Quicker than it takes to double down on an eleven when the dealer is showing a six, some of the leading Mafia members cashed out. The FBI's dogged scrutiny into casino skimming had taken the fun out of the business, and it was time to retire anyway. Some illegal activity masterminded by younger, more aggressive Mafioso, like Frank Rosenthal at the Stardust, continued. But with deeper pockets than the Teamsters, who had financed building and development in Las Vegas for years, the multinational hotel chains bought in and slowly took over, claiming the spoils that go to the victor.

CHAPTER 3

Glitzy, Glamorous, and All Grown Up

GETTING BIGGER ALL THE TIME

Unlike Howard Hughes, Kirk Kerkorian made his fortune himself, every penny of it, rather than inheriting it. Like Hughes, however, he began his professional life as a pilot, sold his interest in an airline, and invested the proceeds in Las Vegas. For a start he bought the Flamingo in 1968. The aging resort was beginning to show signs of wear and tear, so Kerkorian fixed it up, turned it around, and used it as a springboard for his next project, the International Hotel.

When the International opened in 1969, it had 1,500 rooms, half a dozen restaurants offering American and ethnic fare, scores of fashionable boutiques, and three major facilities for entertainment—a lounge, a theater, and a showroom. Everything about it was huge. Elvis biographer Albert Goldman was impressed not only with its size, but also with the amenities it provided. "It was not so much a resort hotel as it was a resort in a hotel: a totally self-contained, round-the-clock pleasure dome," he commented, "where one could check in for a weekend or a week and never once feel the need to step out the door."

Kerkorian did not stop there. Selling both the Flamingo and the International to the Hilton Corporation, he was able to finance his next project, the construction of the MGM Grand (now Bally's), named for the classic MGM movie *Grand Hotel*. When it opened in 1973, it was housed in a twenty-six-story building with 2,100 rooms, and it replaced the International (now known as the Las Vegas Hilton) as the largest hotel in the world, at least until the Hilton added another 1,000 rooms.

Not that the town was standing still for Kirk Kerkorian, or anyone else. In the seventies Caesars Palace built three towers fourteen stories or taller. The Tropicana added some guest wings and built a larger, grander theater to seat 1,150. The Riviera, too, added rooms, as well as championship tennis courts for professional tournaments, while the Aladdin was transformed into a first-class Strip resort by new owners. Even the downtown area known as Glitter Gulch got into the act. In 1971 the Union Plaza on Fremont Street opened on the spot where at the turn of the century the Union Pacific Railroad had auctioned the property that became the town of Las Vegas. At the time the Union Plaza had the world's largest casino, and its showroom specialized in Broadway productions. In 1973 the up-and-coming Steve Wynn came along and revived the Golden Nugget, turning it into a popular, profitable showplace.

ACROSS THE CULTURAL DIVIDE

Visitors crowded the city. From 1970 to 1980 the number of tourists doubled to over 11 million. In 1977 they passed the billion-dollar mark in cash left behind. However, change was in the air. Jet planes made Las Vegas as easy to reach for people on the East Coast as for those on the West Coast, as well as for everyone in between. When *The Merv Griffin Show*, a daily talk program that mixed political guests with Hollywood stars, went on the road and broadcast from Caesars Palace, Las Vegas became psychologically accessible to a wider audience as well. "Yes, the high rollers still come, brought in on free junkets, wined and dined on the cuff," Robert Alan Aurthur wrote in a 1974 *Esquire* article. "But the overwhelming bulk of today's visitors is increasingly Middle America on a spree, paying prices for rooms and meals no less than at any other resort."

And so began the clash between the big gamblers at the craps tables and the small gamesters at the slot machines. At least the faces onstage were familiar to most, or some of them were for a time. On March 23, 1971, Frank Sinatra announced he was quitting the business. He would replace singing, recording, and performing, he insisted, with the quiet, reflective life. Now, who was kidding whom? Three years later he was back. Retirement at 55 had been a mistake he told an audience at Caesars Palace. Dean Martin, star of his own television variety show, was paid $200,000 a week, top dollar at the time, to open the MGM Grand Hotel. Sammy Davis Jr. was also around, although he was wearing Nehru jackets and love beads. Over at the International, Elvis continued to electrify audiences of 30-year-old groupies from his early days even long after he had gotten bored with the whole deal.

The old guard was still around, but they were being nudged out of the spotlight. Johnny Cash, Glen Campbell, Charlie Pride, and other country-and-western stars had arrived in town and found a following, as had rock 'n' rollers. Paul Revere and the Raiders played the lounge at the Flamingo. Sonny and Cher, getting their act together, performed at the Sahara. "Vegas became a city divided," Mike Weatherford noted in his book *Cult Vegas*. Those left standing were "the middle-of-the-road pop stars—the Jacksons, the Carpenters, Donny and Marie—who didn't have enough rock credibility to worry about the stigma of playing a casino and who made the guys in gold chains and pinky rings feel hip and with it."

Michael Mann's television series *Vega$*, which aired from 1978 to 1981, showcased a Las Vegas in transition, probably without meaning to. Robert Urich played Dan Tanna, a private eye with a soft spot for vulnerable showgirls. He drove a vintage 1957 T-Bird from the good old days, but he was aided by two of his Vietnam buddies, suggesting an up-to-the-moment sensibility. The detective always dressed in faded blue jeans, so he had some counterculture credentials, but he donned a sport coat when it was absolutely required, so he fit in anywhere. Old-style Vegas shone through every time Tanna's boss at the Desert Inn, played by Tony Curtis, showed up or an aging guest star had a bit role. Morey Amsterdam, Shelly Berman, Sid Caesar, and even Dean Martin were some of the old-timers that passed through. Then again, Kim Basinger, Lisa Hartman, and Tanya Roberts, playing damsels in distress, were some of the newer guest names on the show's celebrity roster.

"The more popular a mecca it became," Nick Tosches wrote in the introduction to *Literary Las Vegas*, "the less cool Vegas got." Celebrities sensing the change in temperature stayed away, and the healthy stream of celebrity weddings dried up to a trickle. After casually dating, Diana Ross, no longer of the Supremes, and Robert Silberstein, a young Jewish entrepreneur, eloped to Las Vegas, surprising family and friends. At the time those in the know assumed that she was pregnant by Motown's Berry Gordy. Melanie Griffith and Don Johnson married the first time at the Silver Bell Wedding Chapel, but they were young and relative unknowns in the midseventies. They had met three years earlier, when Melanie was 15 years old and Don was costarring with her mother, Tippi Hedren, in the movie *The Harrad Experiment*. Television comedy star Freddie Prinze of *Chico and the Man* chose to get married in Las Vegas in 1975, as did comedian Redd Foxx of the hit sitcom *Sanford and Son* in 1977. Then again, Foxx had performed in the showrooms on the Strip for years and had made Las Vegas his home. Suiting the times, he founded the Fred G. Sanford New and Used Store to commemorate his show. Among those interested in the wacky side of Las Vegas, only the Liberace Museum surpassed its popularity.

DOWN, BUT NOT OUT

It was no longer hip to be hep, not that Las Vegas was considered to be either anymore. Around town anything polyester was the costume du jour, unless it was a velour jogging suit in the cooler winter months or a beaded jersey jumpsuit for the evening disco look. The impersonal corporations that now set the tempo projected a safe, staid environment and one much closer to mainstream America. Once known as Sin City for good reason, the town these days was not so sinful and a lot less fun. Even the quality of the entertainment was suffering. In *Cult Vegas*, Mike Weatherford described the state of the showroom in the early eighties: "Aging headliners were demanding more money than hotels wanted to pay," he wrote. "Small, often amateurish drag and nudie revues were thrown together to fill the smaller rooms."

While Las Vegas might have been suffering from changing tastes and lack of imagination, some of its problems were beyond the control of those in charge. With the legalization of gambling in Atlantic City in 1978, Las Vegas faced competition for the first time since Castro took over Cuba in the late fifties and banished the gambling halls of Havana. Now the major populaces from New York City and other Northeastern cities had access to Vegas-style action within an easy drive, and recession forced many former patrons to stay closer to home. Loss of social status was one thing, but the loss of gaming revenues or a slowing rate of increase was serious.

On a graver note, there was catastrophe in the 1970s followed by tragedy. A flash flood caused more than $1 million in damage on the Strip. Hundreds of cars were swept away in the raging waters. Then in 1980 eighty-four people died and seven hundred were injured when a roaring fire broke out at dawn and quickly swept through the MGM Grand Hotel. It was the second deadliest hotel fire in this country. Optimistic that guests would return, Kerkorian rebuilt and reopened the facility eight months later. But another deadly fire at the Las

Although seventies Vegas had a case of the blahs, the roulette wheel still went round and round.

Vegas Hilton put a damper on the town. To rebuild public confidence, stricter fire regulations were imposed on all high-rise hotels.

However, it wasn't all doom and gloom. Fresh new comedians like the outspoken Roseanne Barr and soft-spoken Louie

Anderson kept the crowds laughing in the aisles of comedy clubs with their unique styles of edgy humor about family life. Andrew Dice Clay and Sam Kinison, in turn, stirred up audiences with in-your-face jokes and controversial dialogue that was liberally sprinkled with sexist comments and doses of profanity. Championship fights were popular also, and brought in fans. When Larry Holmes kept Muhammad Ali from regaining the heavyweight title at Caesars Palace in 1980, sports history was made. In 1981, when the Riviera paid country music star Dolly Parton $350,000 per week for two weeks as a headliner in their showroom, entertainment history was made. Siegfried and Roy first performed their magic show in Vegas at the Frontier. In 1983 the Imperial Palace presented its ongoing "Legends in Concert," featuring celebrity look-alikes of such stars as Marilyn Monroe, Judy Garland, Buddy Holly, and Elvis.

Frank Sinatra look-alikes needed not apply, because the real Frank was still going strong, bucking the downward trend for singing senior citizens. In the mideighties a new crop of admirers was discovering the great crooner, now in his seventies. They were not concerned that he was losing his voice, or that he would occasionally hit the off note. They liked his attitude, and they wanted to see the living legend for the first time, or possibly the last time. And Frank obliged. He not only did sixty appearances a year at Bally's Atlantic City and in Reno and, of course, Las Vegas, but he also toured the country, giving concerts in sports arenas, just like any other rock star.

Slowly but surely, younger, hipper Hollywood couples were again finding their way to Las Vegas to say "I do." Actress Joan Collins eloped with Peter Holm in 1985. Okay, she was over 50, but he was under 40. She was also hot. Playing Alexis Colby on the nighttime soap opera *Dynasty*, she had become the television celebrity the world most loved to hate. Conversely, beloved Bob Geldof, the man called "Saint Bob" for organizing the Live Aid concerts, took the lovely Paula Yates for his wife in 1986. The next year, Bruce Willis of the hit show *Moonlighting* and Brat Pack actress Demi Moore traveled to Vegas to take their wedding vows.

The next generation of celebrities, barely old enough to say "I do" without parental permission, were also discovering Las Vegas as a cool place to take their vows. In November 1987 Lisa Bonet eloped with rocker Lenny Kravitz. At the time Lisa was a star, while Lenny was a struggling musician, so this is her story. She went from playing a supporting role as Denise Huxtable on the number one rated *The Cosby Show* to the lead on the television show *A Different World* while still in her teens. Wanting to cast off her too-good-to-be-true on- and offscreen image, she took the big step with Lenny, got pregnant, left the show after one season, separated after three years, and eventually divorced. She has been trying to live a happy, normal life ever since. Lenny, all the while, claims she will always be the love of his life.

Corey Feldman was another of the teen idols of the 1980s who lost his way in the desert before he grew up. He had been in show business since he was three years old, first in commercials, then in movies such as *Stand by Me, The Goonies*, and the 1987 cult classic *The Lost Boys*. With his popularity at a high even if his maturity was at a low, he married Vanessa Marcil from the show *Beverly Hills 90210* in Las Vegas in 1989. He was 18 years old; she was 20. Amazing! They split two years later. Corey, derailed by drugs and rehab, has been trying to resurrect his career ever since. Vanessa, ironically, returned to Las Vegas to play a casino hostess to VIPs on *Las Vegas*, the 2003 television series with the tagline "Fast. Furious. Fun." If only life were that fabulous.

AS THE WORLD TURNS

Nighttime soap operas were hugely popular in the go-go eighties. *Dallas, Dynasty,* and *Falcon Crest* magnified the excesses of the time, particularly as exemplified by the very rich, and audiences loved watching the mess the characters made of their lives. Except for a false veneer of middle-class ordinariness, *Knots Landing*, a *Dallas* spin-off, was much the same way. It had the special characteristic, however, of taking place on a quiet cul-de-sac in an unassuming suburb of Los Angeles, putting it within driving distance of Vegas.

Although Las Vegas was struggling to regain its former renown, and its image still connoted a certain amount of tackiness, there wasn't a better place for plotlines involving love and marriage to be resolved. It was so easy to get there! There were so many chapels! There was no waiting period! And as much as soap operas themselves, getting married in Las Vegas had become part of the popular culture. It spoke volumes in shorthand about acting rashly and eventually paying the price for one's actions. And the young and the restless as well as their parents could behave badly and live to regret it or, if they were lucky, live happily ever after.

Take Karen and Mack MacKenzie, the heart and soul of *Knots Landing*, for example. Karen was everybody's best friend, loyal to the end, always there when needed. She was also a loving mother, a working woman, and an active environmentalist. Mack was a good guy, a straight shooter, the neighbor others turned to with their problems. He believed no crime should go unpunished, and he pursued all crooks at all costs. They met when Mack in his role as a federal prosecutor was investigating the death of Karen's first husband. How did this goody-goody twosome end up getting married in Las Vegas, contrary to all stereotypes? It was a practical matter. Their wedding plans were not coming together, and they were tired of trying to please everyone but themselves over the details. So they up and eloped.

Karen and Mack said their vows at the Bridal Veil Chapel, a garish place modeled on the common perception of a Las Vegas chapel. It resembled a tawdry Valentine's Day card, with fire-engine red carpet and pastel pink flowered wallpaper. Waiting for the minister, the couple quibbled in their usual manner. "This place is so ridiculous," Karen fretted. "Look at us." Mack, not noticing anything wrong, responded, "Hey, hey, you look beautiful." Not letting it go, Karen lamented, "Well, you should have worn your blue suit, brown suit." Mack, still calm, stated the facts: "You're wearing a dress. We're getting married, and I'm wearing the tuxedo. That's it." "With brown shoes," Karen said, getting in the final word. Then she giggled through the whole ceremony. Regardless of the experience, it worked for them. Despite an argument every other season or so and a brief separation near the end, the marriage lasted through the series.

Karen's daughter Diana's elopement to Las Vegas was another matter. Diana had gotten involved with Chip Roberts, a houseguest of neighbors on the cul-de-sac. Chip, also known as Tony Fenice, was a rather unsavory character with an unctuous manner. And that description is a compliment for someone wanted for murder. When the young couple went on the lam, they stopped in Las Vegas to marry so that Diana could not be required to testify against her husband. Her mother, frantic with worry, found out about the marriage at the same time the police did. "Call me Mrs. Fenice," Diana haughtily instructed everyone within hearing as her husband was being led away in handcuffs. Whether she was rebelling against parental authority or she had truly fallen in love, we will never know. Her husband of a few weeks died in an ugly accident—a pitchfork driven through his heart.

The high-priced, high-powered lawyers at McKenzie, Brackman, Chaney, and Kuzak on television's *L.A. Law* also had easy access to Las Vegas, a point demonstrated during the show's 1986–87 premiere season. Nebbishy attorney Stuart Markowitz had been courting his classy colleague Ann Kelsey for six months when he proposed. "Will you marry me?" he asked over a bottle of champagne at a Beverly Hills restaurant. "Marry you?" she replied, pausing. "Yes. Stuart, this is so exciting. We'll have to set a date." Afraid she would change her mind, Stuart suggested, "How about tonight?" "Tonight?" "Yes, we'll fly to Las Vegas."

As they waited for the reverend at the Chapel of Love later that night, the somewhat seedy atmosphere in the waiting room put a damper on Ann's attitude, and she started to get cold feet. "Stuart, this is terrifying," she fussed. "I mean it. If I don't get out of here first, I'm going to be Mrs. Stuart Markowitz for the rest of my life." Well, Ann had found her soul mate, and she was Mrs. Stuart Markowitz for as long as the show was on the air. However, as impulsively as they had rushed to Vegas, they returned home to tie the knot in a formal ceremony at another time.

In a case of art imitating life, a Las Vegas wedding took place (off-camera) on *Moonlighting* later the same season that Bruce Willis had gotten married in Las Vegas. To the disappointment of the show's loyal fans, Cybill Shepherd's character, Maddie Hayes, did not marry Bruce's character, David Addison, but Walter Bishop, a man she had only recently met. "David, I'm married," Maddie announced, breaking his heart. "I met him on the train. We stopped in Las Vegas. We were there a night." Maddie, one of those people who never did anything without obsessive analysis and almost neurotic planning, had the ultimate Las Vegas wedding, at least according to the popular stereotype. It was spontaneous and short-lived.

The decision to divorce was mutual and amicable. Walter even learned a lesson from the experience. "You know, I haven't even gotten back the pictures from the wedding chapel in Vegas," he told Maddie. "If I'd known then what I know now, I'd have sent them to One Hour Photo." As for the marriage itself, Walter professed, "You know, being married to you was the greatest two weeks of my life." "Yeah, it's the best two-week marriage I ever heard about," Maddie replied. "Besides, we'll always have Amtrak."

The volcano at the Mirage spews fire a hundred feet into the air, lighting up the night sky and attracting tourists to its stretch of the Strip.

TIGERS, TIGERS, BURNING BRIGHT

Almost overnight Las Vegas changed. It was as if someone flicked the switch and the lights went on. Neon had always been part of the street scene, but its glow now seemed brighter than ever, a symbol of the city's once again limitless prospects.

Steve Wynn's Mirage started the revolution when it opened in November 1989. The $600 million hotel with more than three thousand rooms was envisioned as more than a resort with a casino, but rather as a tourist attraction in and of itself. The towering volcanic inferno in front of the building erupted every fifteen minutes, spouting steam, water, and fire, but no ash. And every fifteen minutes crowds gathered to ogle the spewing spectacle, the first step to being drawn in. Inside, more wondrous sights awaited gamblers and bystanders alike. A make-believe tropical rain forest with profuse foliage and cascading waterfalls graced the entry. A fifty-seven-foot-long aquarium holding pygmy sharks and tropical fish behind the registration desk amused those waiting to check in. Nature lovers could watch a family of bluenose dolphins in a specially designed marine environment, or Siegfried and Roy's disappearing white tigers displayed in the Secret Garden. Even the $500-a-pull slot machines in a specially reserved section of the casino were something to see, if not play. Capping off the lush surroundings, the resort offered superior guest amenities, setting a world-class standard for service for all the resorts that followed.

Critics were underwhelmed by Wynn's efforts. Believing that the market had moved on, not only to Atlantic City but to the Indian casinos that had begun to open across the country, they thought that Wynn suffered delusions of grandeur, overbuilding and overspending on his illusion in the desert. They were wrong. The Mirage was successful as soon as it opened its doors, proving that the town still had the ability to reinvent itself by knowing what people wanted and then giving them a little bit more. The competition, while not irrelevant, operated on a different plane. Las Vegas had the advantage and it always would. When it came to gaming, which gambling was now known as, it was the real thing.

In June 1990 the Excalibur was the next supercasino to open on the Strip. It had a thousand more rooms than the Mirage and carried the theme of the King Arthur legend throughout the resort complex. Visitors crossed a moat to enter the castle. Guests were addressed as "lords" and "ladies." Medieval troubadours and playful minstrels wandered the premises by day. Knights on horseback jousted at a dinner show at night. The Canterbury Wedding Chapels were available for couples wanting to marry in a merry olde-fashioned atmosphere, adorned in crowns and capes, if that was their pleasure. While not as upscale as the Mirage, the Excalibur was popular among another market segment—parents traveling with children. To meet the needs of families, a video arcade and amusement-park rides were placed in the basement under the casino.

In 1993 growth exploded on the Strip. Steve Wynn blew up the fabled Dunes to make room for the Bellagio (which would be ready for the public in 1998) and welcomed guests to the recently completed Treasure Island, decorated with pieces of eight and fragments of gold. For those wanting to believe that a jackpot of riches came with that one lucky pull at the slots or throw of the dice—and that was just about everyone—the trinkets and trimmings appeared authentic enough. Every ninety minutes, pirates battling sailors on a British man-of-war on a man-made lagoon in front of the hotel provided free entertainment for passersby. As Wynn once instructed, "If you want to make money in a casino . . . the answer is to own one." What he did not say but what became clear over time was that the more extravagant the investment, the more profitable the enterprise.

Kirk Kerkorian apparently agreed with this philosophy, because that same year he completed the new and improved MGM Grand. With five thousand rooms it was huge, much larger than any other hotel-casino in Las Vegas and, therefore, in the world. Circus Circus Enterprises, the corporate owner of the original Circus Circus Hotel and Casino and the Excalibur, also expanded its holdings when it opened the Luxor. The four-thousand-room, thirty-story-high pyramid guarded by a colossal sphinx at the front door immediately became a landmark at the southern end of Las Vegas Boulevard. Entertainment was no longer the enticement that drew visitors to Las Vegas and differentiated one casino from another; the buildings that were cities in and of themselves were the lure. They were expensively built and offered fun and features found only in never-never land. Who would have imagined that the best was yet to come?

By 1996, 30 million visitors crowded casinos and filled ninety-four thousand hotel rooms. Over the next few years, capacity increased 25 percent with the opening of New York New York, Monte Carlo, and Mandalay Bay, among others. These megaresorts were more than just space to be filled with blackjack tables and roulette wheels. They were the means that brought the fantasy of Las Vegas back to life. Once again nobodies could feel like somebodies and middle-class vacationers could live in the lap of luxury, at least for a few days. It might cost more to leave one's cares behind than in the past, but who cared as long as you were having a good time?

As Las Vegas took on an aura of respectability, so did its wedding industry. The Flamingo tore down **Bugsy Siegel's** private suite, a historic reminder of the city's criminal past, to make room

Why visit Paris, France, when Paris Las Vegas is just as romantic and everyone there speaks English?

for a wedding chapel in the garden. At the gigantic theme-based resorts, weddings became larger and more formal, taking on the theme of the setting. The Bellagio, the first of the billion-dollar-plus resorts, has an Old World sophistication, and so do the ceremonies that take place on its premises. Its dancing fountains on the ersatz Lake Como are a tailor-made background for wedding-party pictures. The Paris Las Vegas holds ceremonies with picture-perfect views from atop an exact half-size replica of the Eiffel Tower. Farther down the Strip at the Venetian, gondoliers serenade newlyweds on a gondola ride with nary a pigeon in sight at St. Mark's Square to mar the proceedings.

HIP TO BE SQUARE

"Suddenly the same things I was doing five years ago that were considered pure corn are now perceived to be in," songmeister Wayne Newton quipped in a 1994 interview with a *Time* magazine reporter. "It's a wonderful satisfaction to finally be hip." The independent wedding chapels lining Las Vegas Boulevard north of Sahara, full of kitsch and cupids and a little bit much, were also hip. Rather than being pushed out of business by the upscale, full-service resorts, they found a second life. Sometimes their clients were looking for a second or third (or fourth?) chance at love and marriage. Other times they just wanted to have fun or to take their vows in the presence of Elvis, which had become an industry in and of itself. Business was so good that chapels added rooms and services, such as banquet facilities. A few, like the Viva Las Vegas Wedding Chapel, were completely overhauled, while new chapels, like A Special Memory Wedding Chapel, were constructed from the ground up.

Celebrity marriages that started in Las Vegas and usually ended elsewhere continued to be entertainment newsworthy, generating headlines for the celebrities and publicity for Las Vegas. Shortly after high-fashion model Cindy Crawford settled into wedded bliss with high-profile actor Richard Gere in 1991, she was on *The David Letterman Show* and talked about her wedding. That was good for a few million exposures for the Little Church of the West, where the ceremony was held. Nine years later Oscar winner Angelina Jolie discussed her marriage to Oscar winner Billy Bob Thornton with Jay Leno on *The Tonight Show*. It, too, took place at the Little Church of the West, a picture of which appeared in *People*. Even *Time* rang in with an assessment of how long the marriage would last. Probably not very long, given that Billy Bob has been married four times already, he's twenty years her senior, he's kind of creepy looking, and they got married in Las Vegas. But that's cool.

Movies, not just movie actors, also played a role in making Las Vegas weddings such a hot topic. The 1992 romantic comedy *Honeymoon in Vegas*, for example, starred Nicolas Cage and Sarah Jessica Parker as the young lovers Jack and Betsy. Typical of the times, he does not want to get married; she does. When he has an inexplicable change of heart, there's no time to waste. "Let's get married tomorrow. Let's just do it. Get on a plane. Get to Vegas, and do it. Now," Jack beseeches her. "You're serious?" Betsy questions him. "I must be," Jack responds. "My legs are paralyzed." "Oh, sweetie," she murmurs agreeably. Then in voice-over, Jack continues, "The die was cast. If I had just said city hall, the story would end here. But I didn't, and Betsy and I took our fateful trip to Vegas." With that line Las Vegas is set up to take the fall for everything that follows. Everything includes Jack losing Betsy in a poker game to a high roller with mob connections, to his having to hitch an airplane ride back from Hawaii. But the fanciful adventure has a happy ending. Jack, in a white skydiving jumpsuit, and Betsy, wearing a showgirl costume, take their vows at the Chapel of the Bells in front of a dozen or so "Flying Elvii" as witnesses. Only in Las Vegas, as they say.

As Clark Griswold in the 1997 movie *Vegas Vacation*, Chevy Chase sends up Las Vegas and all that it stands for. Pitching the town as the ideal family vacation spot, Clark says to his skeptical wife and reluctant teenage children, "I'll tell you what there is. There's first-class entertainment, beautiful scenery, bowls of shrimp cocktail, all you can eat. Listen, everybody. Who knows how many more chances we'll get to do something together as a family? I mean, Ellen, you and I are always working. You guys are growing up so fast that I hardly recognize you anymore. Okay, there's one more reason why you should all go. I'm going to remarry your mom, if she'll have me." Again, after a series of misadventures whereby the parents lose their life savings, the children break the bank, and Wayne Newton comps the family to his show, the movie closes on Clark. Down on one knee, he proposes a renewal of vows in front of the neon sign at the Chapel of the Bells. Mom had no idea what they were in for when she said, "I think this will be the greatest vacation, ever." But the funny thing is, it probably was.

Las Vegas weddings got another boost in the 1997 movie *Fools Rush In*, named from the lyrics of the Elvis song "Can't Help Falling in Love." And with all the impetuousness of youth, that's exactly how Alex (Matthew Perry) and Isabel (Salma Hayek) get married: they rush in. Since they are living in Las Vegas, they do not even have to pack a bag to act on their impulse. They just have to get themselves to the chapel.

The chapel itself is quaint, even charming, but the Elvis impersonator who escorts Isabel down the aisle is a bit of a letch, giving the bride a big kiss on the lips and not letting up until Alex grabs his arm. Then Alex runs into problems with his new father-in-law, who believes his daughter has been stolen from him. Too, the couple split for a while over disagreements about careers and babies. Still, this is another romantic comedy, and they eventually make up and remarry on a desert mesa surrounded by loved ones and presumably go on to live in a big house with lots of beautiful, bright children in Vegas, happily ever after.

READY FOR PRIME TIME

When the top-rated television shows among the trendsetting 18- to 34-year-old market segment lampoon a person, place, or thing, that person, place, or thing has been blessed with being "in." And so it came to be with Las Vegas weddings.

In the 1993–94 season of *Beverly Hills 90210*, Brenda Walsh, a 19-year-old college freshman, eloped with Stuart Carson, 24, the wealthy son of one of her father's clients. Only a few weeks earlier they had gone on a blind date arranged by their parents. Who could have imagined this outcome? Certainly not their friends, who followed the capricious couple to Las Vegas to get them to change their minds. The whole gang went—Brenda's twin brother, Brandon, as well as Dylan, Steve, David, Kelly, Donna, and Andrea, too. When they couldn't stop the couple from doing the deed, they accompanied them to the Silver Bell Wedding Chapel, hoping for a last-minute reprieve. But first there was the selection of wedding music and souvenirs.

"Now on to the music. I have Hawaiian, the War Chants, inspirational, 'Love Me Tender,' traditional, the 'Wedding March,'" the receptionist-organist announced.

"The 'Hawaiian War Chants'?" Donna whispered in the background.

"How about if we just take the 'Wedding March,'" Stuart answered in a daze.

"Yeah, that's good. That sounds good," Brenda chimed in, also in a daze.

"And, as an extra touch, we also offer celebrants to throw rice as you leave the chapel," the receptionist-organist continued.

"I don't think we need any more celebrants," Stuart said, looking about.

"Oh, but you do want the rice," states the receptionist-organist.

"Rice. Rice sounds good," Brenda quickly concurred.

"Good. Okay. That's $55 for the license and the silver mock license holder, $40 for the ceremony, $15 for the audiocassette, $40 for the videocassette, $25 for photos, $40 for the live organist and the rice, which makes a grand total of $215. Will that be cash or charge?"

Now, if that was not enough to throw some cold water on what the twosome was undertaking, the minister about to unite them forever and a day just might have been. "In the world of alienation and poverty and war and misery, perhaps we most truly reveal our belief in possibilities when we make the commitment to share our lives forever," he thundered. "It is not a decision entered into lightly, for marriage is not a gambol across sunlit meadows. Oh, no. It is a long and arduous journey through a dark forest fraught with unseen dangers and sometimes disappointments." That did it for Brenda, anyhow. Later, dancing with Stuart, she said, "Just because you're not my husband doesn't mean I don't love you." Calling to mind not Amtrak, but another romantic destination, he replied, "Yeah. Well, we'll always have Vegas."

The friends of *Friends* also went to Las Vegas. Just like their younger counterparts but a few years later, they went to rescue one of their own in the cliffhanger episodes of the 1998–99 season. Joey's role in an independent film in Las Vegas had fallen through, so to save face he had become one of the Caesars at Caesars Palace, a job requiring him to parade around the casino in a plumed helmet and metal breastplate as part of his costume. (This is saving face?) The gang wanted him home and went to retrieve him.

While in Las Vegas, just about everyone behaved badly, which is what you are supposed to do in Las Vegas. Having some free time, Phoebe played the slots, but got into an argument with some "lurkers," old people who pounce on slot machines others have given up. Monica and Chandler had an argument, but made up while winning throw after throw at craps. Believing their streak was a sign, they decided to get married at one of the wedding chapels on Las Vegas Boulevard. Rachel and Ross got drunk and joined them at the wedding chapel. Which couple got hitched? Why, the dynamic duo that had had a few too many, of course. According to popular mythology, it couldn't have happened any other way. By the way, Rachel and Ross got divorced by the end of the next season. Monica and Chandler, having made the mature decision and waited, got married after several seasons.

There were plenty of laughs in a 1999 episode of *The Simpsons* when both Homer and his next-door neighbor Ned

Reflecting the Roman Empire in its heyday, fighting gladiators and warring centurions line the corridors at Caesars Palace.

got married in Las Vegas. No, they did not marry Marge and Maude, their respective wives. And, no, they did not marry each other. Having gone to Las Vegas so that Homer could teach Ned how to have fun, they had gotten drunk and married some bimbos they had met in a bar. At least that is what they were informed when they awoke the next morning. They couldn't remember a thing, but the videotape labeled "Precious Memories—Impulse Weddings" seemed genuine. Run out of town for "dishonoring their marriage vows," they returned to Springfield, telling

Marge and Maude that they had been abducted by aliens at Wal-Mart.

Such is life in prime time, to be repeated in perpetuity on reruns and in syndication, maybe even making a "Best of" DVD, and winning over future generations of fans.

FOR BETTER OR FOR WORSE

Through the ages Las Vegas has been concerned about the image of its wedding industry. It is an important source of income for the city. By some estimates it accounts for 10–12 percent of the city's annual gaming revenues, when food, lodging, and entertainment expenses of the newlyweds and their guests, along with the marriage-license costs and chapel fees, are taken into account. Unfortunately, when money is to be made, there will always be someone eager to get his or her hands a little dirty to land a share.

The scams went as far back as 1939, when the Gable divorce set the wedding industry on its future course. One enterprising promoter sat around the courthouse after hours waiting for the lovelorn in search of the marriage license bureau. He told them that the bureau was closed, but he would find someone to issue a license "for a consideration." Technically, the promoter was not acting illegally, because the bureau was closed. On the other hand, it was the policy of the county clerk's office to issue licenses out of hours as a service to out-of-town visitors, so the promoter was not doing much of anything for anyone. He was picked up, given a lecture on civil service, and sent on his way. The fleecing of love doves, as easy as shooting clay pigeons and a whole lot more profitable, had begun.

Sometimes simple misunderstandings between the wedding chapel and the betrothed grew into incidents. Or were they really simple misunderstandings? In a story reported in the *Las Vegas Evening Review-Journal* in July 1941, a Bakersfield couple deposited $14 with the proprietors of a chapel for a service to be performed by a Methodist minister. When the best man located the minister in question, the marriage was performed elsewhere. After trying without success to get their deposit back from the original chapel the newlyweds turned the matter over to the police, who in turn passed it along to the city attorney. Having some clout, the city attorney convinced chapel management to split the difference. All was not lost, except possibly later at the gambling halls.

The city attorney saw it all. Six months later, concerned about wedding chapels charging exorbitant rates for minimum services, he went in front of the city government and proposed raising the quarterly fee on wedding chapels from $25 to $250 as a means of exerting some control. To support his plan, he was armed with numerous protests from couples who claimed certain wedding chapels had conned them. "Something should be done to see that these marriage couples are protected. The marriage business is one of the most lucrative in the community, but it won't be for long if the racketeers invade the wedding chapel business," he prophesied.

The cry for legitimacy and respectability for the wedding-chapel business was taken up once again in a July 1945 *Las Vegas Evening Review-Journal* editorial. The occasion was the issuance of the one hundred thousandth marriage license by the Clark County clerk. Noting that the wedding business would grow rapidly with the end of the war and the subsequent easing of travel restrictions, the writer remarked that now was the time to pass rules and regulations for those wanting to open a wedding chapel. "There was too much stigma of a racket attached to the operation of some of the marriage chapels of the past," the writer put forth, "and Las Vegas' name as a friendly city was attacked time after time by honeymooners who were gouged."

In a 1947 editorial, new issues raised the hair on the back of the necks of community watchdogs. One issue concerned $2 kickbacks that were dispensed by wedding chapels, justices of the peace, former district judges, and some ministers to taxicab drivers and other "runners" for directing customers to their door. Another question was the ordination of ministers for the single purpose of being able to perform marriage ceremonies and "getting in on the system." After all, "the marriage business should have some sacredness at the time it is performed," the author pointed out. "The marriage business is plentiful to take care of everyone without having to develop angles by which more revenues can be steered into one person's pockets."

"Oh, to be 'Marry'n Sam' in Las Vegas," a newspaper reporter wrote in 1950. "Even performing the one dollar special, a person could get rich." Yes, being a Marry'n Sam was nice work if you could get it. The term came from the *Li'l Abner* comic strip, where the preacher by that name specialized in $2 weddings. In Las Vegas it referred to a justice of the peace, who by statute could charge $5 for each civil ceremony and, in addition, usually received a tip. It was an elected position for which eager candidates who could do the math would lay out several thousand dollars to support their campaigns for the job. And the demand was there. In 1952, the United Press dubbed Las Vegas justice James Down the "Marry'n Sam of the United States." Conducting approximately six thousand nuptials annually, he "had hitched more people than any other one person in the country."

The justice of the peace wedding business went out of business with the creation of the Office of Civil Marriages in 1969. The process was modified because the number of marriages was so great that it slowed down the running of the courts. They were replaced with commissioners on paid salary who collected the fee and conducted the ceremony. The fee was established at $25 during weekdays, $30 after 5:00 p.m. and on weekends, and the revenues went to fill the county coffers. As a service, the commissioners worked in pairs, so one could act as witness if the couple hadn't brought their own. Today the fee is $50, as is the cost of the marriage license, but the commissioners still work in pairs. For the graveyard shift, the security guard at the building will lend a hand. By state law the office is to provide a "tranquil atmosphere" and to conduct the ceremony "in a dignified manner without haste." And it does.

Ministers working in wedding chapels, religious Marry'n Sams, if you will, also had a good thing going. In 1960 the top five ministers carried out more than a third of the twenty thousand marriages that year, for which they received $3 to $5 plus tip. In order to be qualified by the state to preside at weddings, they were required to have an active ministry. This was generally interpreted as having a congregation for whom they regularly conducted bona fide church services. But someone was not paying attention. That same year a grand jury was convened to look into the complaint that a number of unqualified individuals, somehow, some way, had received state certification to conduct weddings. The community was aghast, particularly as the investigation came on the heels of another scandal, the revocation of the Reverend Glynn Wolfe's certification for having been married too many times. As reported in the paper, "Twelve wives was a few too many to maintain the moral standards of a minister."

Let's jump ahead thirty years. In 1990, twenty-three wedding chapels lined Las Vegas Boulevard, twice as many as a decade earlier. Competition was fierce, so the chapels did everything they could to attract couples seeking to tie the knot. For those wanting something wet and wild, the Villa Roma Hotel arranged weddings in an open-air Jacuzzi built into the trunk of a thirty-two-foot-long limousine. The $350 package included a ride down the Strip while drinking champagne and listening to the "Wedding March." For the romantically inclined, a simple ceremony for two at the Candlelight Wedding Chapel could be set up, just as it was shown on NBC's *Today* show on Valentine's Day. Despite the state of California having relaxed its marriage laws in the early eighties to match Nevada's, business could not have been better.

But little else had changed. Wedding chapels were under attack for the shoddy way they treated their clientele. Rush, rush,

Elvis lives! And he works in a Las Vegas wedding chapel.

rush down the aisle because the chapel had overbooked was one objection. Ring, ring, ring of the cash register because the newlyweds had been pressured into signing up for live organ music and other extras was another. Failure to disclose that the minister's fee was extra or that tips were the sole compensation for the limousine driver was also aggravating and ended up on the bottom line. Ministers did not fare any better in the latest harangue. Are the ministers who perform chapel ceremonies "more men of business than men of God?" questioned a newspaper reporter for the *Las Vegas Review-Journal*. "We have a number of ministers throughout the state who think of nothing but how much money they will make performing marriages," stated one of their own.

In the new millennium the issues have not changed, although they have taken on new, and in some cases otherworldly, dimensions. "Some chapels don't treat weddings seriously," Kent Ripley, an Elvis impersonator at the Graceland Wedding Chapel, lamented to a staff reporter for the *Washington Post* in May 2001. "They're giving Elvis a bad name." Passionate about the subject, he continued, "I don't know where to draw the line, but we need some oversight."

Clark County clerk Shirley Parraguirre thought her office could provide the appropriate guidance. While not concerned with protecting the image of the King, she wanted to shield consumers from fraud perpetrated by those who called themselves ministers but did not have any ministerial functions. It had become too easy to go on the Internet and become ordained for a fee. So she dusted off the twenty-person congregation rule plus an almost unknown mandate that a criminal background check be conducted on anyone applying for certification to marry others. No matter how well intentioned her actions, the American Civil Liberties Union made such a fuss decrying the lack of separation of church and state that the matter went to the Nevada legislature to sort out. Until there is a resolution, buyers should beware of the bogus minister looking to separate them from their money. Hey, isn't that what casinos are for?

HAPPILY EVER AFTER

As freewheeling and happy-go-lucky as ever, the Las Vegas wedding industry continues to thrive. It was certainly to the town's benefit when Barbara Tober, the longtime editor in chief of *Bride's* magazine, in 1994 anointed it an official wedding destination. "Getting married in Vegas used to be a tawdry thing to do," she declared, "but now people look at a wedding day as fun. Las Vegas takes all the angst and difficulty out of getting married." Most couples are thrilled with their marriage ceremonies, even if their marriages lack the excitement they found, if just for a moment, in the self-proclaimed Wedding Capital of the World.

Charlotte Richards, the self-proclaimed Queen of the Las Vegas Wedding Industry, reigns over this world, or at least the old-fashioned part north of the resort casinos on the Strip. The owner of four wedding establishments, including the famed Little White Wedding Chapel, she proudly carries on the tradition of quickie weddings in surroundings of questionable, if not tacky, taste. Not that her clientele, caught up in the emotions of the day, seem to mind the heavy gilded mirror frames, the elaborate crystal chandeliers, and the oversize arrangements of fake flowers. Besides, it is all part of the atmosphere.

Charlotte, an ordained minister, started in the business over forty years ago with her late husband, Merle. Claiming to have conducted hundreds of thousands of ceremonies herself, she has probably seen everything there is to see walking down the aisle, from pregnant, barefoot brides to couples dressed in gorilla suits. Expanding her business with innovative alternatives, she has contributed to the perception of contemporary Las Vegas weddings as being weird and wacky, according to some, and wonderful and fanciful to others. The drive-up wedding concept, whereby couples stay in their cars to say their vows, was hers. Then she expanded it in 1998 with the Tunnel of Love, a partially enclosed driveway that has been painted and decorated. "It's going to be simply beautiful," she declared shortly before its opening. "Stars will twinkle. Birds will float on ribbons, and there will be signs everywhere saying, 'I love you, I want you, I need you—I can't live without you.'"

It is hardly surprising that Charlotte turned the three millionth Las Vegas nuptials into a happening. The marriage of Marlen and Alberto Recio of Miami, Florida, first took place on February 9, 2001, but the Clark County recorder's office did not discover the event until March. "We knew it was coming," a spokeman said. "But when you're doing 450 marriages a day, the first priority is to record those marriages." So the Recios, as well as the couples preceding and following them, were invited back to do it again. The second time took place at Charlotte's We've Only Just Begun Wedding Chapel in the Imperial Palace Hotel Casino on July 3, ninety-two years to the day after Clark County's first recorded wedding. Television cameras and news crews turned out en masse to capture the celebration for posterity.

Showgirls dressed to the hilt served as attendants. An Elvis impersonator gave away the bride. Celebrity look-alikes from James Brown to Madonna acted as witnesses. Was it over the top? Most definitely. Could anything remotely like it be found anywhere else? Definitely not. Will it happen again, say for the four millionth wedding couple? Bet on it.

"The Wedding Place of The Stars"

2

STAR LIGHT, STAR BRIGHT

Hollywood stars have always found their way to the Little Church of the West, despite its having been moved three times.

JUST AS BUGSY SIEGEL had predicted, celebrities have been drawn to Las Vegas like moths to a flame. Sometimes they come for the lights, action, and excitement. Other times they come to rest and relax. And sometimes, just like anyone else, they come to get married.

As a group, the rich and famous are notorious for marrying often, if not always choosing well. Some might call it a character flaw. For Hungarian beauty Zsa Zsa Gabor, known for her eight trips down the aisle, it was part of her personal philosophy. "A girl must marry for love," she once pronounced, "and keep on marrying until she finds it." For Cary Grant, who did it five times, it was part of his boyish nature. "When I am married, I want to be single, and when I am single, I want to be married," he charmingly explained in an interview. Las Vegas was convenient to reach from Hollywood, the other center of the universe where starlight has the highest wattage of all, and it was tailor-made for any well-known figure seeking privacy, or publicity, or who was just in a hurry.

In all probability the more times a celebrity has been married, the greater the chances that at least one of those marriages took place in Las Vegas. Four of Mickey Rooney's eight marriages happened in the City of Lights. So did one of Frank Sinatra's four, two of Judy Garland's five, and one of Elizabeth Taylor's eight, but neither of the two times she married Richard Burton. Richard Burton, as it happens, also got married one out of five times in Las Vegas.

While chances are better than fifty-fifty—the national divorce rate—that a celebrity couple will split up, there is no way of predicting which couples will make it or how long the union might last. Indeed, some very happy, long-lasting celebrity marriages started in Las Vegas. Kirk Douglas and Anne Buydens, Paul Newman and Joanne Woodward, Michael Caine and Shakira Baksh,

85

and Bette Midler and Martin von Haselberg—these are a few of the high-profile names that come to mind. All right, very few names come to mind, but Bette and Martin felt their marriage was strong enough to withstand being the focus of a television situation comedy some sixteen years after the fact. The marriage survived, even when the series did not.

Every wedding tells a story, not only about the celebrities involved, but also about the town in which it took place. Even a little bit about ourselves can be found between the lines. Lana Turner, who twice eloped to Las Vegas before she was 21, once asked, "How does it happen that something that makes so much sense in the moonlight doesn't make any sense at all in the sunlight?" It seems to be the eternal question, one passed down from generation to generation. Over fifty years later in 1992, 16-year-old model turned up-and-coming actress Milla Jovovich eloped to Las Vegas with Shawn Andrews, her 21-year-old costar in the movie *Dazed and Confused,* only to have the marriage annulled two months later. Then she did it again with movie director Luc Besson, 43, in 1997. Her second marriage lasted seventeen months.

CHAPTER 4

In the Heat of the Night

Couples have been eloping for as long as girls have had fathers who did not like their beaux. Add the rashness of youth and the thrill of illicit love, and it is easy to understand why the road to Las Vegas has become a well-traveled one. Yet of the celebrities discussed in this chapter, all had left childhood far behind. Only Linda Darnell was a couple years shy of her twenty-first birthday when she ran away to get married to a much older man. So it would be too glib to say that the others only acted as youngsters. Each had his or her own unique agenda. John Huston was seduced, Nelson Eddy was on the rebound, and Richard Gere was under the gun.

JOHN HUSTON

Movie director John Huston, 39, married for the third time on impulse. He had been dating Marrietta Fitzgerald, an unhappily married New York sophisticate, when Evelyn Keyes, 26, who had played Scarlett O'Hara's younger sister on the silver screen, proposed over dinner. She was young, attractive, and companionable, and he had been drinking, but he still hesitated a moment or two. "Hell, Evelyn, we hardly know each other," he protested. "Do you know of a better way for us to get to know each other?" she countered. Apparently not, for John called a stunt-pilot friend of his to charter a plane and fly them from Los Angeles to Las Vegas. By four o'clock that morning he and Evelyn were married in front of a justice of the peace.

87

It was 1946. John had spent the war years making documentaries for the army, and he was eager to resume his career as a moviemaker, as well as the pursuit of his many outdoor interests, including breeding Thoroughbreds. These were busy years, and he had several box-office winners, including *The Treasure of the Sierra Madre* and *Key Largo* in 1948, and a winning filly named Lady Bruce. When John was not acquiring screenplays, scouting locations, or shooting film, the couple spent much of their free time on his ranch, home to not only horses and dogs, but cats, monkeys, parakeets, pigs, goats, and a mule or two as well. Evelyn pluckily tried to fit into his life, but her animal allergies, among other problems, made it difficult and uncomfortable for her to do so. In 1950 they were granted a Mexican divorce.

MARC ANTHONY

"We're getting married tonight," pop salsa singing sensation Marc Anthony, 31, told his surprised fiancée, Dayanara Torres, 25, a former Miss Universe, on May 9, 2000. The couple had been inseparable ever since they had met two years before in a nightclub in her native Puerto Rico. Neither had been married before although Marc had a 6-year-old daughter from a previous relationship. He had surprised Dayanara once before—with a five-carat engagement ring he had designed. This time he planned on carrying out his honorable intentions.

After Marc performed at the Blockbuster Entertainment Awards in Los Angeles, the couple and about fifteen guests boarded two rented jets to whisk them off to Las Vegas. At midnight in the penthouse at the Desert Inn they said their vows in front of a minister. The reception afterward was romantic. Marc serenaded his bride with his hit "You Sang to Me." Then a food fight broke out. When dancing their first dance together, friends pelted the couple with chunks of frosted wedding cake. Wasn't anyone familiar with the custom of throwing rice?

The honeymoon lasted two years. Marc continued to tour, often with Dayanara standing stage right during concerts. He was so happy that he would introduce his ballads moaning lost love by apologizing. "When I wrote this," he would say contritely, "I have no idea what the hell I was thinking." And when he wasn't touring, he was recording. But Dayanara was not happy. Although they had had a son together, she felt that she could not compete with his all-consuming career. So she walked.

The split lasted three months. To celebrate their reunion, they had an elaborate $500,000 renewal ceremony and reception in the Puerto Rican town where they had first met. The beautiful bride wore an exquisite off-the-shoulder white wedding gown. The groom looked spiffy in his tuxedo. "It was the most nerve-racking moment of my life," Marc declared, teary-eyed. "I could not contain everything I was feeling." Over two hundred guests attended. Throngs of fans greeted them as they emerged from the church. They partied with dancing and singing. It was a fairy-tale wedding, and no one threw cake. Some things are better left in Las Vegas.

NELSON EDDY

Nelson Eddy was one-half of the romantic duo known as "America's Singing Sweethearts" during Hollywood's golden age. From 1935 to 1942 he and Jeanette MacDonald made eight movie blockbusters for Metro-Goldwyn-Mayer, thrilling millions of fans around the world with their on-screen, passionate relationship. Away from the camera, too, Jeanette was the love of Nelson's life. "No woman has ever satisfied me as she does," he declared to friends. "It goes beyond sex."

Jeannette reciprocated his feelings. Their relationship, deeply emotional and strongly physical, lasted throughout their lives; however, they never married. Louis B. Mayer, the tyrannical head of MGM, refused to allow it.

While Mayer had always been fond of Jeanette (in fact, it

was rumored that they had had an affair early in her career), he despised Nelson, calling him "that goddamned baritone." He knew Jeanette placed her career front and center of her life, and he had the power to use this insight to get Jeanette to do what he wanted. In this case, he wanted her to marry Gene Raymond, another MGM actor, and to stay married. He believed that this was the best way of assuring the box-office appeal of Nelson and Jeanette as a couple.

Three years after Jeanette's marriage, Nelson came to the realization that he would never be able to make her his wife. In desperate straits, he took desperate action: he eloped to Las Vegas with another woman.

And so on January 19, 1939, Nelson and Ann Franklin, his bride-to-be, took the train to Las Vegas. Nelson had been drinking so heavily that he later claimed that the judge must have been paid off, "because no one could have ethically performed the ceremony seeing the shape I was in." His mother, hoping to dissuade Nelson from what he was about to do, had accompanied the couple. She later described the service as taking place in "a rough, bare room without one item of beauty around." On the return train trip Nelson awoke from a nap without any recollection of where he had been or what he had done.

Unfortunately, the events of the day were an omen of the days to come. At 44 years old, Ann was seven years Nelson's senior, and she had had him in her sights since her divorce six years earlier. Nelson had thought she was compassionate and understanding, particularly as it concerned his feelings toward Jeanette. In reality, Ann was mean and vindictive, with little or no consideration for her husband or anyone else.

Once Ann had snared Nelson, she was not letting go. No, he did not love her. Yes, they fought all the time. But he was hers. A few months after the wedding, he asked for a divorce and offered her a nice settlement. She turned him down. On their one-year anniversary, he tried again, to no avail. And if he pushed too much, she would bring out compromising pictures she had taken of him and threaten to ruin his career.

Nelson survived his marriage by working hard. He made several more pictures with Jeanette before they both finally left MGM, bitter over their treatment. When his movie career was over, he resumed his singing career. When he died in 1967 at the age of 66, following Jeanette to the grave by two years, his widow, Ann, knew that he had finally slipped out of her control. She startled other mourners at his funeral by commenting to Jeanette's widowed husband, "Now they can sing together forever."

LINDA DARNELL

American beauty Linda Darnell was living the Hollywood dream. As a shy, introverted 14-year-old, she was spotted by a talent scout and given an all-expenses-paid trip from her Dallas home to California for a screen test. When she was 15, she was put under contract at Twentieth Century Fox. At 16, she starred in her first film, *Hotel for Women*. At 17, she showed off her youthful charm in *Star Dust,* an autobiographical coming-of-age story about a poor girl making it big in the movies. Tyrone Power, Henry Fonda, and John Payne were among her leading men. In 1943, at the age of 19, she married J. Peverell Marley, 42, the cameraman on most of her early films.

A sergeant in the army for the past four months, Pev was home on a three-day pass when he proposed. Linda immediately accepted because his absence had made her realize how much she missed and needed him. They hurriedly made arrangements to pick up Private Bill Heath to be Pev's best man, and Ann Miller, Linda's fellow actress and best friend, to be the maid of honor. By four o'clock on the afternoon of April 18, the wedding party was on the road to Las Vegas for a simple ceremony in front of a justice of the peace.

The elopement shocked Linda's family; her mother began ranting and raving when she heard the news. The studio was so concerned about the impact on her image of her marrying a much older man that they suspended her. Columnist Louella

Parsons rallied the public to her cause. "Little Linda Darnell deserves happiness," she wrote. Eventually, Twentieth Century–Fox recanted, casting her in a cameo as a radiant Virgin Mary in the Oscar-winning *The Song of Bernadette.*

For a time the marriage served them well. Pev, entranced by her beauty, loved her very much. Linda, in turn, appreciated his kindness and warmth. He also had a mischievous, fun side, and he was able to draw her out. Yet they both had busy professional lives and were seldom between movies at the same time. As Linda matured, becoming more sophisticated and self-reliant, she began to wean herself from her husband. In 1950 they officially separated.

Shortly before her death at 42 in fire, Linda was reminiscing with friends and fondly recalled the marriage. "I used to wait for him after we'd finished shooting and spill my guts to him. I sure never thought I'd end up marrying the guy," she mused. "Pev may not have been the most polished man in the world, but he was dependable and honest. And he understood Hollywood. He taught me a lot." Sometimes one can't ask for much more than that.

BETTE MIDLER

"Oh, nev-air, nev-air!" summed up Bette Midler's views on marriage for nearly forty years. Life was pretty good for the pop diva known to her fans as the Divine Miss M. She even was an Academy Award nominee for her performance in *The Rose.* Then she met commodity broker–performance artist Martin von Haselberg, better known to his audience as Harry Kipper of the Kipper Brothers. One Saturday night he proposed, she accepted the proposal, and they took off for Las Vegas.

The four-hour drive was fun, a lark. Arriving at two in the morning, they got their marriage license right away. Then they checked into Caesars Palace and changed clothes. They were going to do this in style! Bette had brought a dress, presumably something slinky and showing lots of cleavage, which she had worn to a movie premiere. Martin had brought two suits. The one Bette nixed was a houndstooth check straight out of *The Music Man*. The other, a plain black suit, was not very interesting, but acceptable.

The next stop was the Candlelight Wedding Chapel. With a tape of *Juliet of the Spirits* playing in the background, a minister, who moonlighted as an Elvis impersonator, joined the two as man and wife. The date was December 16, 1984.

On the ride back to Los Angeles, the high spirits of their wedding day dissipated as the impact of what they had done hit them. Although Bette and Martin had been dating steadily for the past two months, they really did not know each other that well. Bette later admitted in an interview, "For the first couple of weeks after we got married it was 'Uh-oh, what did we do?' There were some rough spots, but we did our talking, we did our compromising. Fortunately, we liked what we got to know."

In fall 2000 the union was immortalized in the situation comedy *Bette*, in which Bette played a version of herself in a version of her life complete with a loving and levelheaded husband and a feisty teenage daughter. Although the program was taken off the air after one season, the couple plays on.

JOAN CRAWFORD

Glamorous Hollywood movie actress Joan Crawford and the high-powered president of Pepsi-Cola, Alfred Steele, eloped to Las Vegas after determining that their wedding plans had gotten out of control. So instead of a New Jersey garden party for five hundred of their closest friends, relatives, and associates at the home of the friends who had introduced them, the couple opted for a private affair without press, photographers, or television cameras intruding on the moment. They made their decision over a business dinner on May 9, 1955. A few hours later in the penthouse suite at the Flamingo Hotel, a municipal judge pronounced them man and wife.

Although the nuptials had been toned down, the honeymoon was not. The Alfred Steeles sailed on May 26 on the *United States* to Europe. Joan's luggage consisted of four enormous trunks constructed in a way so that nothing in her wardrobe needed to be folded or ironed, plus several boxes to carry hats, shoes, and cosmetics. She needed everything she had brought, too. They were feted everywhere they went—London, Paris, Rome, and the Isle of Capri.

When Joan married Alfred, her fourth and last husband, she was 50 years old and had four adopted children. He was 55 with two children from two previous marriages. They not only loved each other, but also admired and respected one another. Although she was still involved in the movies, the films that had made her a star, including *Mildred Pierce*, for which she had won the 1945 Best Actress Oscar, were behind her. She had time to devote to the man in her life. In this case, this meant not only Alfred's home life, but also his business life. By the time he died four years later, Joan had become so enmeshed in the soft drink business, using her celebrity status to garner publicity and promote Pepsi, that she was given his seat on the board of directors by a grateful company. After logging 125,000 miles, signing autographs for hours at a time, and attracting tens of thousands of fans to bottle-plant openings, she had certainly earned it.

RICHARD GERE AND CINDY CRAWFORD

For beautiful people, superstar Richard Gere and supermodel Cindy Crawford met in the most traditional of ways: standing over the grill at a backyard barbecue. Good friend and celebrity photographer Herb Ritts had hosted the party. Herb's mother introduced them and encouraged them to go out. They dated for over three years, keeping their relationship secret for most of that time. Shortly after Richard made his triumphant return to movies, first with the 1990 cop thriller *Internal Affairs*, followed soon afterward with the megahit *Pretty Woman*, Cindy gave him an ultimatum: marry me or leave me. Truly in love, Richard arranged for the Disney studio, for whom he was in the middle of making a picture, to fly them to Las Vegas on a company jet so that they could tie the knot that night. It was the first time he had made such a commitment.

And so on December 12, 1991, at 11:00 p.m. at the Little Church of the West, Richard, 42, took Cindy, 25, to be his lawfully wedded wife. It was another casual Las Vegas affair for one of Hollywood's most glamorous couples. Richard hadn't shaved. Cindy wore a pantsuit. The $510 nondenominational ceremony required his and her rings, which, because of lack of preparation, were sculpted out of aluminum foil. Yet Richard personalized the vows, promising to serve the bride breakfast in bed for six months. Before returning to Los Angeles so that Richard could make his 5:00 a.m. call, the wedding party, including Herb Ritts, who took pictures, and Ed Limato, Richard's agent, proceeded to a Denny's Restaurant for a late dinner.

The couple appeared happy, and the marriage seemed off to a good start. On *Late Night with David Letterman*, Cindy professed, "I've wanted [marriage] for a while. It feels nice." She added, "It wasn't so scary after all." Yet there were signs that not everything was as it appeared. Richard opted for touring Buddhist sites in India as a vacation, while Cindy's ideal holiday was getting sand between her toes on the French Riviera. They spent over a year and a half house hunting, usually separately. And everywhere they went, they had to listen to rumors that Richard was gay, Cindy a lesbian, and their marriage a sham.

While nonplussed at first by the gossip, the couple had a change of heart and felt compelled to address it. They placed a $30,000 advertisement in the *London Sun* on May 6, 1994. "We are heterosexual and monogamous," they proclaimed. "And take our commitment to each other very seriously."

Maybe so, but by the time their $5 million, ten-thousand-square-foot Georgian-style mansion in Bel Air was decorated, Cindy was seeking comfort in the arms of her former flame, Rande Gerber. By the end of the year, their marriage was a bust.

Richard and Cindy could not overcome their personality differences, and the union was officially dissolved in 1995. Reflecting on his friends' divorce, Herb Ritts mused, "In terms of life experiences, she is very different from where Richard is. He's spiritual. Cindy gave it a try, but she's not into eating yak butter." He went on to say, "I've been on the phone with both of them in tears. It's really sad." When good marriages go bad, it usually is.

CHAPTER 5

In Love and in Town

Convenience has always been among the reasons couples marry in Las Vegas. The 24/7 open-door policy has been the modus operandi since the first chapel opened for business in 1933. It has meant a welcoming smile and a congratulatory handshake regardless of the time of day or day of week a couple arrive in town and want to say their vows. When busy work schedules prevent more opulent nuptials, celebrities derive a similar benefit from marrying in Las Vegas. Whether they have a third performance scheduled for the middle of the night or give encores until the wee hours of the morning, they can simply walk into a chapel afterward. Nothing, however, beats the convenience of living in town. Just ask Wayne Newton.

NANCY SINATRA JR.

The September 1960 nuptials of Nancy Sinatra, 20, and Tommy Sands, 23, was front-page news in the *Las Vegas Review-Journal*. NANCY, TOM WED IN GALA CEREMONY, proclaimed the headline. Not only was the groom a teen idol whose song "Teen-age Crush" had sold a million copies, but earlier in the year the bride's father, Frank, and his friends had been firmly ensconced in the Copa Room at the Sands Hotel and Casino. Making the movie *Ocean's Eleven* by day and partying in front of a live audience by night, the Rat Pack had focused the attention of the entertainment world on the town and made the Strip the most happening place.

The four o'clock Sunday afternoon service and reception

were held in the specially decorated Emerald Room at the now established, hip Sands Hotel. Nancy wore a street-length gown of white lace and carried a white orchid bouquet. Tommy, serving a six-month reserve tour with the air force, wore his uniform. Among the thirty-five guests celebrating with the newlyweds were the bride's divorced parents; her brother and sister; the groom's parents; Sammy Davis Jr. and his fiancée, actress May Britt; ex–baseball players Joe DiMaggio and Leo Durocher; and songwriter Jimmy Van Heusen.

Frank and his daughter were very close, and he frequently spoiled her with presents. For her sixteenth birthday, he gave her a mink coat. For her seventeenth birthday, it was the first pink Thunderbird in the United States. As a wedding gift, he gave her little diamond star earrings, and he cried when he walked her down the aisle. To reporters afterward, he publicly welcomed Tommy into the family, announcing that he was glad to have another singer in the family because "I'm getting tired." He wouldn't pose for pictures, however, saying, "This is Nancy's day and I don't want to horn in."

Proud papa Frank Sinatra escorts daughter Nancy down the aisle at her nuptials to pop singer Tommy Sands.

Throughout their five-year marriage, Tommy frequently found himself competing with Frank for Nancy's attention and admiration. One Christmas Frank gave her a $10,000 leopard coat, an extravagant item that Tommy could not have afforded. Tommy, hoping to escape Frank's influence, convinced Nancy to move to New York. Yet wherever they were, Nancy sought out her father's advice. Tommy eventually tired of the situation and simply left.

At first Nancy was devastated by her husband's decision to split, but she was tough. She screwed up her courage and got married for a second time. Her nuptials with Hugh Lambert were also in Las Vegas. Moving along with her life, Nancy began a pop singing career, and her 1965 song "These Boots Were Made for Walkin'," an anthem for the recently liberated, was a hit. In 1967 her father once again stood by her side, and not just to walk her down the aisle. Their duet "Somethin' Stupid" was the number one best-selling song in America and England that year.

REDD FOXX

After Redd Foxx had worked his way up from the "Chitlin' Circuit," the trade name for the black clubs and music halls around the country, with his rather blue, down-and-dirty brand of stand-up comedy to the glamorous venue of Las Vegas showrooms, he thought he had it made. However, he found even greater success playing Los Angeles junkman Fred Sanford on television's *Sanford and Son*. It seemed as if he had spent his entire career preparing for the role of "an old black dude" who "don't take no stuff." But Redd loved Las Vegas and always found reasons to return.

In 1977 in the middle of the show's six-season run, Redd, 54, was in Las Vegas and got married for the third time. His new wife, Korean-born Yun Chi Chung, 34, was immediately incorporated into his routine. "Do you want a license?" the clerk at the Las Vegas marriage bureau asked. "I don't," the comedian responded. Then he added, "But I think she does." Later performing at the Thunderbird Hotel, Redd described to the audience how the couple had met. "I just opened my wallet," he said with a surprised look on his face, "and there she was." And then, there she wasn't, possibly because of the jokes that Redd made at her expense.

In 1991 Redd did it again. A couple of years earlier the IRS had caught up with him. His high-rolling, big-spending ways had not left him with enough resources to pay the tax man, so the tax man came calling at his three-bedroom Las Vegas home and stripped it clean. Not one to stay down for very long, he landed the lead role as patriarch Al Royal on a new television situation comedy, *The Royal Family*. And in July he married again in Las Vegas. His fourth wife, Kaho Cho, thirtyish, was also Korean-born.

Redd Foxx felt fortunate. Della Reese, his TV wife on *The Royal Family* and a pal from his early club days, says of that period in his life, "He was always speaking to me about how happy he was. He said he was a man with two new wives and a TV series." Clutching his heart as he had done so many times before for laughs on *Sanford and Son*, Redd died of a heart attack during a rehearsal for *The Royal Family* in October of the same year.

WAYNE NEWTON

Wayne Newton grew up in Las Vegas. When he arrived in town with his brother, he had only $20 in his pocket. When he played his first singing gig in the lounge at the Fremont Casino in Glitter Gulch downtown in 1957, he needed a work permit because he was only 15 years old. By the time he married Elaine Okamura at the Little Church of the West in 1968, a mere eleven years later, he had moved uptown, professionally, financially, and socially. As the headliner in the main room at the Flamingo Hotel on the Strip, he was earning $25,000 per week. His friend and sometime employer Kirk Kerkorian, owner of the Flamingo, hosted their reception.

Wayne and Elaine were married for fourteen years. From the start they had problems. Her middle-class Japanese American family looked down on his Indian heritage and poor southern background, while his parents disliked her because she was Japanese. Eventually his grueling performance schedule served to distance them from each other, and other women began to catch Wayne's eye. However, before the passion ran out, Wayne and Elaine adopted a daughter. Wayne raised her near Las Vegas on the Casa de Shenadoah, his fifty-two-acre ranch named for his Virginian birthplace.

In the years following his divorce, Wayne continued to perform regularly, earning a hefty paycheck that appeared to support his extravagant lifestyle. However, Wayne had never learned how to manage his money. After several bad business managers had gotten him involved in a series of bad investments, he was forced into Chapter 11 bankruptcy. Keeping his morale intact while he put his affairs in order was Kathleen McCrone, a woman whom Wayne had first seen in the audience at one of his performances at the Las Vegas Hilton. In a lavish candlelit ceremony at the Casa de Shenadoah on April 9, 1994, the blond, blue-eyed 30-year-old Cleveland lawyer became the second Mrs. Wayne Newton.

Today Wayne reigns once again as the King of Las Vegas, and the boulevard leading to McCarran International Airport bears his name. He has performed live before over 30 million people, with over twenty-five thousand shows in Las Vegas alone. On New Year's Eve 2000 Wayne kicked off his landmark contract, worth a reported $250 million, with the Stardust Hotel and Casino. Forty weeks a year for the next ten years, Wayne will be snapping his fingers, flashing his pearly white teeth, and giving it everything he's got, with nary a hair of his pompadour-styled head out of place. *Danke schoen*, Wayne Newton, for singing your heart out and keeping us smiling.

NATALIE MAINES

Wedding bells rang for Dixie Chicks lead singer Natalie Maines, 25, and actor Adrian Pasdar, 35, at 12:10 a.m. on June 25, 2000. After the Dixie Chicks concert earlier that evening, the couple had been on their way to the gaming tables to join their friends when they took a detour into A Little White Wedding Chapel on the Las Vegas Strip for a cut-rate $55 ceremony. The couple had met a year earlier and had been immediately attracted to each other. Although they had been discussing marriage, they had not set a date because of conflicts in their busy schedules. She was traveling extensively on her Fly 2000 Tour; he was usually in Vancouver filming the new PAX TV series *Mysterious Ways*. With the Las Vegas marriage business open twenty-four hours a day, seven days a week, there was nothing mysterious about their finally making their way down the aisle.

Less than a year later Natalie missed the Academy of Country Music Awards at which the Dixie Chicks won three honors because she was taking care of her newborn baby. Some things are blessed from the beginning.

RICHARD BURTON

Many years after world-renowned stage and screen superstar Richard Burton had married and divorced Elizabeth Taylor and then remarried and once again divorced her (as well as married and divorced someone else), he agreed to perform with her in Noel Coward's *Private Lives*. Despite unfavorable reviews, audiences everywhere loved it. After all, it was another public opportunity to glance into what was believed to be the ongoing, behind-the-scenes affairs of this infamous duo. The couple played to packed houses, first on Broadway and then on tour.

A young woman whom Richard had been seeing since filming the epic *Wagner* a year earlier, Sally Hay, 34, accompanied them on the road trip. Sally always appeared more amused than threatened by ex-wife Liz's constant presence in their lives. It turned out Sally had every right to feel comfortable, as Richard was devoted to her. "She can do everything," Richard proudly proclaimed to a friend. "She looks after me so well. Thank God I've found her." Later recounting his proposal, Sally recalled, "Elizabeth was off sick. Richard had five free days. 'Let's get married,' he said. I didn't think he meant it. I couldn't believe life could be so good to me." Near Las

Vegas, Sally and Richard married there in 1983. It was his fifth marriage. She was his fourth wife.

When the tour ended later that year, the newlyweds returned to Europe, settling in at Richard's home in Céligny, Switzerland, and officially began their life together. Tragically, Richard was not a well man. Years of self-inflicted bodily abuse had done irreparable damage, and in 1984 he died at the age of 58 of a cerebral hemorrhage. Liz, graciously complying with the widow's wishes, did not attend the funeral and thereby avoided feeding the media frenzy that would have ensued.

Eventually, Sally Hay Burton overcame the emotional toll of losing her husband so early in her marriage. She moved to London, where she pursued a career as a writer and television journalist.

MICHAEL JORDAN

Michael Jordan's fiercely competitive spirit might have earned him his reputation as the greatest basketball player who ever played the game as well as six NBA championships in a decade as a member of the Chicago Bulls, but it was his big heart that won over his wife, Juanita Vanoy.

Michael and Juanita met at a party hosted by a mutual friend in February 1985. At 22 years old, he was midway through his rookie year. He already had a few select product endorsements to his name and no intentions of settling down. Juanita, a onetime model, was four years his senior. An independent sort, she knew how to take care of herself. She was initially reluctant to get involved with a professional athlete, a species heretofore unknown for their emotional maturity on or off the court. Yet, she later recalled, "The more time we spent together, the more our personalities just clicked."

The relationship, enlivened by romantic dinners when Michael was home and sustained by flowers sent when he was on the road, grew stronger and stronger. Michael first proposed on New Year's Eve in 1987 although they subsequently postponed the engagement for over a year. When they decided to pick up where they had left off, Juanita discovered she was pregnant. The first of their three children was born in December 1988.

Michael was participating in a celebrity golf tournament, and he and Juanita were in Las Vegas. Accompanied by four friends, they strolled into A Little White Wedding Chapel to be joined in wedlock on September 2, 1989, at 3:30 a.m. The bride wore blue jeans. So did the groom. The vows were sealed with a kiss and a five-carat diamond ring worth about $25,000. For their honeymoon, the newlyweds went to La Costa, California, for the first Michael Jordan Celebrity Golf Tournament.

While the wedding was a casual affair, there was nothing casual about the marriage, or at least the image of it Michael created for the public. "There was a reason for me getting married and having children. That experience of being a husband and a father provided a balance and a focus away from basketball," Michael mused in his autobiography. "I could have gotten in trouble. I don't know what kind of trouble, but if I had been single, playing basketball, and making a lot of money, I could have made some wrong decisions."

Well, it turned out that Michael did make some wrong decisions. From his perspective, the first was to retire from the NBA in 1993. He corrected that by returning to play, then retiring a second time in 1999. At the age of 38, he was still itching to run up and down the court, so he resigned his executive post with the Washington Wizards and joined the team roster in September 2001. From Juanita's perspective that was another mistake. She begged him not to return to the road, and if he went on the road, to behave himself. Since she filed for divorce for irreconcilable differences a few months later, Michael probably chose incorrectly and behaved badly. But even Juanita was not immune from the charms of the superstar, for they reconciled soon thereafter and were together again. But with Michael's $400 million estate plus advertising endorsements and business deals at stake, is it only love in the air?

CHAPTER 6

"*I Do. I Do. I Do.*"

or some Hollywood stars once is not enough. So they return to Vegas to do it again. And again. Take Tony Curtis, for example. He loves women. And he loves Las Vegas. Why wouldn't he get married there as often as he can?

MICKEY ROONEY

If you are an impetuous person who falls in love easily and wants to get married quickly, there's no better place to go than Las Vegas to say "I do." And that's what Mickey Rooney did four out of eight times he took a bride.

In 1942 he married his first wife, Ava Gardner, when he was 21 years old and under contract to MGM. Because he was its "child" star in the Andy Hardy series, the studio took propriety interest in his welfare and decreed that the ceremony take place in Ballard, California, a small town high up in the mountains of Santa Barbara County, far away from the curious public and inquisitive press.

Two years later it was love at first sight when Mickey was introduced to his second wife, Betty Ann Rase, Miss Birmingham of 1944, at a party in Alabama. Drinking bourbon and branch, he proposed and she accepted. As he was with the army's 6817th Special Services Battalion and about to be shipped overseas, they married the following weekend in her hometown.

Sin City did not play a role in Mickey's marital adventures until 1949. Six hours after picking up his divorce papers in Los Angeles, he married his third wife, Martha Vickers, in Las

Vegas. Ever the romantic, Mickey arranged a double-ring ceremony followed by a champagne reception.

Mickey flew his soon-to-be fourth wife, Elaine Mahnken, to Las Vegas after they had been dating for a month. They were married at the Wee Kirk o' the Heather wedding chapel in 1952. In his memoirs, *Life Is Too Short*, Mickey recalled, "They knew me there. Maybe they recognized the rice marks on my face." The newlyweds celebrated with an extended honeymoon at the Hotel El Rancho Vegas.

Mickey delayed divorcing Elaine on the advice of his psychiatrist, who thought that the actor's serial marriages and divorces were having a negative impact on his self-esteem. By the time the marriage was officially over, the next Mrs. Rooney, Barbara Ann Thomason, was five months pregnant. Without missing a beat, Mickey whisked her off to Las Vegas in 1958 to become wife number six.

Mickey adored Barbara, and they were very happy for several years. Yet Mickey's roving eye gave Barbara a reason to stray. In 1967 she was murdered by her lover, who then killed himself.

In shock from the death of his wife and the mother of four of his children, Mickey married her best friend, Marge Lane, a few months after the tragedy, in a ceremony close to home. Marriage number six, a mistake from the start, lasted only a hundred days.

In 1969, Mickey returned to Las Vegas with Carolyn Hockett for his seventh walk down the aisle. They had met when he was playing in a celebrity golf tournament in Miami. He proposed while she was visiting him in Los Angeles to meet his seven children from previous marriages. As soon as she accepted, they were up, up, and away on a chartered plane to Vegas.

It took Mickey Rooney a long time to grow up. When he was 28 years old, he was still playing boys in the movies. When he was 58 years old, he was still playing the groom. However, the eighth time appears to be the last time. He has been married to Jan Chamberlin, a country-and-western singer-songwriter, since 1978. They wed in a religious ceremony near their home about thirty miles northwest of Hollywood.

In a 1996 interview with the London *Daily Telegraph,* Mickey reflectively gave this insight: "Don't marry anybody you love; that's the secret of a happy marriage. Marry somebody you like. Love is sex, love is drunkenness, but it never lasts. But when you marry your best friend, love grows." For anyone who questions this advice, he added, "And people that follow what I tell them end up happily married."

JUDY GARLAND

The girl next door eloped to Las Vegas for the same reason many girls next door elope to Las Vegas: to assert her independence. For Judy Garland this meant being allowed to grow up off-screen and to play grown-up roles on-screen. She needed to convince her domineering stage mother that she had the emotional maturity to successfully manage her own life. Simultaneously, she wanted to persuade the paternalistic, if not dictatorial, head of MGM, Louis Mayer, that she was more than a girl singer, albeit a very popular girl singer. She had to show him that she could be a box-office sensation in romantic, glamorous roles.

Judy was just seventeen and a half years old, with box-office hits in *Babes in Arms* and *The Wizard of Oz* to her credit, when she met David Rose, the first of her five husbands. He came into her life shortly after Artie Shaw, her first serious love, had eloped to Las Vegas with Lana Turner (a marriage which lasted a scant four months). Like Shaw, Rose was a well-regarded and successful musician. Twelve years her senior, he had the maturity and experience working for him to win Judy's heart. However, his separation and eventual divorce from his first wife, comedienne Martha Raye, did not boost his ratings in the minds of Judy's mother or the studio. Judy was forbidden to see him.

Ignoring numerous ultimatums, the couple dated for over a year, wearing down her elders with their persistence. They began planning their nuptials with at least the support, if not the blessings, of her mother and the studio. In fact, Mayer had come around. He now hoped to give the bride away in a fabulous wedding, generating lots of publicity for the studio.

Louis Mayer was denied his moment in the sun. At 1:20 a.m. on July 28, 1941, Judy Garland, wearing a pink one-piece knitted outfit with white accessories, married David Rose in front of a justice of the peace at the Las Vegas courthouse. At a Sunday evening dinner at the Brown Derby in Beverly Hills only a few hours earlier, they had decided in a romantic moment to elope that night rather than waiting several months for Judy to complete filming *Babes on Broadway*. They invited her mother and stepfather, who had originally opposed the relationship, to join them and serve as witnesses.

After the ceremony Judy cabled Mayer with the following message:

I AM SO VERY HAPPY. DAVE AND I WERE MARRIED THIS AM. PLEASE GIVE ME A LITTLE TIME AND I WILL BE BACK AND FINISH THE PICTURE WITH ONE TAKE ON EACH SCENE. LOVE. JUDY.

Furious at the turn of events, Mayer responded with a resounding no. The Roses immediately returned to Los Angeles, and the bride was back in the studio within twenty-four hours. By the time they took their honeymoon six months later, the marriage was already on shaky ground. They announced their separation the following year. In June 1944, just before she turned 22, Judy testified that after the first months "our careers began to conflict," and she was granted a provisional divorce decree. The divorce became final twelve months later.

YEARS later, following her subsequent marriages to Vincente Minnelli, father of her daughter Liza, and Sid Luft, father of Lorna and Joey, Judy at 43 years old married Mark Herron, 33, at the Little Chapel of the West in Las Vegas on November 14, 1965. None of her children were present at the impromptu, middle-of-the-night ceremony. The witnesses were her press agent and his wife.

Mark wanted to be an actor, while Judy was approaching the end of her extraordinary screen and stage career as both a comic and dramatic actress and a singer. They had met at a party soon after *The Judy Garland Show* was taken off the air. They separated only several months after the wedding when he learned that under California law he could be liable for half her debts, including $400,000 she owed in taxes.

In 1969 Judy died in London of a pill overdose. She was married to Mickey Deans, another young actor, at the time.

LANA TURNER

As legend has it, Lana Turner, Hollywood's "Sweater Girl" of the thirties turned femme fatale in *The Postman Always Rings Twice* in the forties, was discovered at the soda fountain across from Hollywood High School when she was 15 years old. Soon under contract to MGM, Lana started in small roles, playing innocent teenagers in Andy Hardy films, before advancing to gold-digging gangster molls in movies for a more mature audience. The camera loved her radiant good looks and exuberant personality, and she was on her way to becoming a star. But first she met, married, and soon divorced her first husband, America's King of Swing, big-band leader Artie Shaw.

Lana and Artie met while making the movie *Dancing Co-Ed*. Lana played a professional hoofer; Artie played himself. Lana thought he was self-centered, and she was not shy about saying what she thought. Artie, in turn, was contemptuous of the movie business and everyone in it, and he did not care who knew it. Six months later, they renewed their acquaintance when Artie visited the set of Lana's new film, *Two Girls on Broadway*. This time Lana was flirtatious, Artie was pleasant. She gave him her telephone number despite being involved with Greg Bautzer, a successful attorney.

If Mr. Attorney had not stood her up on February 12, 1940, presumably because he had stomach problems, possibly because he had a date with Joan Crawford, whom he was also seeing, events of the day might have turned out differently. As it was, when Artie called, Lana accepted his invitation to dinner. However, instead of dining, the couple went for a drive along the ocean, sharing dreams about a house with a white picket fence and lots of children. Somewhere along the road to nowhere, they decided to fly to Las Vegas to get married.

Later that night, Lana, 19, and Artie, 30, became husband and wife in front of a justice of the peace in the living room of his home. Given the hour, the justice was wearing pajamas and a bathrobe. Lana, dressed for a date, was wearing a little navy blue dress trimmed in red with matching jacket and suede shoes. Artie, apparently unconcerned that both Betty Grable and Judy Garland thought they were his one and only, was cool and collected, as he had done this twice before. When a ring was called for, he calmly used his own blue star sapphire. It was the last tranquil moment the couple ever had.

The crowd of reporters awaiting the couple when they returned home clamored for comments. They enraged Artie, as did Lana, whose style of dress, makeup, and manner were no longer to his liking. Artie did not mind his wife working, but he expected her to prepare his meals and clean his clothes, no excuses. Although Lana knew she had made a big mistake three days after eloping, she waited four months before walking.

Lana's second marriage was just as sensational. Once again on the party circuit, she met a tall, dark, and handsome stranger by the name of Stephen Crane. Although Louis B. Mayer of MGM warned Lana of Stephen's underworld connections, she was too taken with his witty charm and displays of wealth to care. Three months later on July 17, 1942, the couple, accompanied by fellow actress Linda Darnell and friend Alan Gordon, eloped to Las Vegas. After a simple ceremony before another justice of the peace, the small group, happy and carefree, went out for a champagne brunch before returning to Los Angeles.

The first five months of marriage were blissful. Finding out she was pregnant only added to Lana's feelings of well-being. Then the bad news arrived: Stephen, who thought he was divorced, found out he was still married, so the marriage was immediately annulled. The couple remarried on March 15, 1943, in Tijuana, Mexico, primarily to protect Lana's reputation. Their daughter was born a few months later, but the relationship was doomed.

Lana's private life was as dramatic as some of her movie roles. She married a bankrupt millionaire and a billionaire real estate tycoon. Her fourth husband, Lex Barker, who played Tarzan, molested her daughter, while her daughter later stabbed and killed Lana's fifth husband, mobster Johnny Stompanato, to defend her mother. After two more husbands, Lana once reflected, "I always wanted to have one husband and seven children. Not the other way around." Some things just aren't in the script.

JOHNNY WEISSMULLER

Hollywood's best-known Tarzan, Johnny Weissmuller, winner of five Olympic gold medals in swimming, was married five times. At the age of 29 he met his second wife, "the Mexican Spitfire" Lupe Velez, 23, a fellow MGM contract player, while promoting his first film, *Tarzan, the Ape Man*. With studio approval, they had a secret wedding in Las Vegas in October 1933. It was so secret that they denied getting married, even after the press had confirmed that the couple had driven all Saturday night, taken out a marriage license early Sunday morning, and driven back to Hollywood the same day. The Clark County clerk, who had been called to the office to issue the license at 3:30 a.m., had been sworn to secrecy, while the Las Vegas justice of the peace refused to comment. If the stars had been as good at keeping their mouths shut as the supporting players in this melodrama, Johnny and Lupe's frequent fights, both public and private, fueled by their explosive personalities, might not have led to a divorce in 1938.

Thirty years later the mob and the Mormon moneymen had brought great changes to Las Vegas, yet it was still the most convenient place to marry quickly. The King of the Jungle returned to marry his fifth wife, Gertrudis Maria Theresia Elizabeth Bauman, a titled descendant of Bavarian nobility. He was now 59, and she was 42. Johnny was more forthcoming about this marriage, and many details of the event were reported in the newspaper.

The nuptials were held in a garden suite of the Dunes Hotel at six in the evening on April 24, 1963. The bride wore an oyster pearl wedding gown. The groom wore a conservative business suit. Forrest Tucker, the stage and screen actor, was the best man, returning the honor, since Johnny had once stood up for him. Champagne, hors d'oeuvres, and a big wedding cake were served at the reception following the ceremony.

Johnny told reporters that he and his wife did not have immediate plans for the future except for a possible trip to Acapulco or perhaps Europe. Apparently the couple bonded on the honeymoon, for they remained together until his death in 1984.

TONY CURTIS

Tony Curtis's fifth wife, horse trainer Jill Vanden Berg, is big (five feet eleven inches), blond, and beautiful. She is also young, at least relatively speaking. On November 6, 1998, the day they walked down the aisle, Tony was 73; Jill was 28, twelve years younger than the second of his five children, actress Jamie Lee Curtis.

The couple had met in a Los Angeles restaurant. Never shy, Tony asked for her telephone number and called her twenty minutes later. Five years and another marriage later (to lawyer Lisa Deutch), they tied the knot at the MGM Grand in the new Las Vegas, home of billion-dollar super-resorts that cater to every conceivable whim and fancy. The couple dressed to the nines, just what you would expect from a Hollywood legend—star of such movies as *Some Like It Hot* with Marilyn Monroe and

Tony Curtis looks fit, his bride looks fabulous, and the wedding cake came compliments of the MGM Grand.

Jack Lemmon and *Operation Petticoat* with Cary Grant—and his much younger bride. Tony wore a tux by Armani. Jill wore a skin-revealing dress of her own design. After the ceremony she sported a diamond-studded ring on her finger, and they celebrated with their seventy-five guests before leaving on their European honeymoon.

As an honorary member of the Rat Pack in the sixties, Tony also knew the old Las Vegas. Shortly after his eleven-year marriage to Janet Leigh broke up, he married German actress Christine Kaufmann on February 8, 1963, at the Riviera Hotel in Las Vegas. Kirk Douglas, his *Spartacus* costar, was his best man, and Kirk's wife, Anne, was matron of honor. At the time Tony was 38; Christine was 18.

When his second marriage failed as well, Tony took a third

bride, Leslie Nelson, a 23-year-old model whom he had met in New York. The nuptials on April 20, 1968, four days after Christine had gotten her divorce in Juárez, Mexico, were held at the Sahara Hotel in Las Vegas.

This marriage, needless to say, was another miserable union, albeit one that lasted over a decade. Tony's foray into drugs had taken the edge off his unhappiness and removed any motivation he had for changing his situation.

Tony's love affair with Las Vegas has endured longer than his marriages, possibly longer than all of his marriages combined. "I loved Las Vegas. I still love it," he rhapsodized in his 1993 autobiography. "It's a wonderful environment—carefree, gay, bigger than life. It's got a vitality like no other city in the world."

Still, Tony's latest marriage seems to be working. If life starts getting tough, he should remind himself of what he avowed after his last trip to the altar: "I'm good-looking, got a beautiful girl, I'm known all over the place, I mean, how bad can it be?" And this one just might last.

ZSA ZSA GABOR

As much as Zsa Zsa Gabor wanted to, she did not sleep with her third husband on the night of their nuptials at the Little Church of the West on April Fool's Day 1949. "I don't know if I can ever sleep with you again," he told her. "Yesterday you were the glamorous Mrs. Conrad Hilton. Now you are just plain Mrs. George Sanders."

George Sanders was a well-respected British actor, who would win the 1950 Best Supporting Actor Oscar for *All About Eve*. He was the great love of Zsa Zsa's life. He would torment her with his infidelities with socialites, such as Doris Duke, and starlets, such as Marilyn Monroe, while flying into a jealous rage if she showed even polite interest in someone else. But George was her dream man, charming and intelligent with an elegant, aristocratic demeanor. She proposed to him the night they met. At the time she was 30 years old; he was 43.

Inadvertently, George Sanders's behavior propelled Zsa Zsa to instant stardom. After he refused to take her to London, where he was to film *Ivanhoe*, because she would "spoil his fun" (presumably with other women), Zsa Zsa leaped at his brother Tom Conway's invitation to be on the popular TV talk show *Bachelor's Haven*. As a panelist answering questions from the audience, she had an opportunity to be herself, saying what she thought without regard for the consequences. She was a hit. Soon after her first appearance, she graced the covers of both *Life* and *Cosmopolitan*. In short order, she made her way to Las Vegas nightclubs, one time appearing with her sisters Eva and Magda (who, by the way, became George Sanders's fourth wife), and pursued a movie career.

Wanting a stay-at-home wife, George filed for divorce. When it was granted in April 1954, Zsa Zsa cried throughout the proceedings. George was so moved that he took her home and then straight to bed. Zsa Zsa recalled later, "We may have been divorced, but George and I were lovers again."

ZSA Zsa's wedding to Jack Ryan, husband number six, also took place in Las Vegas. Jack, her neighbor in Bel Air, was an outgoing, fun-loving Irishman. He proposed to her down on one knee in front of a hundred guests at one of his loud and lavish parties. They married October 6, 1976, at the Las Vegas Hilton. Her ex-husband Conrad Hilton graciously catered the affair. Unfortunately, she was initially unaware that Jack vigorously pursued a swinging lifestyle or that he came with a menagerie, a group that consisted of one ex-wife, two mistresses, and assorted hangers-on. She was dismayed when she figured it out. Not surprisingly, this union, one of Zsa Zsa's shorter ones, lasted less than seven months.

Zsa Zsa's seventh husband, Michael O'Hara, was the lawyer who handled her divorce from Jack. Once she received her papers, they, too, married in Las Vegas at the Las Vegas Hilton. The newlyweds were happy at first. However, Zsa Zsa found Michael, unlike Jack, to be moody by nature and uncommunicative. They slowly drifted apart, calling it quits after five years. He was the only one of her ex-husbands with whom she did not stay friends.

CHAPTER 7

The Fabulous and the Scandalous

*N*othing gets the media stirred up as much as a celebrity wedding. The press will go to the ends of the earth to get the story. Paparazzi will hang out of helicopters to get a shot of the bride and groom. And if there's a touch of scandal or a hint of the sensational, watch out. You could get hurt if you get in the way.

These stories involve at least one big star, juicy gossip, and over-the-top antics, all the ingredients that ensured they lingered in our collective consciousness and stayed in the headlines longer than they warranted. Enjoy!

ELIZABETH TAYLOR AND EDDIE FISHER

Before there was Princess Di, there was Elizabeth Taylor—the most famous woman in the world. Appearing in *National Velvet* in 1944 at the age of 12, the raven-haired, violet-eyed beauty captured the public's imagination and never let go. She lived boldly and loved passionately, tantalizing millions with the alluring lifestyle of a Hollywood movie queen.

When Liz became romantically involved with Eddie Fisher, she was 26 years old. Although she hadn't yet won an Oscar, she had been nominated twice. She had three children, and had been divorced twice and widowed once. In fact, it was her third husband Mike Todd's unexpected death in a plane crash that drove her to seek solace in the arms of his best friend, Eddie Fisher.

Eddie, 30, was a popular crooner who had had twenty-two consecutive songs hit the top of the pop charts. He had his

117

own television show, *Coke Time*, and was a regular headliner at venues such as the Desert Inn and the Tropicana in Las Vegas. However, when Eddie and Liz began "shacking up," as they said in 1950s parlance, they created a headline-grabbing, rumor-laden scandal, since Eddie was married at the time to Debbie Reynolds, with whom he had two children.

When they decided to marry, Liz pronounced to a reporter that she expected to be married to Eddie for no less than a century. But Eddie first needed a divorce, and he needed it quickly. The bad press their affair had generated turned friends and fans against them, and Eddie's career, in particular, was sustaining irreparable damage. So Eddie, along with Liz and her children, moved to the Hidden Well Ranch about five miles from Las Vegas to meet Nevada's six-week residency requirement. On May 12, 1959, the day Eddie received his divorce papers, he married Liz, who earlier in the year had converted to Reform Judaism, at Temple Beth Shalom.

It was a traditional Jewish wedding somewhat at odds with the Las Vegas setting. For the ceremony the couple stood under a chuppah, or canopy, and the groom stomped on a wineglass to demonstrate the fragility of life, if not the vagaries of fame. Eddie wore a white yarmulke and navy blue business suit. Liz wore a Jean Louis moss green chiffon dress with a loosely draped hood, a high neckline, and long sleeves. The intimate circle of invited friends and family gathered around them included their parents, her brother and sister-in-law, her stepson Michael Todd Jr., and his mentor, Eddie Cantor, with his wife. Outside, the usual crowd of tourists, reporters and photographers waited for the glamorous, albeit beleaguered, newlyweds to appear.

After an extravagant honeymoon that included a Mediterranean cruise on a private 120-foot yacht, Liz returned to work. Despite everything that had been printed about her, her star was rising higher and glowing brighter than ever before. She made *Suddenly Last Summer*, for which she received her third Academy Award nomination, and *Butterfield 8*, for which she finally won the elusive Oscar. And she was signed to do the highly touted Twentieth Century–Fox epic *Cleopatra*.

The Taylor-Fisher union was over by the time the lavish production of *Cleopatra* was completed in 1963. When Liz left Eddie for Richard Burton, whom she had met on set and fallen in love with between takes, she outdid the scandal caused by Eddie leaving Debbie for Liz. Once again, Liz was news.

CLARA BOW

Appropriately, the "It" girl of the 1920s, the quintessential flapper and silent silver screen star Clara Bow, got married in Las Vegas before it was fashionable to do so.

On-screen, Clara was an idealized, modern every girl, playing manicurists, waitresses, and department store clerks. Audiences loved her energy and vitality, her independence and high spirits. "She danced even when her feet were not moving," enthused Adolph Zukor, president of Paramount Studios. "Some part of her was always in motion, if only her big rolling eyes."

Off-screen, she was Hollywood's first sex symbol. Her love affairs and gambling exploits were tabloid headlines, and the public couldn't get enough of her private affairs. But as Clara lamented in correspondence with Rudy Behlmer, a film and television writer and director, "A sex symbol is always a heavy load to carry, especially when one is very tired, hurt, and bewildered."

In 1930 an ugly court trial, in which she sued her private secretary, Daisy De Voe, for blackmail and embezzlement, generated lurid charges on both sides and bad publicity for the onetime party girl. Although she won the case, she was physically and emotionally exhausted and had the first of a series of nervous breakdowns. Wearing a white hat and riding a white horse, cowboy movie actor Rex Bell came to her rescue. He stood by Clara through her trials and tribulations and carried her off to the Walking Box Ranch, his 350,000-acre ranch in Searchlight, Nevada.

In Las Vegas on a legal matter, the couple married on the evening of December 4, 1931, in the chambers of Judge William E. Orr. Clara, 26, wore a wine-colored dress covered by an expensive fur coat. Atop her head, she sported a Princess Eugenie hat. Rex, 28, wore a brown business suit. They had wanted to keep the wedding a secret, and Rex, in fact, denied that it had even taken place. However, a search through marriage licenses by reporters at the county clerk's office revealed the truth.

After spending the night in town, the newlyweds returned to the ranch, their home for the next fifteen years. Lionel Barrymore, Errol Flynn, Clark Gable, and Norma Shearer were among their celebrity guests. Sadly, however, Clara never really recovered from her work-hard, play-harder lifestyle and was in and out of sanatoriums for the rest of her life. Rex pursued a political career and was elected Nevada's lieutenant governor in 1954 and 1958. Upon their deaths in the 1960s, the ranch went to their two sons. In November 2000 it was auctioned off for $650,000.

RITA HAYWORTH

Love goddess Rita Hayworth was lucky at neither love nor marriage. Although GIs bought into the image on her erotically charged World War II poster, even pasting it on the first atom bomb detonated at Bikini Atoll, that image was a myth. Nor was she anything like her signature role, the provocative, sultry temptress Gilda in the film of the same name. Instead she was shy and vulnerable. Men, particularly husbands, were constantly taking advantage of her, betraying her innate sweetness.

Her first husband, businessman Eddie Judson, was intent on making Rita a star, pushing her to sleep with other men if it furthered her burgeoning film career. Although her second husband, boy genius cum director Orson Welles, adored her, he put his career above attending to her emotional needs, while his extramarital affairs left her unhappy and depressed. To Prince Aly Khan, husband number three, she was simply a part of his entourage. In 1953, when Rita, 35, met her fourth husband, Dick Haymes, also 35, her self-esteem, never very robust, was all but decimated, and it was relatively easy for another manipulative charmer to make his moves on her.

Dick had been a popular crooner, singing a few years earlier as a soloist with the best of the big bands, including those led by Tommy Dorsey, Harry James, and Benny Goodman. Yet he had squandered $4 million in earnings and had developed a reputation as a lush and a loser, with two going on three ex-wives and three children to provide for and back taxes to pay. To Rita, however, he appeared sensitive and understanding, listening to her talk about her troubles for hours and taking her side in her battles with her ex-husbands for alimony and child support. And with Rita by his side or sitting ringside when he performed, he began to rebuild his image.

The height of the orchestrated publicity that Dick was able to garner came with the Hayworth-Haymes wedding on September 24, 1953, at the Sands Hotel and Casino in Las Vegas. Curious guests crowded the pathways, and the media and press lay in wait for the wedding party. The excitement grew as the procession went from Rita's bungalow through the casino (although not even one of the great screen beauties of the day could slow the place of a bet or the roll of the dice) to the Gold Room. When the couple reached their destination, the media were ready. Flashbulbs flashed, television cameras whirred, and the ceremony was saved on film for posterity.

"Will you love, honor, and cherish each other throughout your married life?" were not vows, however, intended to last a lifetime. After two years of persistent public and private verbal and physical abuse, Rita gathered enough courage to leave Dick and dissolve the marriage. Her divorce in Reno on December 12, 1955, was granted on grounds of "extreme cruelty."

DENNIS RODMAN

The bad boy of basketball and former Madonna boy toy, Dennis Rodman, 37, liked gambling and drinking. And he particularly liked gambling and drinking in Las Vegas. So it was no surprise that his surprise wedding on November 14, 1998, to the buxom babe of *Baywatch*, Carmen Electra, 26, took place at the Little Chapel of the Flowers on Las Vegas Boulevard.

Neither the bride nor the groom wore a traditional satin and tulle white wedding dress and veil (as the groom had done at a book signing). Instead, the multitattooed, bejeweled NBA star, who had been married once before for eighty-two days, was decked out in what appeared to be a police uniform. Carmen, her lips freshly plumped from an emergency collagen treatment the week before the blessed event, wore a dark-colored pantsuit. In a playful moment before the ceremony, he carried her piggyback into the chapel.

Upon hearing the news, Dennis's agent, Dwight Manley, immediately hit the airwaves, denouncing the legitimacy of the union and accusing the five-foot-four-inch-tall actress of taking advantage of the six-foot-seven-inch-tall athlete. "From what I can determine, it's not legal," he was quoted as saying. "It sounds like he was deeply intoxicated." But Dennis rebounded, insisting, "I love Carmen and am proud to be married to her."

Still, it was a marriage that one suspected was not going to last as long as the news it generated. Nine days after saying "I do," the Worm filed for annulment because the goddess herself, the love of his life, the woman he had been dating since the summer, refused to sign a postnuptial agreement.

But, wait. The NBA lockout gave Dennis lots of free time for contemplation, and he, once again, reconsidered. "I'm still married," he announced on December 9. Two days later, in her own interview, Carmen confirmed that they were working on strengthening their relationship. "I am still in love with him," she declared. In January, while Dennis terminated his relationship with his agent and the union of Dennis and the

Chicago Bulls appeared on the rocks, Dennis and Carmen were still together.

The cutting of the knot did not officially occur until April 1999, when Carmen sadly filed for divorce for irreconcilable differences. Fortunately for sports fans and celebrity watchers everywhere, the couple remained a couple and continued to generate headlines. In August of the same year Dennis, who was fired from the Los Angeles Lakers after less than two months with the club, announced that he wanted to make a commercial sex video with Carmen. Unfortunately for sports fans and celebrity watchers everywhere, this never happened. In November 1999, they were arrested in a domestic squabble after a noisy fight. This fouled-up marriage had officially run out of free throws.

CELINE DION

Some people really know how to party. International pop diva Celine Dion, 31, and her manager-husband, René Angélil, 57, renewed their vows after five years of marriage in a quiet, private ceremony at Caesars Palace on January 5, 2000. They then threw a $2 million extravaganza for two hundred friends and family members.

The Moroccan-themed event was part Marrakesh street scene and part desert nightlife. The walls of the hotel ballroom housing the event were draped in jewel-toned fabrics, fostering the fantasy of being inside the tent of an Arabian prince. For the five-course meal guests were seated on cushy pillows at lowered tables and served on china flown in from Morocco. For entertainment belly dancers danced, snake charmers charmed, and magicians made magic while a camel caravan paraded around the perimeter of the room. Not even Malcolm Forbes could have staged a more elaborate spectacle.

When she was 12 years old, Celine, the youngest of fourteen children from a musical but impoverished family from Quebec, had a singing audition in front of the man who would become her husband. She was so good, so moving, that he signed her up immediately. Under his tutelage her career took off almost from the start. It culminated in her heartrending delivery of the hit ballad from the film *Titanic*, "My Heart Will Go On." The song made both the movie sound track album and her own album *Let's Talk About Love* the top sellers of 1998.

Romantically, Celine had a schoolgirl crush on her future husband from the moment they first met. She was 20 years old when René's marriage fell apart and old enough to finally make the moves on her beloved. They have been together ever since.

The year prior to their Las Vegas celebration had been a difficult one for the couple. René had to drop out of Celine's fourteen-country world tour when cancer was discovered on his neck. Celine canceled a month of performances to be at his side through his surgery and radiation therapy. However, René regained his strength, and Celine started a two-year retirement, giving the couple time to concentrate on their next project: having a baby. Thanks to in vitro fertilization, their efforts came to fruition a year later.

With so much good fortune coming their way, one can only wonder how over-the-top their tenth-anniversary celebration will be.

ELVIS PRESLEY

Elvis called her "Baby," "Honey," "Sweetness," "Cilla," "Little One," and "Little Girl." But on May 1, 1967, Priscilla Beaulieu was introduced to the world as Mrs. Elvis Presley. On the day they married, she was 21 years old; Elvis was 32.

The couple had known each other since she was a 14-year-old air force brat, living in Germany with her family at the same time Elvis was stationed there. They had lived together for five years, after she moved into Graceland during her senior year in high school. While Elvis was making one movie after another and being romantically linked with his leading ladies, she was waiting patiently for him to decide the time was right to tie the knot.

Shortly before Christmas 1966, Elvis made his move. He got down on one knee and held out a small black velvet box containing the most beautiful diamond ring Priscilla had ever seen. The stone was three and a half carats, encircled by a row of smaller, detachable diamonds that could be worn separately. "We're going to be married," he told her.

The King takes a bride and gets a cake befitting royalty.

To keep the wedding as private as Elvis's popularity allowed, the couple stayed at their Palm Springs retreat the night before their wedding. Arising before dawn, they flew to Las Vegas, arrived at the city clerk's office at seven in the morning to get their marriage license, and then rushed to dress for the 9:00 a.m. ceremony.

Priscilla wore a floor-length gown of white silk chiffon that she had designed herself. It was topped with a three-foot tulle veil held in place by a rhinestone crown. The headlines of the times later described the bride as a brunette beauty despite the heavy Cleopatra-style makeup she wore at Elvis's behest. Elvis wore a black brocade silk tuxedo and Western boots.

The eight-minute nuptials took place in a private suite at the Aladdin Hotel in front of a few friends and family.

Afterward the newlyweds were joined by a hundred guests at an elaborate breakfast banquet, dining on ham, eggs, southern fried chicken, oysters Rockefeller, roast suckling pig, poached and candied salmon, lobster, and champagne. Together they cut their six-tiered wedding cake.

As expected, photographers and reporters kept pace with Elvis and Priscilla throughout the day. They greeted the couple with flashbulbs after they said their "I do's," at the airport upon their return to Palm Springs, and in the driveway of their home. As befitted the King of Rock 'n' Roll, Elvis handled the media graciously, posing for pictures and holding a press conference. Playing to the crowd, he carried Priscilla over the threshold of their house and upstairs to their bedroom singing "The Hawaiian Wedding Song." They were alone at last—but not for long.

The following February, their daughter, Lisa Marie, was born. Then in the summer of 1969, his manager, Colonel Tom Parker, arranged a monthlong engagement for Elvis to be the headliner at the new Las Vegas International for an unheard of half-million-dollar salary. It was such a success that he was signed to a five-year contract to appear twice a year for a million dollars a year.

In Vegas, surrounded by adoring fans and ardent friends, Elvis was happy, performing his music and perfecting his style. Meanwhile, at home in Bel Air with the baby, Priscilla began moving outside the enchanted Elvis circle for the first time in her adult life. Meeting new people, developing self-confidence, and maturing as a mother, she became her own person, one who no longer needed Elvis to tell her how to dress or what to think.

Although their love story ended in divorce in October 1973, Elvis and Priscilla's relationship endured. Based on a shared history of living in the high beams of the celebrity spotlight and a mutual devotion to their daughter, they remained close until Elvis's death in August 1977.

CLINT EASTWOOD

Despite his movie image as a no-name cowboy in the Sergio Leone spaghetti flicks or as the hard-boiled cop Harry Callahan, Clint Eastwood is really a romantic at heart. How else can the surprise wedding ceremony he arranged in Las Vegas for newscaster Dina Ruiz be explained?

Clint pulled it all together the weekend Dina was vacationing there with six girlfriends, a school reunion of sorts. Thanks to his friend Steve Wynn, he was able to forgo the typical chapel wedding for the picture-perfect and very private patio of the casino magnate's Shadow Creek golf course home. Dina's companions were her bridesmaids, and Clint flew his and her families to Vegas to join them. His adult son, Kyle, was his best man. And so on March 31, 1996, Clint, 65, handsome in a navy blue suit, and Dina, 30, beautiful in a long white silk gown, exchanged vows. Clint obviously knew his bride well. "It was my dream wedding," she happily proclaimed afterward.

Although this is only Clint's second marriage, a surprisingly low number for such a powerful Hollywood icon, his numerous relationships and bitter breakups have provided fodder for the gossip mill for years. His divorce was rancorous, and it cost him $25 million. His involvement with costar Sandra Locke resulted in an unsuccessful but all too public palimony suit, and he was living with actress Frances Fisher, the mother of one his children, when he met Dina.

No one can control when and where they fall in love, or with whom. Certainly, when Dina was sent by her television station two years earlier to interview Clint after he won the Best Picture and Best Director Oscars for his movie *Unforgiven*, she was only doing her job. Upon meeting him, she found him charismatic, but she was not attracted to him. For his part Clint thought the young woman bright and articulate, but his mind was on his next film, *The Bridges of Madison County*, with Meryl Streep. A year later they met again when she was seated next to him at a civic function in Carmel,

California. The conversation flowed as easily as the wine served at the banquet, and Clint asked for her telephone number.

From that point, the relationship blossomed. Caught kissing by a photographer, the couple generated some buzz, but Clint initially asserted that they were just friends. Subsequently, Dina, concerned about his reputation if not her own, politely but adamantly maintained, "We didn't become a couple until he was free." Whatever. The Eastwoods, so very much in love, became the proud parents of a baby girl that December.

CHAPTER 8

I've Got a Secret

Some in the public eye value their privacy more than anything else. When Tom Selleck got married in 1987, he was at the height of his popularity. He had become a household name as star of the hit action series with a sense of humor *Magnum P.I.* On top of that, he had been voted *People* magazine's sexiest man in the world. He was so concerned about keeping his impending nuptials to English actress Jillie Mack secret that he arranged the ceremony under false names and bypassed Las Vegas in favor of Lake Tahoe, a more out-of-the-way location. Such a good job was done keeping quiet about the marriage that the local paper did not report the event until twenty-seven days later.

The celebrities here were just as concerned about their privacy as Tom Selleck was, yet they did not take the same extreme measures. Instead they braved running into a freelance photographer or an out-of-town stringer and took their chances on quietly getting married in Las Vegas. They had various degrees of success. The same can be said of their marriages.

CARY GRANT

On July 22, 1965, Cary Grant, as debonair and dashing as ever at 61, married for the fourth time. He was at a stage in his career when he thought that his romancing of much younger leading ladies on the screen no longer had any credibility. On a personal level, however, there was no such reluctance. His bride, Dyan Cannon, was thirty-five years younger than he was.

129

Four years earlier, Cary had spotted Dyan on the short-lived television series *Malibu Run* and contacted her through her agent. When she finally responded to his attentions, they dated on and off while he continued to delight his fans in such films as *Charade* with Audrey Hepburn and *Father Goose* with Leslie Caron. Cary finally felt the time was right to try marriage again. He charmed Dyan's parents in Seattle, Washington, while she won his mother's approval in Bristol, England. They then went to Las Vegas for a wedding ceremony conducted in utmost secrecy from the press.

For subterfuge the couple obtained their marriage license in Goldfield, Nevada. The nuptials took place at the Dunes Hotel, owned by Cary's lifelong friend Charlie Rich. Their efforts at privacy were so successful that the press did not learn of the event until the eleventh day of their English honeymoon. Cary announced it himself during an interview and created the media frenzy he had originally hoped to avoid.

Whatever one might think of May-December relationships, the marriage, which lasted only seventeen months but produced a daughter, did not break up because of the difference in their ages. Rather, Dyan felt overwhelmed by Cary's domineering personality and left. Barbara Harris, the fifth Mrs. Grant, was forty-seven years his junior. They were happily married for five years until his death in 1986.

SIR BOB GELDOF AND PAULA YATES

Once was not enough for the British rock couple Sir Bob Geldof and Paula Yates. They first said "I do" in a secret, simple ceremony at the Little Church of the West in Las Vegas in June 1986. Back home in England two months later, they did it again. The second time, despite the traditional church setting, was neither secret nor simple. The bride wore a red satin gown with a twelve-foot train. The groom sported top hat and tails with an array of medals blazoned across his chest. Paul

McCartney, David Bowie, and Sting were among their wedding guests.

Bob Geldof had come a long way from his modest success with the Irish punk group the Boomtown Rats. He was honored with knighthood and anointed with the nickname "Saint Bob" for his efforts organizing the 1985 Live Aid concerts featuring every single rock star with even a modicum of fame and raising more than $100 million for Ethiopian famine relief. Paula, a peroxide blonde with a quick wit, had gotten her start as a groupie, taking up with Bob in 1977 at the age of 17. A few years later she, too, became a celebrity, first hosting a British television show featuring top pop musicians and later interviewing a range of personalities from a king-size bed on a morning program called *The Big Breakfast*. In both positions, she fed the public's growing appetite for melodrama and soap opera among the mighty and the mighty sexy.

For a while it seemed as if this were one of those matches made in heaven. Notwithstanding Paula's penchant for flirting and Bob's ego-driven need for control, the marriage seemed to work. They were both committed to their three beautiful daughters, Fifi Trixibell, Peaches Honeyblossom, and Pixie. Bob took care of them financially, having a real knack for business, while Paula lovingly managed the household, determined to make every day a holiday. Then nine years into the marriage, she fell in love with someone else, Australian Michael Hutchence of the band INXS, one of her interviewees.

This modern morality tale played out in public across several continents, with tragic results. The press sided with Bob, who got custody of his daughters, and crucified Paula. He had powerful friends in the media, and she was pregnant with another man's child. For the new couple, the daily replay in the tabloids was stressful to say the least, and when they adopted a high-profile rocker lifestyle, taking up drinking and drugs, they found little support anywhere. In the end, Michael, in 1997, was a possible suicide, and Paula, in 2001, overdosed on heroin, less than six years after they had begun. Their daughter, Heavenly Hiraani Tiger Lily, joined her half sisters in Sir Bob's care.

JON BON JOVI

Like many other young couples in love, Jon Bon Jovi, 28, and Dorothea Hurly, 28, decided to get married in Las Vegas. They were childhood sweethearts and had dated for ten years with only a few minor interruptions. Because of Jon's high regard for Elvis, they selected the Graceland Wedding Chapel as their venue and arrived there by taxi one spring night in May 1989. As a sign of the times or an indication of his profession, the groom wore black leather, but then, so did the bride. Afterward, Dorothea had a few moments of remorse, wanting to undo the whole thing. Jon, meanwhile, called his mother in New Jersey at 3:00 a.m. to share the good news.

Of course, Jon and Dorothea were not quite like any other young couple. Although Jon went unrecognized by the chapel's minister, he was the hard-playing lead man of the hard-rock band bearing his name, a band at the peak of its first wave of popularity with hits such as "I'll Be There for You." His manager, concerned that a married rock star would lose his sex appeal, asked the minister, still not sure what the big deal was, to keep the marriage secret. He needn't have bothered, because Jon's mother, so happy at the surprising event, excitedly announced her joy to the world. "Staying with one girl is totally against the ways of Hollywood and show business, I think," she said in an interview with *People* magazine. "But Jon is his own man, and that I'm proud of."

Jon keeps returning to Graceland. A few years after his nuptials, he arranged the wedding of a crew member at the chapel, flying in the twenty-five-guest wedding party and dressing everyone from grandmothers to babies in Elvis costumes. On Jon and Dorothea's tenth anniversary, Jon was best man at his brother's wedding there. But his coup de grâce took place the following year.

In Las Vegas for their One Wild Night tour, Jon and band member Richie Sambora agreed to serenade seventy-five couples, winners of radio contests across the country, as part of a group marriage ceremony. To accommodate the crowd, the Graceland Wedding Chapel erected a large tent in its parking lot. And that's where everyone gathered for the 11:30 p.m. nuptials. And that's where everyone anxiously waited until well after 1 a.m. Jon and Richie had been waylaid after their concert for a private performance by the cast of the show *The Rat Pack Is Back*. Despite the late hour, not really that late for a rock 'n' roll star, Jon, a big fan of Frank and friends, was pumped up and sang his heart out. It was a memorable day and night for everyone. Now if only some of those newlyweds can keep it going as long as Jon and Dorothea.

KELLY RIPA

"Hey, we both have off tomorrow," Mark Consuelos noted on a Tuesday evening over pizza. "Wanna fly to Vegas and get married?"

"Sure," Kelly Ripa, 25, responded. "Let me run home and get a dress."

And so it came to pass that on May 1, 1996, two of the stars of the daytime drama *All My Children* went from New York to Las Vegas to tie the knot at the Chapel of the Cheese. Chapel of the Cheese? Kelly professes that she simply does not remember the name of the chapel where her nuptials took place (although Chapel of the Bells claims the couple as one of theirs). The made-up name is probably not an indictment of the wedding business, but one of the typical sassy, off-the-cuff comments for which she has become known. It might be. They wanted to get married quietly so their secret relationship would not impact their work situation, and that's what they did.

It was the first marriage for both Kelly and Mark. Conversely, when their television alter egos, Hayley Vaughan and Mateo Santos, had a formal wedding in their hometown of Pine Valley in June 2000, it was her fourth marriage and his third. She had once eloped, once been conned into marriage, and once before married her current husband. The latter marriage turned out to be illegal because Mateo's first marriage had not been annulled, as he had thought. His first wife also surprised him with a young son he had not known about.

"When your TV character is married to your real-life husband, it makes the kissing scenes easy," Kelly once cheerfully said. For now, however, all kissing and other displays of affection will be off-camera when the couple can find the time. Mark quit *All My Children* to pursue a movie career. Kelly, too, said good-bye to Hayley, but she is still a working mom. Her other job as Regis Philbin's cohost on his morning talk show, now called *Live with Regis and Kelly*, keeps her busy. Real life might not be as torrid as a soap opera, but it can be just as eventful.

BORIS KARLOFF

Englishman William Henry Pratt, better known as Boris Karloff, the stage name he took for himself, or as Frankenstein's monster, the movie character he brought to life, was a very private man. It is known that he loved cricket, his national sport, but he was not particularly fond of Hollywood parties, the local pastime. On the other hand, few people know anything about his first wife or why he divorced his second wife or when he fell in love with his third wife, countrywoman Evelyn Helmore.

As reported on the front page of the evening edition of the *Las Vegas Evening Review-Journal*, Boris, 58, married Evelyn, 42, in Las Vegas on April 11, 1946, the day after he met his six-week state residency requirement and had obtained his divorce decree. About noon Boris, wearing a plain dark suit, and Evelyn, in a black and red ensemble, casually strolled from their hotel to the flower shop next door and asked the proprietor, J. P. Hayward, a justice of the peace, if he would do the honors. Although the justice was knee-deep in fertilizer tending a store full of lilies at the time, he shook himself off, cleaned himself up, and graciously agreed to conduct the service then and there. His wife stood up for the bride and presented her with a complimentary six-flower corsage. A passing state ranger with a revolver strapped to his leg was the best man.

Following the ceremony Boris did not grant any interviews, and the newlyweds went on their honeymoon, destination unknown. If the popular actor wanted to keep news of his nuptials from spreading like a brush fire across the dry Southern California landscape, he succeeded, at least for a while. The first marriage announcement in a Los Angeles paper did not appear until three weeks later, on May 2.

In 1951 the couple left the West Coast for New York City, from where they could be "home" in London overnight by air. They liked that. In 1959 they repatriated to England, and they liked that even better. Boris continued to play menacing monsters and mad scientists until his death in 1969.

ANDRE AGASSI

When hometown boy Andre Agassi, 31, took Steffi Graf, 32, to be his lawfully wedded wife, he did so as quickly and privately as possible. After making several public statements that they would not wed until they had recovered from the birth of their child expected in December, the ceremony was quietly held on a Monday afternoon, October 22, 2001, at the couple's Las Vegas home. Other than the fact that Andre was seen rushing around town that morning, lining up the district judge who would make the pronouncement and tying up some loose ends, no details of the event got out to the press. Only their mothers were present when they said "I do." If you can't trust Mom to keep a secret, whom can you trust?

The couple began dating after each had won the 1999 French Open singles titles. Andre and his first wife, actress Brooke Shields, had recently filed for divorce, and he was a free man. Similarly, Steffi was just coming out of a seven-year relationship with German racing-car driver Michael Bartels. The tabloids were on top of the relationship from the very beginning. Then again, when one of the world's leading men's tennis players, and a popular one at that, is frequently seen with the dominant women's tennis player of the nineties, there is bound to be interest and, possibly, some unwanted attention.

Marriage was first rumored in January 2000, when the couple spent some time in Hawaii before going on to the Australian Open. Despite paparazzi following them around the island of Kauai, there were no wedding pictures because there was no wedding. In Australia, the newspaper the *Melbourne Age* asked readers to report any sightings of the couple, particularly near any churches or registry offices. It didn't happen then and there, either.

In July 2001 Andre announced that he and Steffi were expecting a child, and the question of when wedding bells would ring was raised once again. His spokesman, Todd Wilson, would say only, "I do not know what their plans are for marriage." Andre, using the opportunity to change the subject, joked that his and Steffi's offspring would beat his rival Pete Sampras's future offspring. Pete wasn't worried and replied, "My parents didn't pick up a racket, and I turned out all right."

Still, a strong case can be made for genetics. Jaden Gil Agassi was born four days after his parents' wedding, beating all previous estimates by a good six weeks. Confounding the fourth estate once again, the boy is already taking after dear old dad.

CHAPTER 9

Never Mind

If no one was in a forest when a tree fell, did it make a noise? If a marriage lasted only a few months, did it really happen? Was it really a marriage? If it lasted a year? If it lasted two years?

These celebrity marriages were short, if not sweet. Yes, they really happened. There are pictures to prove it!

SHANNEN DOHERTY

Celebrities like Shannen Doherty give Las Vegas weddings a bad name. It is not because she acted out when she was in town. Nor did she have a barroom brawl with her boyfriend like the ones she had when she was a teenage star on *Beverly Hills 90210*. Nope, she did not endanger any of Vegas's denizens or visitors by driving under the influence, a charge she faced while playing one of three sister witches on the television show *Charmed*. So what did she do that was so terrible? She had a quickie wedding.

On January 25, 2002, Shannen, 30, married Richard Salomon, 32, a movie producer. Four months later it was over. It lasted two months less than her 1993 marriage to Ashley Hamilton. "Her husband said things started going bad between 'I' and 'do,'" joked Craig Kilborn on his after-hours television show *The Late Late Show with Craig Kilborn*. Not that Richard was entirely blameless: someone who was kicked out of a New York club for allegedly trashing the place presumably has some of his own anger-management issues to work out. Maybe the third time will be a charm for Shannen. Let's just hope she doesn't do it in Vegas unless she means for the marriage to last.

CHER

Cher, best known in the early seventies for being the taller, better-looking half, in her belly-baring slinky dresses, of the pop singing team Sonny and Cher, met Gregg Allman, of the popular Allman Brothers Band, at the Troubadour, a small Hollywood nightclub. At the time Cher was 29 years old and legally separated from Sonny. Although she was no longer performing weekly in front of a national audience, she still had the cachet of a television glamour queen. Gregg, himself twice divorced at 28 years old, was a rock star. That night he was playing with his friends in the band, just for fun. He spotted her in the audience and sent her a flowery note, asking her out. Being a sucker for flowery notes, she accepted.

It was the date from hell. Gregg took her to a couple of doper parties and then to a restaurant on Sunset Strip. The whole evening dismayed the drug-free Cher, and she could not wait to go home. But being a sucker for down-home country boys who wrote flowery notes, Cher said yes when he suggested that they try again. The next time Gregg took her dining and dancing, and they talked and talked. It was much more to her liking, and Cher fell in love.

The couple married in a small, private affair at Caesars Palace in June 1975, a mere three days after Cher's eleven-year marriage to Sonny officially ended. Her sister stood up for her as matron of honor, and the couple's business managers attended. Cher looked lovely in a sleeveless white floor-length outfit. Gregg, also in white, appeared serious and sincere. So why did she cry all the way home to Beverly Hills? Or file for divorce nine days later?

Cher believed a sensitive soul lay underneath Gregg's long, golden locks and bad boy façade, and he was undeniably good in bed. So the marriage did not end immediately. They gave it a go, but the going was tough. Gregg was a heroin addict, something that Cher had naïvely refused to acknowledge, but possibly sensed, before the marriage. When he quit, he became an alcoholic and gained weight. The first year they were together, Gregg's band broke up, and his fans unfairly blamed her. With her television show *Cher* sinking in the ratings, Cher re-upped with Sonny for the second incarnation of *The Sonny and Cher Show*. She was now spending more time with her ex than with her husband. Gregg, lost without his band and unhappy with the turn of events, filed for divorce in 1976.

It still wasn't over. They had a son, Elijah Blue, together and made an album, *Allman and Woman*, together. And then in 1977 they were done. "We were a disaster waiting to happen," Cher wrote introspectively several years later. "I think I was looking for someone who wouldn't try to dominate me. And I never felt that Gregory would try to box me in, because it wasn't in him to put that box together." Cher has had her share of boy toys and love affairs, but Gregg was the last person with whom this sexy lady took the plunge.

ANGELINA JOLIE AND BILLY BOB THORNTON

The couple took the $189 Beginner's Package at the Little Church of the West for their Friday afternoon wedding on May 5, 2000. The bride carried red and white roses and walked down the aisle as "Here Comes the Bride" played over the chapel's sound system. Afterward she posed with her new husband, sporting his trademark baseball cap, for the traditional wedding portrait. At the conclusion of the ceremonies, "Unchained Melody" played. There was one witness.

This time the couple were not acting out a movie script, as they had in the 1999 film *Pushing Tin*. For Oscar winners Angelina Jolie, 24, and actor-director-screenwriter Billy Bob Thornton, 44, it was the real thing. "I'm madly in love with this man," she said, referring to Thornton, "and will be till the day I die."

It was her second marriage, his fifth. "I view marriage," Angie stated a year earlier, "as an amazing, wonderful thing." In a hurry to wed, she had petitioned the court to speed up finalizing her divorce from British actor Jonny Lee Miller, whom she had married in 1996. Billy Bob, in turn, had abruptly broken off his engagement to Laura Dern, for whom he had left his most recent spouse. Laura's take on the situation was, "I left home to work on a movie, and while I was away, my boyfriend got married, and I've never heard from him again."

Pundits, noting that the couple had married in Las Vegas, gave the marriage until the end of the year. This in spite of the fact that Angie had recently added her second Billy Bob tattoo on her right biceps, visible to the world whenever she went sleeveless, which was quite often. "The other one is in a place where nobody's ever seen," she told an interviewer for *Us* magazine. The couple, seeing greater long-term potential for their union, purchased a sprawling $3.8 million eight-bedroom, seven-bathroom Beverly Hills home three months after the wedding. They took up wearing vials of each other's blood around their necks, purchased joint grave plots, and adopted a baby from a Cambodian orphanage. Then, just over two years after they had started, they ran out of steam. What were the odds of that?

Billy Bob took off on tour to promote his rock album *Private Radio*, generating unwanted rumors of infidelity for himself, as well as much needed publicity for his band. At home minding the baby, Angie stated, "Let's just say that I'm not OK with certain kinds of behavior." Now if only tattoos were as easily dissolved as marriages.

DARVA CONGER AND RICK ROCKWELL

Most people don't become celebrities by getting married in Las Vegas. Either they are celebrities before they get married in Vegas or they are not. Occasionally, a couple will get their fifteen minutes of fame by marrying on New York New York's roller coaster or while free-falling from the Big Shot, a thrilling ride atop the Stratrosphere Tower. But this type of fame, if it can be called fame, is fleeting, usually worth no more than a mention in the hometown paper. So the world was unprepared for the *Who Wants to Marry a Multi-Millionaire?* Las Vegas wedding of Darva Conger, 34, emergency-room nurse, and Rick Rockwell, 42, stand-up comic and real estate developer, on a live Fox television special on February 15, 2000.

Before the part game show, part beauty pageant took place, host Jay Thomas said, "I don't think anyone will watch it." Well, he was not even in the ballpark. The 10 million viewers watching during the introduction of the fifty contestants at the beginning of the show grew steadily through the personality test and the swimsuit competition. There were nearly 23 million viewers as the bachelor, who had been waiting and watching in the wings, picked the one lucky lady to wed on the spot and then sealed it with a kiss.

That kiss was the kiss of death for the groom because his new bride deemed it overly intimate for having just met. Returning alone from her chaperoned, no-sex honeymoon in the Caribbean, Darva announced she would seek an annulment and proceeded to plead her case before a public eager to hear all the intimate details. On ABC's *Good Morning America* she confided to Diane Sawyer that she went on the show as a lark, never expecting to be picked. Rick, not seeing the maelstrom about to engulf him, defended himself on NBC's *Today* show. About the kiss he claimed, "I didn't mean any offense by that. I was just ecstatic."

In July word of Darva's impending appearance in *Playboy* began to seep out. It was rumored that she had secured a $400,000 fee plus bonus if her issue sold an unspecified number of copies. News clips showed her dancing at Hugh Hefner's Los Angeles mansion. She decided to do Howard Stern's radio talk show because many of his listeners read *Playboy*. She told Larry King that her ex-husband would not buy her *Playboy* issue because he's notoriously frugal.

Not to be outdone, Rick used the publicity he was getting to resurrect his stand-up routine. From his partisan vantage point, he joked, "This might be the first *Playboy* where men actually read the articles." He bantered with Joy Behar on ABC's *The View*, "Just call me old-fashioned, but I think it's important to see your wife naked at some point in time."

Nevada marriage laws made it possible for the first instant celebrity newlyweds to find some degree of notoriety, if not love, from two hours on a Las Vegas stage. Alas, they were bumped from the headlines at the end of the summer by the survivors of CBS's *Survivor*, who had spent up to forty days on a quasi-deserted island off Borneo competing for $1 million.

JOAN COLLINS

More than any other actress, Joan Collins embodies the excesses of the eighties. Joining ABC's hit nighttime soap opera *Dynasty* in its second season, she played the career-defining role of Alexis Carrington Colby Dexter to the hilt. Part predatory femme fatale, part glamorous businesswoman, she married richer and richer men until she had enough money and power to control not only her own fate, but also the lives of all around her, making them miserable in the process. She became television's favorite wicked witch.

On a personal level, Joan professed, "I believe in marriage, good old-fashioned marriage." While manipulating the lives of her television family, she married her fourth husband, former pop singer and Swedish businessman Peter Holm, in 1985. She was 51 years old; he was 37. A couple of years earlier they had met at a mutual friend's pool party in England. She told him to look her up if he was ever in Los Angeles, and he took her at her word. After dating for a while, Joan decided that she wanted to introduce Peter as her husband rather than her boyfriend. She skipped a day's shooting, and they slipped off to Las Vegas to walk down the aisle at A Little White Chapel.

Everything seemed to be going great the first few months. On summer hiatus from *Dynasty*, Joan and Peter were in Venice and Paris filming a $14 million made-for-TV movie called *Sins*. She was the star. He was the producer. Beautiful locations. Luxurious sets. They were together. What could be better? Yet it all fell apart a short time later.

Joan claimed that Peter became abusive toward her and her children, and she reportedly had to see a doctor about heart palpitations. Then there was the small matter of a million dollars that Joan alleged was missing, rather than merely misplaced. Whatever caused the split, comments came from all directions once the marriage was over.

Joan Collins and Michael Jordan were married at A Little White Chapel, though not to each other.

"We were very happy together, and I treated her like a goddess," protested Peter.

"The only things he's interested in are money, sex, and prestige—in that order," proclaimed one of Peter's former girlfriends.

"I never liked him from the beginning," Joe Collins, Joan's 83-year-old father, declared.

"He can barely write his name, let alone a book," Joan scoffed after learning that Peter was hoping to publish his account of their marriage gone bad.

But it is A Little White Wedding Chapel that has the last word on the matter. Although Joan's marriage to Peter Holm lasted only thirteen months, its marquee on Las Vegas Boulevard South has proudly proclaimed that "Joan Collins Married Here" for over thirteen years.

FRANK SINATRA

Frank Sinatra never liked anyone—anywhere, for any reason—telling him what to do. So when friend and producer Brad Dexter suggested that marrying Mia Farrow was not a good career move, Frank immediately got on the horn and directed his wiseguys to make plans for a Las Vegas wedding in forty-eight hours. Never mind that he was in the middle of filming *The Naked Runner* in London.

It therefore came to pass that two days later, at 5:30 p.m. on July 19, 1966, Mia Farrow became the third Mrs. Frank Sinatra. The four-minute civil ceremony was held in a private apartment at the Sands, a casino in which Sinatra had a 9 percent interest. Frank's newest record, "Strangers in the Night," played faintly over the hotel's loudspeaker system. To Mia's distress, no family was present. Frank's longtime valet, George Jacobs, and A-group friends Bill Goetz and his wife, Edie, the daughter of Louis B. Mayer, served as witnesses and shared a good-luck bottle of champagne. No one touched the wedding cake. The newlyweds had their honeymoon in London, where Frank had the movie to complete.

Frank Sinatra, 50, and Mia Farrow, 21, were an odd couple. It wasn't so much their ages that made them an unlikely match, although two of his three children were older than she was, as much as the different generations each represented. At the time they got together, Sinatra was the hip leader of the Rat Pack, the Chairman of the Board. He hung out with Dino and Sammy and went to Las Vegas for fun and games, games that included high-stakes gambling, hard liquor, and wild women, the type of "broads" who usually came with a price tag.

Mia Farrow was a blossoming flower child. She disliked the big hair and heavy makeup currently in style. While starring on television's *Peyton Place*, she had shorn her long blond locks in favor of a short, elfin cut. She smoked marijuana, used words like "groovy," and practiced transcendental meditation.

Yet Mia loved her husband, at least his private, gentler side. While she enjoyed spending long, quiet weekends alone with Frank, she was also proud to accompany him to concerts, basking in the audience's adoration of him. However, she was young, ambitious, and not about to forsake a promising film career. When she accepted the lead role in *Rosemary's Baby* with the internationally respected filmmaker Roman Polanski, she assured her husband she would also be able to work with him on *The Detective*. This never happened.

Rosemary's Baby fell behind schedule, and Mia refused to follow her husband's instructions to walk off the set and join him. Infuriated, Frank had his lawyer draw up divorce papers and serve her at the studio during production.

After a quick divorce in Juárez, Mexico, in 1968, the couple resumed their separate lives. Mia went on a retreat with the Maharishi Mahesh Yogi in India, crossing paths there with John, Paul, George, and Ringo, who had just completed their album *Sgt. Pepper's Lonely Hearts Club Band*. Frank filmed *Lady in Cement* in Florida during the day and performed at the Fontainebleau at night. To fill in his free time and stay out of trouble, if that was possible, Frank also became seriously involved with Hubert Humphrey's presidential campaign. He never spoke of Mia again.

BRITNEY SPEARS

It is lonely at the top. At 22, Britney Spears probably felt like she was never going to find love, let alone marriage. As a pop icon since she was in her teens, her every move has been calculated and evaluated, and her handlers have handlers. Her very public three-year relationship with fellow singing sensation Justin Timberlake ended badly, with accusations of infidelity and cries of foul play. She did not return Limp Bizkit frontman Fred Durst's high regard, and her liaison with wildman actor Colin Farrell was fun but fleeting. Is it any wonder that she found comfort, however briefly, in the arms of a man she has known since kindergarten?

New Year's Eve weekend began innocently enough. Britney, her entourage of friends, dancers, and bodyguards, and her older brother, Brian, checked into the Palms Casino Hotel, the hopping hip place for Hollywood celebrities, on Wednesday, December 31, 2003. They had booked several rooms, including a $5,000-a-night penthouse and the $10,000-a-night "Real World" Suite. That night they ate at the Palms's N9ne Steakhouse before going on to the hotel's ritzy nightspots, Ghost Bar and then the club Rain. Tired, Britney retired early.

New Year's Day was rather uneventful, but that night at about 10:00 p.m., it was back to Rain. Enter Jason Allen Alexander, 22, the future groom. Jason is a good ol' boy from Britney's hometown, Kentwood, Louisiana. He seems like a nice guy, and nice-looking, too, with the build of a professional football player he hopes to become. He was there at Britney's invitation and wanted to do nothing more than "have a good time and relax." The couple was seen canoodling and kissing, and they left together at about two in the morning.

Friday evening started off in much the same way. There was dining and dancing and later some quiet conversation while looking out at the city lights. "It was real pretty, a beautiful night," Jason attempted to explain later. "We were looking at each other, and it was, like, let's go do something wild and crazy. Let's go get married." So they did.

The adventure, such as it was, was not without a few stumbling blocks. The soon-to-be Mr. and Mrs. first had to find a chapel that was open in the middle of the night and then learned that they needed to go to the courthouse for a marriage license. The Palms bellman, doubling as chauffeur of the hotel's lime-green courtesy limousine, readily helped out. He drove the twosome up and down the Strip and escorted Britney down the aisle. Finally, at 5:30 a.m. on Saturday, January 3, at A Little White Chapel, the couple, young and undaunted, said "I do." The bride, hardly looking like a teen queen, wore a crop top, torn jeans, and a white baseball cap.

And then it was over—except for the fallout. When Britney and Jason announced their news, the proverbial stuff hit the fan. Lynne Spears, Britney's mom, was immediately on a plane to Vegas, arriving just hours later. On Sunday an annulment was agreed upon and a course of action for securing that annulment put into play. The strategy worked. At approximately 12:30 p.m. on Monday, a district court judge determined that the couple did not "have a meeting of the minds," and the union was no more. From a legal standpoint, the fifty-five-hour hour marriage never happened. Fans, however, will never forget.

CHAPTER 10

Better Luck Next Time

Some things are just not meant to be. These celebrity marriages lasted for a while. Several of them produced children. Then the parties involved moved on.

BARBRA STREISAND AND ELLIOTT GOULD

Long before Barbra Streisand had become the biggest multimedia star of her generation, even before she had recorded a single note or recited a single line for the camera, she fell in love with Elliott Gould. And Elliott Gould fell in love with her.

Barbra and Elliott were both cast in the Broadway musical *I Can Get It for You Wholesale*. Elliott at 23 had the lead role as a brash young man who rises to the top of the garment industry. It was 19-year-old Barbra's debut. After auditioning five times before the producer David Merrick was convinced that she was neither too ugly nor too weird for the part, she won the role of Miss Marmelstein, a put-upon, harassed secretary. Her solo literally stopped the show night after night, and a star was born.

When the show closed in December 1962 after a successful, though unspectacular, run of nine months, Barbra's career took off. She appeared on *The Ed Sullivan Show*, recorded her first album, and went on a nationwide concert tour. Elliott eventually got a gig in a poorly received revival of *On the Town* in London. When he returned to the United States, he joined Barbra's entourage and accompanied her to Los Angeles, where she bowled over the Hollywood elite at the Coconut Grove. Then it was on to Harrah's Tahoe near Reno, where she fulfilled the second part of a commitment to open for Liberace; the first had been at the Riviera in Las Vegas a few weeks earlier.

It was then and there that Barbra and Elliott decided to get married. It was obvious that their lives had changed. They would never return to the tiny one-bedroom cold-water flat over a fish restaurant on Third Avenue in New York City, but they could try and hold on to the happy memories of their idyllic lives of only a year before. On September 13, 1963, Barbra and Elliott exchanged vows before the justice of the peace in nearby Carson City. Her personal and business managers, Marty Erlichman and Marty Bregman, pleased that Nevada had no community property laws, served as witnesses.

For their working honeymoon, the couple stayed and played at the Beverly Hills Hotel when Barbra wasn't taping *The Judy Garland Show* or performing at the Hollywood Bowl with Sammy Davis Jr. Then it was back to New York. Rehearsals for *Funny Girl* were about to begin.

Although they had a son together, the Streisand-Gould marriage was almost over before it had begun. Barbra had an affair with Sydney Chaplin, her costar in the stage production of *Funny Girl*, and then with Omar Sharif, her costar in the movie version. Elliott, whose career languished until his 1969 Best Supporting Actor nomination for *Bob & Carol & Ted & Alice*, gambled and smoked dope. Whether it was Elliott's inability to deal with his wife's success or Barbra's unwillingness to sacrifice her ambition or her appetites for her husband, the couple announced their separation in September 1969. They eventually got a quick divorce in the Dominican Republic in June 1971.

As a footnote, Elliott's pregnant girlfriend, Jenny Bogart, had accompanied him to the Dominican Republic when he went for his divorce. Epitomizing the hippie lifestyle, they left the courthouse chanting, "We don't believe in marriage!" Two children later, they had obviously recanted—they got married in December 1973 in Las Vegas. Elliott's second marriage lasted barely a year.

MEL TORMÉ

Mel Tormé really got around. Known as the "Velvet Fog" for his silky smooth vocals, he was a popular singer and songwriter. "A Christmas Song"—"Chestnuts roasting on an open fire"—was one of his. Multitalented, he also played the drums, acted in movies, hosted the first daytime television talk show, and crossed the country again and again, performing pop and jazz melodies for the pleasure of his fans everywhere. He was popular with the ladies, too, dating such sophisticated beauties as Ava Gardner and Marilyn Monroe when he was between wives.

Maybe Mel accomplished so much because he started so young. He was a regular on a weekly Chicago radio soap opera by the age of 4. He wrote his first hit song, recorded by Harry James, "Lament to Love," when he was 15. He went to Hollywood to tour with the Chico Marx Orchestra when he was 17, and he was in his first feature film with Frank Sinatra at 18 before a brief stint in the army. And he was married the first of four times when he was 24 years old.

Mel loved his wife Candy, the mother of two of his children, but the passion was long gone by the time they said "I do." After a multitude of fights, it was over. Still, the divorce was civil; Candy had gone to Las Vegas to get it over with quickly, and Mel was free to move on. "I think a law ought to be passed: minimum legal age for marriage—thirty years old," Mel wrote years later in his autobiography. The only thing wrong with this thinking was that he did it again in 1956, a year after his divorce. He was now 31 years old, and he met with the same disastrous results.

Mel was smitten the moment he laid eyes on his second wife, Arlene Miles. Not only was she a knockout, the type of woman other men followed longingly with their eyes, she was witty and intelligent. Unfortunately, according to Mel, she was also a voracious flirt with a volatile temperament. Although they hooked up immediately upon meeting, Arlene dumping two other beaux to join him on a trip to England, they broke up frequently, including twice in the forty-eight hours preceding their Las Vegas nuptials. And it was her suggestion to get married in Las Vegas, too. Despite the warning bells, the wedding bells rang for the couple on Halloween 1956 at the Little Church of the West. Needless to say, the marriage, while producing a son, lasted only seven years.

It took Mel a while to get it right. His next marriage, to English actress Janette Scott, was equally unsuccessful. Aside from producing two more children, the best thing about his third union was its dissolution, as contentious as it was. On a break from depositions, Mel serendipitously met his fourth and last wife, Ali Severson, in the halls of justice at divorce court in 1976. Although they didn't marry for eight years, they were together until his death in 1999.

DAVID CASSIDY

When David Cassidy, the seventies teen idol with the trendsetting shag cut, married actress Kay Lenz in April 1977 in Las Vegas, he was 27 and no longer at the top of his game. Only a few years earlier, he had been starring in the popular TV show *The Partridge Family* and doing solo concerts before legions of fans. At one time he was paid more than Elvis Presley, Paul McCartney, and Elton John. He hadn't yet lost his entire fortune. That wasn't going to happen for another three or four years, when the Southern California real estate market collapsed and took his investments with it. But he was on his way.

David and Kay tied the knot at the Little Church of the West after dating for six short weeks. Needless to say, it did not work out. Kay was working steadily in a variety of television shows. David was not working at all. Immature and incompatible, the couple separated in 1981. His second marriage did not make it either, but the third time was a charm. Today David is happily married, living and working in Las Vegas. At the approach of the millennium he starred at the Copa in the Rio Hotel and Casino and was the headliner at MGM Grand's multimillion-dollar stage show *EFX*. Knowing only too well the exhilaration of a comeback, he produced *The Rat Pack Is Back* at the Sahara Hotel and Casino.

Happy newlyweds Kay Lenz and David Cassidy leave the Little Church of the West, but the honeymoon was soon over.

"I think I'm gonna stay here," David says of Las Vegas. "I believe this is the entertainment capital of the world, and I'm an entertainer. I could say about myself that I'm an actor, a singer, a songwriter, a producer. But I'm an entertainer, and that's what I do."

As long as David keeps doing it, fans will keep singing his most well-known song, "I Think I Love You." And, David, we do, too.

JANE FONDA

It was the sixties. "Sex, drugs, and rock 'n' roll" was the mantra of the day. In the spirit of the age, Jane Fonda, screen ingenue turned sex kitten, and Roger Vadim, French director of erotic films, were openly living together. Depending on their schedules, sometimes they were in Malibu, sometimes in France, and sometimes they had to maintain their transatlantic relationship over the phone.

On one such occasion, Jane, then 27, was alone in California to film *The Chase*. She and Vadim, ten years her senior, had been together for three years. As he had previously transformed his first wife Brigitte Bardot, his second wife, Annette Stroyberg, and his lover, Catherine Deneuve, into sexy film sensations so he had done for Jane's career with his film *Circle of Love*. He had also urged her to make *Cat Ballou*, which became an enormous box-office success. Jane knew that they were committed to each other, both personally and professionally, and deeply in love, but she had steadfastly rejected the concept of marriage. Suddenly she changed her mind and summoned a surprised Vadim back from Europe for a trip down the aisle.

When asked later why she had decided to get married, Jane's answer was, "Well, I guess because of my father. I knew I was hurting him." Henry Fonda was about to take his fifth wife and learned about the wedding from the newspaper. Although he sent a congratulatory note from New York, where he was in rehearsals, it is unlikely that her marriage did much to allay the friction that had developed between them. In his memoirs Vadim suggested another reason for Jane wanting to formalize their relationship: living with him without the benefit of matrimony had begun to feel like a halfhearted commitment. And Jane never did anything halfheartedly.

On August 11, 1965, three days before the actual event, the couple flew the wedding party to Las Vegas, where they checked in to the Dunes Hotel on the Strip. The evening ceremony was held in Jane and Vadim's six-room suite on the twentieth floor. Peter Fonda, Jane's brother, supplied background guitar music accompanied by six lady violinists. There were a few minor glitches. The couple had forgotten wedding rings, for which the judge chastised them. "It's the best part of my speech," he complained. To compensate, they borrowed those of the best man and his wife. Jane's borrowed ring was two sizes too large so she had to hold her ring finger up in the air throughout the ceremony. Overcome with either emotion or remorse, she cried copiously from start to finish. Vadim's mother, who was to have been the matron of honor, missed the ceremony altogether because she was too engrossed in taking pictures around town.

Afterward, for entertainment the newlyweds and their entourage went first to a burlesque stage revue of the French Revolution complete with a topless Marie Antoinette, who was guillotined in front of a cheering crowd. They then proceeded to the casinos for some baccarat, at which Vadim won $2,000. It was a happy occasion despite the earlier sentimental outburst.

Although Jane was married to Vadim for eight years, her growing involvement in radical politics drove an emotional wedge between them. They separated. However, it was not until she was pregnant and engaged to Tom Hayden, the antiwar protestor and left-wing activist, that she flew to the Dominican Republic for a divorce. It was granted in December 1972, enabling Jane to move ahead with the next phase of her life.

DUDLEY MOORE

When English comic Dudley Moore married for the third time, he was no longer the surprising sex symbol that his movies *10*, costarring Bo Derek, and *Arthur*, for which he had received an Oscar nomination in 1981, had made him. But he was riding high. The sequel *Arthur 2* was about to be released, and he was in love with a woman who called him her "sex thimble."

Dudley had first met his future wife, Brogan Lane, in 1981 on the movie set of *Six Weeks*. At the time he was involved with Susan Anton. A few years later they met up with each other at Ma Maison, the now defunct but once hot Hollywood restaurant, and began dating. After a few short weeks they were living together. The first year was spent in her two-bedroom rented home in the San Fernando Valley. When renovations were completed at Dudley's more palatial Marina Del Rey home, they relocated there.

Although Dudley was initially slow to pick up on Brogan's numerous hints that they get married, he did it up right when the time was right. At his friend and *Arthur* costar Liza Minnelli's suggestion, they went to the Little Church of the West in Las Vegas for a private twenty-minute ceremony in a comfortable setting. At high noon on February 21, 1988, the 52-year-old, five-foot-two-inch groom and 32-year-old, five-foot-eight-inch bride took their vows.

The couple looked the part. Dudley had donned a traditional morning suit, while Brogan was dressed in a low-cut white wedding gown. "Perfect for Vegas" is how she subsequently described it in interviews. The ring Dudley gave her was a knockout, just like his wife—two heart-shaped diamonds separated by an emerald-cut blue sapphire. The Reverend Jim Hamilton, who conducted the ceremony, later commented, "He's very congenial; she's absolutely gorgeous."

Unfortunately, good manners and movie-star good looks were not enough to keep this twosome together. They were divorced in December 1991.

GEORGE HAMILTON

George Hamilton is one of those people who are famous for being famous. While he has been on the small and large screens, appearing in over eighty movies and television shows for more than four decades, he is best known for his fabulous year-round tan and pearly white smile, as well as the many newsworthy women he has dated over the years. He went out with Lynda Bird Johnson to the consternation of her president father, befriended Elizabeth Taylor when she was in between husbands, and squired Imelda Marcos around and about after she had departed the Philippines.

In November 1972, George, 33, married model Alana

Collins, 27, at the Las Vegas Hilton, formerly known as the International, the hotel Elvis was putting on the map with his biannual concerts. Elvis, however, was not in attendance at the time. The marriage was the first for both of them. Before they divorced a few years later, they had a son, Ashley. When Ashley grew up he married Shannen Doherty, one of the teen stars (reputedly the temperamental one) of *Beverly Hills 90210*, after a two-week courtship. Ashley's marriage, which did not take place in Las Vegas, did not last, either.

Alana subsequently married rock star Rod Stewart, while George made movie history by being the first actor to play Count Dracula without his traditional pasty complexion in the 1979 movie comedy *Love at First Bite*. In the nineties he developed a line of skin care products, and he reunited with his former wife to host their own television talk show, appropriately titled *The George & Alana Show*. It, too, was short-lived.

George still pops up in the society columns now and then, visits Las Vegas to tend his cigar bar at New York New York, and lives in New York City six months of the year, occasionally appearing on Broadway. "I had succeeded in creating the perception of great wealth," he reflected in the *National Enquirer*. "And that has been the story of my entire life."

LORENZO LAMAS

Lorenzo Lamas, the handsome hunk who played Reno Raines, a modern-day bounty hunter on a motorcycle, on the cable television series *Renegade*, has a Hollywood heritage with Las Vegas connections. In June 1954 his father, Argentinean heartthrob Fernando Lamas, married his mother, movie beauty Arlene Dahl, in a small, private ceremony at Little Church of the West on the grounds of the Frontier Hotel and Casino. This second marriage for each of them lasted six years.

"I idolized my dad growing up and thought my mother

was a force of nature," Lorenzo confided in an interview, "but I was an overweight kid with a poor self-image and never imagined a glamorous life for myself." Slimming down and shaping up, Lorenzo was encouraged by his parents to take up acting. After a series of small roles, he landed the pivotal part of Lance Cumson, the playboy grandson of Jane Wyman's Angela Channing, on the 1980s nighttime soap opera *Falcon Crest*. When his on-screen mother, Abby Dalton, introduced him to her daughter Kathleen Kinmont, Lorenzo was between wives, but not for long. On January 21, 1989, Lorenzo, 31, took Kathleen, 24, as his third wife at the Graceland Wedding Chapel on Las Vegas Boulevard.

Graceland marked the occasion with a sign that read "Lorenzo Lamas was married here." Amused by the announcement, Lorenzo had his picture taken in front of the sign at a latter date. Sadly, the marriage was less successful than the sign, which was still posted a good ten years after the marriage ended in 1993.

Lorenzo pays tribute to the memory of his father with a tattoo on his upper back of a woman riding a unicorn. It symbolizes two of Fernando's favorite things: women and horses. Lorenzo likes women, too. When he married his fourth wife, former *Playboy* Playmate Shauna Sands, he matched his father in number of wives. With their split, his tattoo for her, a Tahitian eternal love symbol, will last longer than the marriage, and Lorenzo is well on his way to besting his old man.

CHAPTER 11

Close, but No Cigar

These Hollywood twosomes were at the top of the A-list. They were called "golden couples" and described as having perfect marriages. After years of what appeared to be wedded bliss in a happy home, cracks and crevices in the foundation started showing up. Then the façade came a-tumblin' down.

BRUCE WILLIS AND DEMI MOORE

Bruce Willis, 32, was the big man in town. As the sexy and charming leading man in the hit television show *Moonlighting*, he had the pick of the ladies. When he decided to tie the knot with Brat Pack actress Demi Moore, 25, one of Hollywood's most active and sought after bachelors was taken out of circulation.

Demi, in turn, had been married once before, to rock musician Freddy Moore. The previous year she had been engaged to Emilio Estevez, whom she had met on the set of *St. Elmo's Fire*. When she and Emilio broke up, she stopped hanging out at the downtown clubs favored by her crowd and started stopping at the bar at the Improv, a West Hollywood comedy club that Bruce frequented. After knowing each other for a few short but intense months, they headed for Las Vegas.

On Saturday, November 21, 1987, at 11:57 p.m., they picked up their marriage license at the Clark County Marriage Bureau and then returned to their suite in the Golden Nugget Hotel and Casino. It was there that they said their vows in a casual ceremony in front of a small group of friends. He had stubble on his chin. She wore black. Steve Wynn himself, the owner of the Golden Nugget, had made the last-minute arrangements for the event.

It was questionable whether the couple would make it. One observer noted, "He's a real womanizer. Even when he's with Demi you can tell he's fighting temptation at every moment." Yet in the next decade they became one of Hollywood's most visible and bankable power couples. Bruce reached superstardom playing a wisecracking cop in the blockbuster *Die Hard* action series. Demi won hearts in the tearjerker *Ghost*. Seven months pregnant with the second of their three daughters, she garnered more publicity than she could possibly leverage when she posed nude for the cover of *Vanity Fair*. It was quite a media event.

As the 1990s came to an end, so did the Willis-Moore union. In June 1998 they announced their separation. Two and half years later, after finally determining how to divide their $20 million property portfolio, including a forty-acre ranch in Hailey, Idaho, they divorced for irreconcilable differences. Bruce, seen squiring around all the pretty ladies, was the big man in town once again.

MARY TYLER MOORE

Mary Tyler Moore fell in love with Grant Tinker on their first date. She was 26 years old, recently divorced from her first husband, whom she had married when she was 18, and well on her way to becoming America's sweetheart as Mrs. Rob Petrie on *The Dick Van Dyke Show*. As a television network executive, Grant Tinker, eleven years Mary's senior, lived in New York. So for the first six months of their blossoming relationship, Mary and Grant spent a lot of time on the phone and making plans for their future, generating over $300 in monthly phone bills, an enormous sum in those days.

After what felt like an eternity to Mary, Grant moved his career to the West Coast, and they married on June 1, 1962. Concerned that the state of California would not recognize their divorces, his in Alabama, hers in a small Mexican village, they went to Las Vegas. Since privacy was a priority, the couple accepted the use of a friend of a friend's usually vacant one-bedroom suite at the Dunes Hotel for the ceremony. The setting was pleasant enough, but the actual nuptials could have passed as an episode from a television sitcom.

The suite's owner, a local furrier, had replaced the bedroom furniture with racks of fur. Short on time and with no mirror to aid her efforts, Mary made do with the arrangements. Beginning to change into her wedding costume, a dark blue silk dress with a little white hat and veil, she was startled when the owner rushed into the room from the hallway and began looking frantically for some business papers. Reminding him of who she was and why she was there, she quickly finished dressing, the rows of minks and lynx providing coverage so her modesty, if not her privacy, was left intact. Then she joined Grant, the judge, and their friends in the other room.

The judge began speaking, when a knock from the bedroom door temporarily halted the proceedings. The furrier, having come across Mary's bouquet, which she had left behind in haste, entered the room, pushed the flowers into her hands, mumbled his apologies, and left as unobtrusively as he could. After a few more words were exchanged, the ceremony was over and the newlyweds returned to Los Angeles on the next plane.

With MTM Productions, the golden couple of the small screen created what came to be known as the "Camelot" of independent television production, an ideal working environment for writers and producers. However, just as Camelot was not forever, neither was the Moore-Tinker union. They divorced after seventeen years of marriage.

DINAH SHORE AND GEORGE MONTGOMERY

It was wartime when blues singer and radio star Dinah Shore, 25, and cowboy turned leading man George Montgomery, 26, met at the Hollywood Canteen. Friendly and outgoing, she was there to entertain the troops. As a corporal in the Single Corps serving in the First Motion Picture Division, he was there in uniform. Before George left for his first assignment in Alaska, the couple fell in love. When he was back in Los Angeles on three days' leave, they eloped to Las Vegas.

In high spirits the couple drove across the desert with a group of friends and fellow actors and musicians. At three o'clock on a cold and frosty winter morning on December 5, 1943, Dinah and George said "I do" in front of a justice of the peace on the outskirts of town. The celebratory wedding breakfast at an all-night joint called the Failing Elk consisted of damp toast, warmed-over eggs, and cold coffee, yet Dinah recalled, "I ate heartily."

And so began what the press deemed "the perfect marriage." After the war the Montgomerys happily settled down in a ranch house on two and a half acres in Encino in the San Fernado Valley. Dinah successfully pursued her singing career, earning the title Queen of the Jukebox with a string of hit records, and eventually becoming one of the first television personalities as the popular hostess of *The Dinah Shore Show*. George not only continued to act, but opened a successful custom-furniture business. At home they opted for a quiet, family-oriented lifestyle, sharing mutual interests while shunning the Hollywood social scene.

But fissures in the foundation began appearing. Dinah was described as a night person, George as a day person. She was city, he was country. Their personal communication increasingly centered on work, and work was bringing more and more pressures. For business reasons Dinah was spending greater amounts of time away from home, and George, whose film career had begun to falter, had time to take up with other women. Nineteen years later they were formally divorced.

BILLY MARTIN

"Billy the Kid" Martin loved everything about the game of baseball. He loved playing, and he played hard, believing that it was important to win at all costs. He relished his victories almost as much as he enjoyed the celebration afterward. And celebrate he did, by partying heartily and drinking heavily. It is hardly surprising that more than one after-game get-together led to a fight or a brawl. When his first wife filed for divorce, she explained, "You can just say there was too much baseball."

Billy wanted it all—not only a successful career, but a happy home life as well. So while the divorce devastated him, he eventually pulled himself together and, once again, went looking for love. He found it, too, in Kansas City, when he was playing for the Athletics. His intended, Gretchen Winkler, an airline hostess at the time, was an attractive, intelligent woman with a practical nature.

Two years later, at the end of his first and only baseball season with the Cleveland Indians, Billy, now 31, and Gretchen, 24, went to Las Vegas. He had wanted a big blowout surrounded by good friends, such as Mickey Mantle, but scheduling conflicts kept the guest list down. Still, the two-minute ceremony at the Desert Inn on October 7, 1959, came off as planned, and the couple went on a two-week honeymoon in Italy.

Billy had only another two years before his body wore out and he could no longer deliver on the field. After that, he became a coach and then a manager, and one of the best at that, having the unique talent of being able to turn a no-talent team into a force of nature. Sadly, in 1975, when he got the call to manage the Yankees, he moved to New York alone. Gretchen, tired of his unrestrained playboy lifestyle, chose to stay in Texas, where she had made a home when Billy worked for the Rangers, and raise their son.

Billy was renowned in the Big Apple, taking the Yankees to the 1976 and 1977 World Series, winning the latter. His relationship with his boss, George Steinbrenner, was infamous; Billy was fired and rehired five times for what amounted to personality differences. Despite his successes and his numerous girlfriends and two more wives to keep him company, he was a lonely man. He died in a car crash on Christmas Day 1989 at the age of 61.

BELA LUGOSI

Bela Lugosi started as a young matinee idol on the Hungarian stage and became the most famous Count Dracula on the Hollywood screen. He gave what many consider to be the definitive portrayal of the villainous vampire: charming but cold-blooded; erotic yet evil. In his trademark tuxedo and black cape, he was dashing and debonair but somehow threatening, too. Except for drawing two lines on his brow with a grease pencil to convey concentration, he gave eternal life to the gothic melodrama without makeup or special effects.

Women adored him, attracted to his eastern European sensibilities, and he had numerous wives and lovers. Yet those same sensibilities, which today would be considered extremely chauvinistic, coupled with an authoritative personality, led to some very brief relationships. He was married to his third wife, an extremely rich widow, for only four days because he did not approve of her drinking in public. His next attempt at wedded bliss, while not everlasting, was much more successful; he was married to Lillian Arch, the mother of his son, for twenty years.

Lillian was the shy daughter of a respected member of the Hungarian community in Los Angeles. The couple had met in her parents' home following a meeting Bela had attended. Despite their age differences—Bela was 50 to her 20—her father had initially encouraged the relationship, thinking that Bela had money. Once he learned that he didn't, it was too late. Lillian had fallen in love.

"Would you like to go to Las Vegas with me?" Bela proposed one Sunday evening in January 1933 following a movie. Given a resounding yes, Bela set their clandestine plan in motion the very next day. As usual, Lillian went to work, but then met Bela afterward for dinner at a nearby chili parlor. With time to spare, they took a cab to the train station. They didn't know it then, but their taxi driver had identified them, and he tipped off the tabloids for a fee. "Dracula Weds Beauty" announced every newspaper in town upon their return the next day.

Arriving in Las Vegas at six in the morning, they had three hours before the courthouse opened and they could have their five-minute ceremony in front of a judge. When they settled in to wait at a rather run-down all-night café, drinking coffee and happily sharing the moment, they were under the impression that the elopement was a private affair. Bela even denied that he was associated with the movies when questioned by a local reporter. That afternoon the headline of the Las Vegas paper read DRACULA WEDS IN LAS VEGAS THIS A.M.

Fame and fortune followed the newlyweds their first several years together. Then disaster struck. Horror movies, censored in England, fell out of favor at the studios here, and Bela, who was forever typecast as the vampire count, could not find work. Generous to a fault, he had given away huge sums of money to worthy causes, down-on-their-luck actors, and just about anyone who might ask, and they had nothing to fall back on. Yet Lillian stuck by him, through good times and bad, in sickness and in health, until he began drinking. His alcohol consumption was accompanied by false accusations of adultery, and she was granted a divorce on grounds of mental cruelty in 1953.

At 70 years old, Bela, ill and impoverished, could still be captivating and charismatic, and he married Hope Lininger, a lifelong fan. They lived together for two years before he passed away.

BETTY GRABLE AND HARRY JAMES

In the 1940s the movie studio reigned. When Twentieth Century—Fox proclaimed that Betty Grable had the best legs in the land, it became so. To protect their assets, the studio safeguarded

the famous gams with a $1 million Lloyd's of London insurance policy. When she was crowned "the Pin-Up Girl," 10 million copies of the wholesome yet sexy image of her dressed in a one-piece backless swimsuit, smiling coyly over her shoulder, were distributed, and the poster was plastered on billboards and barrack walls everywhere.

When Betty met Harry James at the Hollywood Canteen, she was the number one actress at the box office. He was the leader of the country's hottest band and universally regarded as the

Harry James and Betty Grable eat cake after their fans almost ruined the festivities with their enthusiasm.

greatest trumpet player in the world. They were both 27 years old. Betty was divorced from her first husband, Jackie Coogan, had been jilted by Artie Shaw for Lana Turner (as Judy Garland had been), and was dating George Raft, the matinee idol with mob connections. Harry was still married to his first wife, former band singer Louise Tobin, with whom he had two children.

After falling in love, it was easier for Betty to extricate herself from her relationship with George Raft (a public fistfight he had lost to Harry took care of that) than it was for Harry to leave his wife. When Harry finally got a quickie Mexican divorce, Betty was five weeks pregnant. They immediately made plans to marry quietly at the Little Church of the West on the grounds of the Frontier Hotel.

Filming the movie *Pin-Up Girl* in Los Angeles, Betty was the first to arrive in Las Vegas. She waited in a limousine with her friend and witness-to-be, actress Betty Furness, surrounded by ardent fans and eager photographers, while Harry, taking the train from New York, where he was playing, was hours late. By the time he got there, a loudspeaker system had been installed so that the crowds who couldn't get into the tiny church would be able to hear the ceremony. "This isn't a wedding," Betty, tired and anxious, exclaimed. "It's a three-ring circus."

To salvage the situation, the couple went to their hotel, where they called a Baptist minister and asked him to come to their suite to perform the ceremony. They were officially married in the early hours of July 5, 1943.

After a three-day honeymoon during which they reportedly never left their hotel suite, Betty returned beaming to Hollywood. Although gossip columnists gave the marriage six months at the most, Betty declared, "I aim to stay Mrs. Harry James for the rest of my life." And despite Harry's penchant for drinking, gambling, and philandering, they were married for twenty-two years. Betty, who had eventually quit Hollywood to live in Las Vegas and would stay there until her death in 1973, also got her divorce there.

CHAPTER 12

Till Death Do Us Part

*E*ven some Hollywood marriages that began in Las Vegas were made in heaven. They are not necessarily first marriages for one or both parties, but they are happily-ever-after marriages.

ANN-MARGRET

Ann-Margret's dreams of a fairy-tale wedding were not to be. Instead of a little white church in the countryside or an outdoor garden in her native Sweden, the ceremony took place in a smoke-filled suite in the Riviera Hotel and Casino. Rather than being surrounded by family and friends wishing them health and happiness, they were crowded by reporters and photographers just doing their job. With mascara-laden tears streaming down her face, Ann-Margret said "I do" and then fled back to Los Angeles with her new husband, Roger Smith.

At the time Ann-Margret was 26 years old. She had debuted in the movie *Pocketful of Miracles*, dazzled moviegoers in *Bye Bye Birdie*, and bewitched Elvis Presley on-screen in *Viva Las Vegas*, and off. Roger Smith, 35, was a popular actor, best known for his role as the hip detective Jeff Spencer in *77 Sunset Strip*. He had been married once before and had three children.

After going out for three years, being engaged for one, then splitting up for three weeks over a disagreement about the management of her career, the couple made up by setting a date to get married the next time they saw each other. Later that day, May 8, 1967, Roger picked her up, drove to the airport, and flew them to Las Vegas. Ann-Margret, happy and excited, traveled in her sixties-style wedding attire—a white piqué micro-miniskirt and matching fluffy short shorts. The cloudless blue sky boded well for a perfect day.

Wanting to generate publicity for Ann-Margret's club appearance the next month, the Riviera had put up a banner saying, WELCOME ANN-MARGRET AND ROGER. The world soon knew they were in Las Vegas, dashing their romantic plans for a quiet, private wedding. Ann-Margret could not control her disappointment.

Although this Hollywood twosome did not have an auspicious start, they have weathered the difficulties that come with marriage. Roger nursed Ann-Margret back to full singing and dancing health after her twenty-two-foot fall onstage at the Sahara Hotel in Lake Tahoe in 1972. In turn, she took charge when Roger fell ill with the near fatal disease myasthenia gravis in the eighties. They have been together over thirty years because as Ann-Margret says, "He concentrates on me, while I concentrate on him."

WILLIAM POWELL

Although William Powell started his movie career playing mean and menacing villains in silent films of the twenties, he became best known to an adoring public as the dashing and debonair detective Nick Charles in the *Thin Man* series. His on-screen relationship with his costar, Myrna Loy, who played his wife, Nora, was so believable that many thought that they were indeed married, and happily so.

Bill's personal life, however, was not quite so charmed. He had first been married in 1914 when he was a struggling 22-year-old actor. The second time was in 1931 to newcomer Carole Lombard when he was a successful 39-year-old movie star. Divorced after two years, they remained friends. They even dated for a while after the divorce. Yet Bill felt responsible for the failed union. When he became deeply involved with Jean Harlow, another young and beautiful blond actress, it looked as if he had found the happiness that had been eluding him. However, Jean's sudden and tragic death of cerebral edema at 26 sent him into deep mourning. Only his own successful fight against cancer, almost unheard of at the time, seemed to get him to move forward with his life.

Now 47, Bill was recuperating at his Beverly Hills home when he met the woman who would become the third and last Mrs. William Powell. He had given permission to the MGM marketing department to use his property for publicity stills. Believing him to be out of town, they had set up a photo shoot with a pretty, petite brunette actress, Diana Lewis, 21. When he caught sight of her posing in a bathing suit on the diving board, he decided an introduction was in order. He strolled across the lawn, surprising the MGM personnel with his presence, and asked the young woman to join him for dinner. Despite the difference in their ages, the star and starlet found they had much in common, and one dinner turned into another dinner into another dinner.

On January 6, 1940, less than one month after Bill and Diana had met, they married at a dude ranch in Warm Springs, Nevada, close to Las Vegas. They had been in Palm Springs, at the time a small, unspoiled, and unknown community, with her family so that everyone could get to know each other. With the blessings of her parents, they decided to travel the short distance to Nevada and become man and wife that weekend, avoiding California's premarital waiting period. Making arrangements by phone, they lined up a justice of the peace to administer the vows and some friends to serve as witnesses. Their plans were almost spoiled when their car broke down near Baker, but with the help of a passing driver, they arrived at their destination before noon. The single-ring ceremony was performed outdoors in the bright, warm sunshine.

William Powell knew just what he was doing that day in

the desert. He had finally found lasting love, and he was not about to let it go. Bill and Diana were happily married until he died at the age of 92 in 1984.

KIRK DOUGLAS

The self-proclaimed ragman's son, Kirk Douglas, was also a self-professed ladies' man, at least until he married for the second time. After his divorce from his first wife, Diana Dill, on grounds of infidelity, he was supposedly engaged to Pier Angeli, his Italian costar in the movie *The Story of Three Lives*. It was during this on-again, off-again two-year relationship that he began seeing Anne Buydens.

Kirk and Anne met in Paris where he was filming, in French, *Act of Love*. He first tried to hire her as his personal assistant while he was overseas. She turned him down. He then tried to date her. Again she turned him down. So they became friends. And then lovers. Even after Kirk returned to the States, they kept their relationship going.

Just as one of Anne's Los Angeles visits was about to end, Kirk proposed. It was a clumsy proposal, not really planned. "Uh, uh, I have to talk to you," Kirk, down on one knee, stuttered. "Uh, I think we should get married." Anne was surprised, but thrilled, and they made plans to do just that that weekend.

With a small group of friends, the couple flew to Las Vegas on Saturday, May 29, 1954. The twenty-three-hour-a-day license bureau was closed when they arrived. To wait out the hour, they shot craps at the Golden Nugget. Finally, after getting the license they were married in their suite at the Sahara Hotel by a justice of the peace.

Having to be on the set of *20,000 Leagues Under the Sea* the first thing Monday morning, Kirk had no time to think about what he had just committed himself to. "The ring felt strange on my finger for a few months," he commented in his memoir. "Then, like Anne, it was a part of my life." And, symbolic of the happy union of its bearer to his wife, it has remained so for over fifty years.

BETTY WHITE

Every time Allen Ludden, the bespectacled, gentlemanly host of the popular 1960s television game show *Password*, proposed, and he proposed often over the course of a year, the queen of television, Betty White, just said no. She certainly had plenty of reasons. She had been married and divorced twice before. Approaching 40, she was enjoying the carefree, single lifestyle in California. She regularly commuted to New York to appear on *Password*, but she couldn't imagine living there, even to be with Allen. Becoming a stepmother to his three teenage children, as much as she adored them, was another hurdle she couldn't overcome in her mind. So she said no for so long that when she finally said yes, Allen had used up most of his annual vacation traveling to the West Coast to court her.

Rather than waiting until there was more time to plan a lavish ceremony and go someplace exotic for their honeymoon, the couple opted instead for a quickie wedding in Las Vegas followed by a short holiday in Laguna Beach, California. They were in complete agreement on this. Then they almost split up before they got hitched. Allen, who had never missed a plane in his life, missed his plane from New York to Los Angeles because he got caught in a traffic jam on his way to the airport. Betty, upset and angry, thought it was a bad sign. But Allen caught the next fight out, and the soon-to-be newlyweds were soon on their way to Las Vegas as planned. Betty's parents were witnesses to the ceremony that took place in the wedding suite at the Sand Hotel on June 14, 1963. Eager to catch the plane for their trip back to California, the wedding party left behind a table full of canapés and bottles of champagne, compliments of the hotel.

The Luddens had a strong, happy marriage. It lasted until Allen's death eighteen years later. In her book, *In Person*,

Betty wondered why she hesitated for so long before accepting his proposal. Yet she knows that they stayed together because they thought of themselves as a unit, rather than two separate entities. "All of our problems came from the outside . . . never between the two of us," she reflected. "And we handled those problems together."

BING CROSBY

When Bing Crosby, the 50-year-old superstar who was filming what would become the hit classic *White Christmas*, met Kathryn Grant, a 19-year-old aspiring actress, the widower with four sons fell hard for the young, talented looker. Yet it was three years and four broken wedding dates before the couple actually made it down the aisle. Cold feet coupled with an innate sense of decorum kept the normally nonchalant Bing from consummating the relationship.

Kathryn had just about adjusted to the idea of living her life without the man of her life when Bing conspired with her aunt Mary to get her to Las Vegas for one last go. He was now ready to take the plunge and felt confident that Kathryn would forgive his dallying and dalliances. Not really sure how she felt—she had seen Bing infrequently over the past year—Kathryn let Aunt Mary take charge. And take charge she did! She hurriedly, almost frantically, packed for the trip, quickly putting together a wedding trousseau for Kathryn, and they made it to the airport for their 5:30 p.m. flight with ten minutes to spare. That night before the wedding the ladies stayed at the Desert Inn. Bing was at the Sands.

Bright and early the morning of October 24, 1957, Leo Lyn, Bing's boyhood friend and driver, gathered the wedding party together and chauffeured them first to the county courthouse for the marriage license and then to St. Anne's Church. Despite the lack of time to prepare, Kathryn, at least in appearance, had pulled herself together and looked elegant in a white suit with matching pumps, a string of pearls, and a borrowed mink stole. Her corsage was a white orchid, purchased at the last minute from one of the all-night marriage chapels.

The ceremony was a simple mass with the addition of the marriage prayers. Two candles burned on the chapel altar. Kneeling to pray, Kathryn was overcome with self-doubt. "Can this be the right thing, Lord?" she asked herself. "Will I make a good wife for Bing Crosby?" But it was too late to change her mind; besides, she did not really want to, and the service was under way.

Afterward, Leo, looking out for Bing's reputation, convinced him to call back the press whom he had misdirected to the small desert town of Yerington, a miserable five-hour drive away. Thus forty-five members of the media joined the newlyweds, Aunt Mary, Leo, and the monsignor at a champagne breakfast hosted by the Sands. The festivities weren't over. Going on to Palm Springs, they were greeted there by the mayor, several hundred townspeople, and a band playing "Here Comes the Bride."

Misgivings aside, married life for Bing and Kathryn Crosby was off to a joyous start. They lived together until Bing's death twenty-four years later.

MICHAEL CAINE

British actor Michael Caine always had fond feelings for Las Vegas. He had first visited the Rat Pack's playground in 1966 as the guest of his friend Nancy Sinatra Jr. They stayed at the Sands and had ringside seats with Mia Farrow, Yul Brynner, and other family friends at her father Frank's show in the Copa Room.

Several years later Michael, now 40, was a famous movie star and living the bachelor's life at home in London when he fell madly and passionately in love at first sight with his second wife, Shakira Baksh, 26. After spotting her in a television commercial for Maxwell House coffee, he was ready to pursue her to Brazil, which was where he assumed she lived, when a mutual acquaintance gave him her local telephone

Michael Caine crossed the big pond with his beautiful bride to say his vows in Vegas.

number. When he called, she agreed to go out with him in spite of his reputation as a bit of a rogue. He convinced her of his virtues (no, he told her, he wasn't anything like the character Alfie he had played in the movie by the same name), and they dated exclusively, seeing each other constantly. Then they moved in together. When she became pregnant, their next logical step was to get married. Las Vegas would be perfect, they felt, for a simple wedding ceremony with a few close friends and no fuss. They just needed an excuse to visit the Silver State, preferably before the baby arrived.

As luck would have it, *Sleuth*, Michael's picture with Laurence Olivier, was ready for release, and the studio wanted him to go to America to publicize it. So off the couple went. On January 8, 1973, their first free weekend in Los Angeles, they flew to Las Vegas. Their friend Dennis Selinger accompanied them; he would give the bride away and was paying for the wedding as a gift.

Everything proceeded without a hitch. They made a quick stop at the Clark County Courthouse to obtain their license. Then they selected the Candlelight Wedding Chapel, which Michael nicknamed "the Little Chapel on the Green" for the Astroturf encircling the establishment. Waiting for the justice of the peace, they signed up for some extras—Polaroid pictures, an audio recording of the ceremony, and orchids for the bride and groom. After all, it was Dennis's treat. Finally, they said their vows. This was a very busy Friday night, and it was all over rather quickly. After eating dinner and catching a cabaret performance, they returned later that night to the Beverly Wilshire Hotel in Los Angeles for a working honeymoon.

By the time Michael fell in love, he knew what it is all about. He had gone from bit actor to leading man, from ladies' man to family man, and along the way, he found lasting happiness with Shakira. Their married life continues to this day.

PAUL NEWMAN AND JOANNE WOODWARD

Little is known about the 1958 wedding nuptials of Paul Newman and Joanne Woodward. This is hardly surprisingly, because one of Hollywood's most enduring couples is also one of its most private. What is surprising is that it took place Hollywood-style at the newest and most glitzy Las Vegas hotel and casino at the time, the El Rancho. In front of singer Eydie Gorme, entertainer Sophie Tucker, and comedian Joe E. Lewis, who were performing there, Paul and Joanne became husband and wife. On their honeymoon in London, they posed for pictures in their bedroom suite at the elegant Connaught Hotel. It was almost as if the whole affair from soup to nuts had been planned by their agents to attract publicity for a couple who usually did not like, want, or need publicity.

Paul, 33, and Joanne, 28, were already in the public eye, both individually and as an item. He had been expected to get an Academy Award nomination for *Somebody Up There Likes Me*. He didn't, but his career was flourishing. She had won for the 1957 film *The Three Faces of Eve*. They had acted together on the stage in *Picnic*, in the film *The Long, Hot Summer*, and in the live television play *The 80-Yard Run*. Meanwhile they successfully evaded reporters' queries on their wedding plans while awaiting Paul's divorce from his first wife.

Over forty years later they are still together. Paul became a superstar, part of the most popular screen team of them all, playing Butch Cassidy to Robert Redford's the Sundance Kid. Joanne continued to hone her craft, working on the stage, one of her true loves, and pursuing quality vehicles for her unique talents and special interests. It is possible that their success in their personal lives is due to their keeping the success in their professional lives from going to their heads.

Or the secret for their longevity as a couple might be as simple as a statement Paul once made. "If you have steak at home," Paul reputedly said, "why go out for hamburger?" And if he didn't say it, then he should have.

3

WHAT'S A WEDDING WITHOUT ELVIS?

In Vegas everyone tries to cash in on Elvis, but it is equally unlikely that Elvis slept here or that the Normandie Motel is still in business.

"H OW ARE PEOPLE GOING to remember me?" Elvis Presley lamented to his friend and backup singer Kathy Westmoreland three months before his death on August 16, 1977. "I've never done a classic film. I've never sung a lasting song."

Well, have we got news for him. He is known around the world by his first name, and he still carries the title "the King." Along with presidents, Pulitzer Prize winners, and other Americans of some repute, his picture has appeared on a postage stamp, the selection of which required a national poll conducted by the United States Postal Service. In addition to Marilyn Monroe, Elizabeth Taylor, and Campbell soup cans, his image lives in perpetuity in Andy Warhol's silk screens in the world's best museums. And he has been immortalized in movies and song, just not necessarily his movies or his songs. Paul Simon's 1986 hit rightly claims that "Poorboys and Pilgrims with families" got "reason to believe" they'll all "be received in Graceland," his Memphis home.

Graceland is a symbol of Elvis's enduring popularity. Over 750,000 paying guests visit each year, making it one of the most popular historic homes in the country along with the White House and Mount Vernon. Thousands of fans make a pilgrimage to Graceland on his January birthday to celebrate his life, and tens of thousands more come on the anniversary of his death to mourn his passing. At the same time Las Vegas, sixteen hundred miles away, has become Elvis's living memorial year-round.

Elvis impersonators, or tribute artists, as some prefer to be called, abound around town. By some estimates at least fifty entertainers in Las Vegas make some money each year impersonating Elvis, a threefold increase in less than a decade. At any given time they perform in as many as six or more venues along the Strip and downtown. In the larger casinos such as the MGM

Grand, the shows are often lounge acts. They are located adjacent to the slots and cost the audience nothing except what they lose to the one-armed bandits. Others are held in showrooms for a fixed price of upwards of $30. For the cost of admission fans can also hear Elvis impersonators singing a few songs about once an hour at the Elvis-A-Rama Museum; and Elvises are hired to perform at private parties and pose afterward for pictures with the guests for an up-close and personal experience. In Las Vegas, Elvis truly is everywhere.

And let's not forget the wedding chapels. Elvis is welcome at almost every facility in town where people can tie the knot, from the fancy hotel chapels to the fanciful independents. Some of the uptown Strip hotels, somewhat snobby like uptown hotels everywhere, prefer that Elvis's presence be limited to his voice on a CD of his greatest hits. Otherwise, Elvis impersonators take part in all aspects of the nuptials, from escorting the bride down the aisle to serenading the newlyweds after they are pronounced husband and wife. While there is an impersonator for any celebrity—male or female, tall or short, living or dead—only too happy to grace a wedding with a joke or a song, it is the King that couples clamor for. "Elvis is Las Vegas," a groom noted on his way to the altar. "And since we're getting married in Las Vegas, we have to have him at the altar with us."

CHAPTER 13

To Vegas and Back to Vegas

OFF TO A SLOW START

In April 1956 Elvis first performed in Las Vegas. He played for two weeks for $8,500 a week at the New Frontier Hotel as the opening act for Freddy Martin and his orchestra and the comedian Shecky Greene. Billed as "the Atomic Powered Singer," he bombed big-time. Although teenage America was in the process of turning his first RCA record, "Heartbreak Hotel," into gold, the high rollers, the only demographic that counts in Vegas, just weren't ready for rock 'n' roll.

Not that Elvis was really ready for Las Vegas. The state fairs and other country outlets at which he had honed his act were unsophisticated, requiring Elvis to do little more than show up with his three-piece combo and sing his heart out, and so Elvis himself remained unsophisticated. Even then he would lose himself in his music, letting his "arms and legs just follow the music," as he told one interviewer. But he was only 21 years old and not yet the consummate performer he was to become. He didn't know how to converse with an audience, pulling them in and making each and every one of them feel like he was singing to him or her alone. To the Vegas crowd Elvis simply sang loudly. And then there was the matter of his appearance. Although his Svengali-like manager, Colonel Tom Parker, insisted he wear a bow tie and jacket, an attempt to dress him up, he couldn't do much about Elvis's bushy sideburns and long hair. To the Vegas crowd, Elvis was

With his unique look and distinctive style, Elvis drove the teenagers wild but turned the dice cold, a no-no in Vegas.

simply uncouth, quite a contrast to what would become his Las Vegas superstar image.

Still, the year 1956 was big for Elvis. He made a series of television appearances, first with Tommy and Jimmy Dorsey, famous bandleaders of the big-band sound, on their program *Stage Show* in January, and then subsequently with Milton Berle, Steve Allen, and Ed Sullivan on their respective shows. Ironically, although none of the three maestros of 1950s variety shows thought very highly of him or his talents, they created the public forum from which Elvis shimmied and shook his way into history.

Milton Berle had Elvis on his show to help attract a younger audience. When Elvis showed up without a guitar to mask the way he moved his hips, he created a coast-to-coast controversy over the licentious way he sang "Hound Dog," and his career took off. Steve Allen thought Elvis was a flash in the pan, but correctly believed the ballyhoo his appearance on the Berle show had stirred up could help him in the ratings war with *The Ed Sullivan Show*, which aired at the same time as his. Allen was right, and he clobbered his competitor's show the night Elvis was his guest. Ed Sullivan, meanwhile, who had publicly stated that he would never have Elvis on his program, paid Elvis the astronomical sum of $50,000 for three appearances in order to regain his lock on Sunday-evening audiences. Ed Sullivan could not afford not to go back on his word, and an unprecedented 54 million viewers tuned in to see what the fuss was about. Swiveling his hips and curling his lips, the rockabilly rebel had moved onto the national stage, and in the process set a cultural revolution in motion, changing the world.

Before the year was out Elvis returned to Las Vegas, not as a performer, but as a visitor, and attended Liberace's opening at the Riviera. Liberace, who had first performed in Vegas at the Frontier in 1945 for $400 a week, was now getting $50,000 a week and was on his way to earning the title "Mr. Showmanship" with his extravagant costumes and personal flair.

Elvis joined Lee, as Liberace was called by his friends, backstage afterward, and the two posed for pictures. For something different they traded roles and clothes. Lee picked up the guitar, playing the rock 'n' roller in Elvis's oversize striped jacket. Elvis, looking spiffy in Liberace's gold lamé jacket, sat down at the piano. Elvis took his meeting with Lee to heart, and he brought a touch of the Liberace showmanship, so lacking in early 1956, to his Las Vegas performances thirteen years later.

MAKING MOVIES, MONEY, AND MISCHIEF

The second act of Elvis's career unfolded on the big screen.

After returning home from his hitch in the army, a new Elvis headed to Hollywood. His image was flossed and glossed, groomed and glamorized, and he was cleaned up and grown up. In movie after movie, from *G.I. Blues* in 1960 to *Change of Habit* in 1969, Elvis was the affable hero, the good guy, the one who always got the girl.

Elvis depicted a wide variety of different characters, even if those characters always managed to find themselves in the same situation. He was in the service, not only as a G.I. Joe, but also later as a navy frogman and an air force lieutenant. He piloted planes, helicopters, and boats. Three times he acted as a race car driver. Placed in popular vacation destinations, he was once a tour guide and another time a lifeguard. In more unusual settings, he was a rodeo rider and a carnival worker. Occasionally he had a professional career, as a writer, a photographer, or a doctor in the ghetto. Sometimes he needed extra money, whether it was to buy a car, boat, or plane, a motor for his car, boat, or plane, or just to make ends meet. Then he would take a second job as a singer—in a nightclub or at a hotel, on the cliffs of Acapulco or the beach in Hawaii.

Elvis's leading ladies were even more legendary than the movies he made, and rumors that he had affairs with almost all of them abounded. Titillating the public with his off-screen romances kept the fan magazines busy. On the set of *G.I. Blues* he dallied with Juliet Prowse, right under the nose of Frank Sinatra, whom she was also dating at the time. He met up with Tuesday Weld, who played the town tramp to his troubled young man in *Wild in the Country*. Joan Blackman was his love interest in *Blue Hawaii* and *Kid Galahad*, and Shelley Fabares shared the spotlight with him in *Girl Happy*, *Spinout*, and *Clambake*. But the excitement these relationships generated was nothing but an ember compared to the bonfire produced when Elvis partnered with Ann-Margret in *Viva Las Vegas*.

At this time of his life Elvis viewed Las Vegas as his playground, a great place to impress starlets over a long weekend or blow off steam with his buddies, collectively known as the Memphis Mafia, before going home, just like any other tourist. To film *Viva Las Vegas*, however, Elvis was in town with over 225 cast and crew members for two weeks of location work in July 1963. It was the first time Elvis had worked here since his live-performance fiasco, yet in terms of what the future would bring it would turn out to be a most noteworthy career choice.

In the movie, a good-natured romantic musical, Elvis and Ann-Margret make a dynamic duo, the chemistry between them electric and unmistakable. She meets all his moves, matching him note for note and thrust for thrust. It is only natural that after Elvis wins the Las Vegas Grand Prix, they get married in front of the Little Church of the West before the screen fades to black. Yet the movie is also a travelogue, a tribute to the city that never sleeps. Early on, Elvis is shown in every showroom in every famous casino in town: the Thunderbird, Stardust, Flamingo, Tropicana, and Sahara. He is checking out the showgirls, looking for Rusty, Ann-Margret's character. When they finally hook up, they go water-skiing on Lake Mead, take a helicopter over Hoover Dam, and play shoot 'em up at a Western-styled theme park, presumably modeled after the one at the Frontier Hotel and Casino. Elvis, always in the foreground, enhancing the scenery with his good looks,

While making *Viva Las Vegas,*
Ann-Margret and Elvis danced together
on-screen and played together
off-screen.

becomes inextricably linked to Las Vegas, his image against the neon-lit skyline captured forever in a celluloid memory bank.

For a while the formula worked, the one which called for Elvis to sing and dance his way through a series of silly movie plot twists surrounded by a bevy of beauties. By the time Elvis was 30, he was the industry's highest-paid star, earning the unheard-of sum of more than $750,000 per movie, plus 50 percent of the profits. In 1965 he was paid $5 million for three movies and their sound-track albums, bringing his total earnings from his eighteen movies to date to $150 million.

But times were a-changing. Elvis's fans were getting older, while the hearts and minds of young people were being captured by a new generation of insurgent musicians, like the Beatles and the Rolling Stones, and their feet were dancing to a new beat. With the advent of the sexual revolution, his moves were no longer considered exotic or erotic, but rather tame and tired like the movie characters he depicted. To make matters worse, Elvis was losing his once boyish figure in the battle of the bulge.

Producer Hal Wallis first noticed the problem on the set of *Easy Come, Easy Go,* in September 1966, and he alerted Paramount Pictures. One studio executive urged Colonel Parker to do something, saying, "The clothes keep getting tighter and tighter, and our hero fatter and fatter." Another admonished Elvis, through the Colonel, of course, "Navy men aren't supposed to be fat." Hal Wallis wanted the Colonel to talk to Elvis not only about his weight, but also about his hair. "Fluffed up, in some kind of pompadour," he lectured, "it's beginning to look like a wig."

Elvis's poor eating habits, the lifelong indulgence of an addictive personality, were catching up with him. Gone were the days when munching one more fried peanut butter and banana sandwich wouldn't make much of a difference. Besides, Elvis was bored. He had never been allowed to develop his innate acting talent, noted as early as 1958 in his movie *King Creole.* That would have gotten in the way of the movie moneymaking machine. And as the quality of his movies deteriorated, so did the amount of fun, if any, he derived from making them.

Wrapping another film, Elvis once again turned from Hollywood to his Memphis home, seeking the solace he knew he would find there. In less than a year he was back in Las Vegas for another event that wouldn't soon be forgotten. The King was getting married!

It was none too soon for Elvis's bride-to-be, Priscilla Beaulieu. Priscilla had been living at Graceland for five years, ever since she was 16 years old. She had been hidden from the press, unknown to the public, and a good thing, too, as a scandal would have ensued if word of his underage mistress had ever gotten out. To hear Priscilla tell it, the proposal, whereby Elvis got down on his knee, was heartfelt and romantic. But, she felt, the ceremony was cold, and the reception, planned by Colonel Parker at the Aladdin Hotel and Casino, was an impersonal affair. According to Marty Lacker and others of the Memphis Mafia, however, Elvis no longer wanted to marry Priscilla. The bloom was off the rose, so to speak, but "just saying no" was not an option. Rumors circulated that Colonel Beaulieu, Priscilla's father, had threatened him with the Mann Act, and Colonel Parker had scared him with its consequences. And so with everyone smiling for the cameras one May day in 1967, another knot that bound Elvis to Las Vegas, in general, and the marriage industry, in particular, was tied.

Before the end of the decade Elvis made a few more movies, but he was no longer the leading man at the box office. When he made *Speedway* with Nancy Sinatra in 1968, her recent hit "These Boots Are Made for Walkin'" made her, not him, the star to watch. Elvis had not had a number one recording since 1962's "Good Luck Charms," and he had not performed live or on television since her father, Frank Sinatra, welcomed him home from the army on an ABC variety show in 1960. For Elvis to keep his crown, something had to change.

THE KING IS BACK

It is quite possible that if Elvis had not done "The Singer Special," named after its sponsor, the Singer Corporation, and eventually known as "The Comeback Special," on NBC in December 1968, the Elvis phenomenon, at least as it is incorporated into Las Vegas mythology, might never have happened. Originally planned as a Christmas show by Colonel Parker and network executives, the television program became a one-man production envisioned and developed by the director, Steve Binder, and Elvis himself. The idea was to present the real Elvis, first taking him back to his musical roots and then bringing him into the present with new songs.

Elvis wore a tight-fitting black leather jacket and pants, one of the outfits now copied by Elvis impersonators everywhere. Slimmed down, he looked sensational, and he sang like the legendary performer that he was. One moment he was the sexiest rock 'n' roll star; the next he was the sincerest blues singer. He wooed the live audience, and he won over the home viewers. Bumping and grinding, Elvis shook 'em up, showing everyone that he still had it. His resurrection had begun, and it was on to Las Vegas.

In the summer of 1969 the opening of the International, the newest hotel and casino in Vegas, was an event. Built by business magnate Kirk Kerkorian for $60 million, it was the tallest structure in Nevada, with a thirty-story main tower, and the largest, with 1,519 rooms and suites. Its 350,000-gallon swimming pool was not the state's most massive man-made body of water (those honors went to Lake Mead), but it was in second place. The showroom with seating for two thousand was vast by any standards; its relief carvings of winged gods and goddesses and its statues of George and Martha Washington were considered tacky by most. Only bigger-than-life personalities could succeed on its oversize stage.

Barbra Streisand went first. Colonel Parker had insisted that Elvis not perform until the dust had cleared and the kinks had been worked out of the sound system. On July 31

Elvis's turn came, and he proved that he was more than up to the task. "Well, it's one for the money; two for the show," he began singing, and the crowd went wild. "Three to get ready, now go, cat, go," he continued, only to be drowned out by shouts of "Bravo! Bravo!" No one was able to hear the words to "Blue Suede Shoes," and no one seemed to care. It was almost as if the audience knew history was being made.

Over the next twenty-nine days Elvis pulled in 101,500 paying customers and grossed $1.5 million. "He went in there and just exploded," Lamar Fike, a Memphis Mafia member, declared. "He literally tore the town apart." The Colonel immediately struck a deal with the International's president: for five years Elvis would perform semiannual engagements, four weeks in the summer and again in the winter, at $125,000 per week, earning $5 million. It was a bonanza for everyone. "There has never been an entertainer that did business in Vegas like Elvis Presley," author Frank Coffey observed on E! Television's *The Last Days of Elvis*. "In Las Vegas when Elvis Presley was performing, the entire town saw a 10 percent across-the-board boost in revenues."

Elvis never performed to less than a sold-out house. In the early years of his Las Vegas engagements, a third show at 3:00 a.m. was sometimes added to accommodate the crowds turned away from the 8:00 p.m. and midnight shows. His fans, now more mature and with money to spend, came from as far away as Japan, England, and Germany, and went not to just one performance, but to as many performances as they could get tickets for. They were as adoring as ever, pressing for a kiss or a scarf during a concert, and purchasing souvenir posters, teddy bears, and anything else Elvis afterward.

From the beginning the show was an extravaganza. A rock band, a stage orchestra with lots of brass for newer selections, and male and female gospel vocal groups accompanied Elvis. To announce his entrance, the orchestra played Strauss's "Also Sprach Zarathustra," familiar the world over as the majestic-sounding theme of the movie *2001: A Space Odyssey*. The black karate outfit Elvis wore at the first concert was replaced with the now famous bejeweled and sequined jumpsuit with high collar and wide belt. Sometimes he wore a cape, sometimes he didn't, but he always had diamond-laden rings sparkling on his fingers, probably visible from as far away as the showroom's balcony.

Elvis was so well received in Las Vegas that he took the show on the road, and more fame and fortune followed. In June 1972 he played New York's Madison Square Garden, and became the first artist to sell out four consecutive nights. In January 1973 his show "Aloha from Hawaii" was the first to use satellite to broadcast overseas. It is estimated that up to 1.5 billion people in forty countries saw the show, watching Elvis rocking and rolling in a specially designed white jumpsuit emblazoned with an American eagle on his front and also on the back of his matching cape. But no matter where he was or what he did, he eventually returned to Vegas, where fans from around the world awaited him.

To endure his grueling concert schedule, Elvis took prodigious amounts of prescription drugs, seeking to mask his pain, both physical and emotional. It worked for a time. Some nights he made it through concerts without a mishap, singing well and putting on a memorable show. Other nights he should have stayed in bed. Then his drug abuse threatened his health. Eventually, it took his life. On August 16, 1977, the day before he was to leave on yet another tour, Elvis Presley, 42, died.

LONG LIVE THE KING

"Elvis is very much for real," *Las Vegas Sun* columnist Joe Delaney wrote in his review of Elvis's 1969 opening at the International Hotel. "Elvis is here to stay."

How surreal those words are today! Who could have foreseen that Elvis would play Vegas year in and year out for seven years until he died, or that Elvis impersonators would still be playing Vegas more that twenty-five years after his death? Or

Elvis's sweaty silk scarves became the
ultimate concert souvenir.

that the image of Elvis and the persona of Las Vegas would become intertwined? Elvis living the American Dream went
from rags to riches to more riches, reaching the apex in Las
Vegas, the city of dreams. And when he fell from grace, well,
no one can roll sevens forever.

Elvis impersonators were around almost from the beginning, and Elvis himself saw many of them. He was a good sport
about being copied, once inviting Douglas Roy, a Canadian
singer with an all-Elvis act since the sixties, to join him onstage
for a round of "Hound Dog." As part of his opening act for Bob-
bie Gentry, comedian John Byner did a wicked Elvis impersonation. "We went to see Byner three or four times in a week,"
friend Sonny West recalled. "Elvis just loved it."

In Las Vegas as well as across the country, many Elvis impersonators are not simply mimics. They are performers personally paying tribute to a performer they emulate and a man
they respect, as well as providing a forum for Elvis's devoted
fans to relive the pleasure and excitement Elvis brought into
their lives. "I wanted more than anything to maintain his
legacy," Rick Marino, president of the Elvis Impersonators International Association, declares. The night Elvis died, Elvis
impersonator Alan Meyer asked the audience at the Tropicana for a moment of silence for the King, professing, "This
man meant more to me than anyone who ever lived."

It is not really clear when impersonators moved from the
stage into the chapel. Peggy Johnson, part owner of Graceland
Wedding Chapel, believes that her chapel was getting four to
five requests a month for an Elvis impersonator as early as
1977, a number that has steadily grown to four to five requests a day. The reasons can only be surmised. For diehard
Elvis fans it is a privilege to get married in the presence of
Elvis's kind and generous spirit and an honor to help keep the
legend alive. For everyone else, having a living legend, even if
only an impersonator of a dead legend, stand up for them is a
hoot. Besides, it keeps the proceedings from getting too heavy.

CHAPTER 14

A Day in the Life of a Wedding Chapel

ROCKIN' ROUND THE CLOCK

*R*on DeCar, owner of the Viva Las Vegas Wedding Chapel, believes that weddings should be fun, whether Elvis is involved or not. He specializes in themed weddings, and the list of themes that can be used as a backdrop for a wedding here is extensive. Blue Hawaii, starring Elvis and based on his movie of the same name, of course, tops the list. Also appearing are Knights of the Round Table for a Camelot theme, different generations of *Star Trek* supporting an intergalactic theme, and the Big Kahuna and fellow surfers for a beach party wedding. "Although Elvis plays a part, sometimes just singing a song, in about 40 percent of our weddings, we do a lot of different things here," Ron modestly claims. "But even traditional weddings are done with flair and finesse, making each a real production."

Ron got into the marriage business by way of show business. Hoping for a place in the spotlight treading the boards, he left Kansas for Las Vegas over twenty years ago. The attractive young man with talent to spare (he sounds like Vic Damone) quickly found a role in *City Lights* at the Flamingo before settling in as lead singer at that show of shows, the *Folies Bergere*, at the Tropicana for twelve years. Entrepreneurial in spirit, he formed Wedding Singers of Las Vegas as a second source of income and hired himself out as a soloist. The Carpenters' "We've Only Just Begun" was a much requested favorite, but then the requests for Elvis songs started coming in. When he followed up on a wedding coordinator's suggestion that he dress as Elvis, his second career was born, and his success was just about ensured.

But first Ron had to renovate the Mission of the Bells, the chapel he had taken over on Las Vegas Boulevard South, just north of Sahara Boulevard, where the glamour of the Strip begins to fade. The place needed a lot of work, but nothing that some good old-fashioned elbow grease coupled with the ingenuity of Tom Sawyer couldn't fix. The walls were whitewashed, and a large sign showcasing Elvis and the other characters from the themed weddings was hung. (Ron had sketched it on the back of a napkin one day.) When he was done, the only recognizable features of the adobe building were the bell tower from which the chapel had gotten its original name and the bells carved on the backs of the pews echoing the chapel's theme.

On February 18, 1999, Ron opened the doors of the Viva Las Vegas Wedding Chapel. Ten months later, on the evening of December 31, the chapel was featured on Fox television network when eighteen couples tied the knot there.

Ron DeCar has made the finger wiggle part of his Elvis impersonation.

For the millennial nuptial celebration, hula girls, showgirls, a Merlin, and, of course, Elvis impersonated by Ron joined them. When the mass ceremony was finished at midnight, the couples danced in the New Year to the strains of "Auld Lang Syne."

Within the first two years of its opening, *Nevada* magazine named the Viva Las Vegas as the Best Wedding Chapel in the state for the year 2000 and then again in 2001, while the *Las Vegas Review-Journal* selected it as the Best Wedding Chapel in the city for the year 2000. The chapel was also featured in a host of television stories on *The Oprah Winfrey Show*, the *NBC Nightly News*, the Arts and Entertainment Cable Network, the *Today* show, and E! Television. In 2002 the Viva Las Vegas showed up frequently as the chapel of choice for many couples getting married on the Travel Channel's *Two for Las Vegas*.

It's a new Las Vegas, one people visit for some glitz and glamour, to be amused and entertained. They want to view the neon lights and take in the crazy sights, whether it's a thundering volcano or dancing water fountains in the desert. Ron has taken the pulse of the city and prescribed a champagne cocktail with a pinch of fantasy and a dash of fun for those getting married or renewing their vows. He has replaced kitsch with a touch of class, and quickie two-minute weddings have been eliminated altogether. At the Viva Las Vegas Wedding Chapel, it's a new day.

8:00 A.M.

Las Vegas is experiencing a beautiful autumn morning. After a long, hot summer, which began early and stayed around for eternity with the temperature over 110 degrees on one too many occasions, it feels like fall. The desert air is cool and crisp, and the sky is blue and cloudless.

The breakfast room for guests of the Viva Las Vegas Villas, the motel-hotel behind the chapel, is open. Ron DeCar fashioned it after a fifties diner and decorated it with his personal collection of memorabilia from that decade. For seating there are two dinette furniture sets with Formica-top tables and matching chairs with white seat cushions. A Rock-Ola Hit Tunes jukebox sits in the corner of the room. Among the classics on file are Bill Haley's "Rock Around the Clock," Fats Domino's "My Blue Heaven," and "Sh-Boom" by the Crew Cuts. Authentic metal signs for Royal ice cream, Sun Crown cola, and Howdy Doody Twin popsicles adorn the walls, while a Red Crow gasoline pump serves as a reminder that regular gas once cost 28.9¢ per gallon. The room is the perfect place from which to watch the world awake; and the coffee is hot, the large, 400-calorie muffins are fresh, and the individual-size bottles of Morning Delight orange drink are there for the taking. For those guests who feel they have lingered long enough in the past, there is a computer with an Internet connection on a table on a far wall.

Judy Bates is the chapel's flower lady. On Saturdays as busy as this promises to be she might need to prepare for upwards of thirty weddings. At half past the hour, she makes the first of many trips from her workshop adjacent to the diner across the parking lot to the chapel. She carries as many of the just-prepared bouquets as can safely be managed without dropping any vases or losing even one flower. When she returns, one of the wedding coordinators in the front office accompanies her to pick up more flower arrangements. They will be stored in the cooler near the bride's dressing room off the chapel until they are needed.

Judy has been a florist for most of her life. She was born in La Jolla, California, "when La Jolla was on the ocean," before growth and development extended it inland, and she had her own flower shop when she and her husband lived in Iowa. When he got a job in Las Vegas fifteen years ago, they once again relocated across the country. Today he is retired, and she at 65 continues to work, doing what she loves to do. "Flowers make the wedding," she happily asserts.

Flowers are included in all wedding packages, and everything is color coordinated around red, white, or pink. For themed weddings, colonial-style bouquets that are European hand-tied, per Judy's preference, are the standard. Judy also tries to reflect the theme in each bouquet with a unique touch. Purple and gold ribbons are added for the Egyptian-themed wedding, while sparkling streamers are used for the intergalactic theme. Of course, for a Blue Hawaii ceremony, Hawaiian leis are the preferred floral decorations.

More and more brides customize their bouquets by selecting the type of flowers they want in a specific style and color scheme. "Customers who have already booked their weddings see the variety of florals available on our Web site, and they call in their preferences," Judy explains. "Most of these special arrangements cost over $100, but once people see what they want, they don't care if it costs $3 or $300. Couple that with add-ons, that's boutonnieres for all the men in the wedding party and corsages for the mothers, and whatever else anyone wants, and you can see why I am one busy lady." That she is, answering questions and fielding orders over the phone while she works.

"I've seen big changes in the wedding business here," Judy continues. "It used to be that couples would come in by themselves to get married. Now as soon as family hears that a couple is planning on a Las Vegas wedding, they want to come, too. The whole family. Everyone wants to go to Vegas. So weddings are getting larger. Yes, they are larger and more festive, but also more like home."

The chapel at Viva Las Vegas can handle large weddings—just like at home. About a hundred guests can be seated on the wooden pews aligned on either side of the wide aisle covered in a muted green carpet. The vaulted ceiling gives a spacious feeling, while the stained-glass windows let in natural light. For traditional weddings the stage at the front of the room serves as an altar. It is decorated with silk plants and trees and a working, flowing fountain. For themed weddings the stage, enhanced by theatrical lighting and a professional sound system, is the setting for wedding fantasies brought to life.

To manage the flow of people traffic, first the betrothed and then their wedding party and guests are directed to enter the chapel from the lobby. When the ceremony is over, the wedding party and guests leave first through the doors at the back of the chapel. This puts them in position to greet the newlyweds when they are introduced for the first time as husband and wife. Sometimes wedding parties will bump into each other, reminding the bride that she is sharing her big day with others. Yet the staff's good humor is usually contagious and helps get everyone through any resulting stress or anxiety in a situation when emotions can run rampant.

On this particular day ceremonies have been scheduled in the chapel for every half hour beginning at 9:30 a.m., plus two outdoor weddings at Red Rock Canyon, a scenic desert landscape with impressive sandstone bluffs less than twenty miles from the Strip. There will be thirteen Elvis ceremonies, six themed ceremonies, and three same-sex commitment ceremonies. The remainder will be traditional ceremonies conducted by a minister.

With weddings scheduled one right after the other, many of which require a change of backdrops and props, music and costumes, every minute counts if every couple is to have its allotted time in the chapel. So to keep on schedule the limousine drivers have a very important role in the day in the life of a wedding chapel. They are responsible for making sure that the newlyweds arrive on time. "All couples get a courtesy ride to and from the chapel," Sonny Singer, the head limousine driver, explains. "I pick them up at their hotel half an hour early. As soon as I arrive, I call the couple's room and arrange a meeting place. We all follow the same procedure. It usually works out pretty well, unless the couple isn't in their room or the groom is off gambling. It's been known to happen."

Sonny has been intimately involved in the Las Vegas wedding business for many years, driving limousines up and down the Strip. He met his second wife, Joyce, a county marriage commissioner, at the courthouse, where he daily brought couples to get their marriage license. "I like driving," Sonny confides. "I just drove 3,700 miles to attend my grandson's wedding in Minnesota. My wife doesn't like the way I drive. She says she drives 50 miles while it would take me 55 miles to go the same distance because I weave. Maybe I do. I'm used to driving the superstretch."

As befits his position, Sonny drives the latest and grandest limousine. Like the others in the Viva Las Vegas fleet, it is a white Lincoln Continental stretched out twenty-seven feet. His car holds eight passengers and costs about $70,000. "Come take a look," he urges onlookers. "It still smells new." The seats are white leather, trimmed with gray. A starlit sky is simulated on the ceiling. A bar stretches almost the length of the vehicle and is outfitted with three sets of highball and cocktail glasses. Yet the license plate ELVIS P goes to the 1964 pink Cadillac Coupe Deville convertible with ninety thousand miles on it. It has been beautifully restored and maintained in pristine condition, belying its age.

In the parking lot the drivers with early calls are preparing their limousines to take out. Not that there is that much to do. Every night, no matter how late, the limousines are tidied up after the last ride. The stretches are washed twice a week, more if necessary, and kept in immaculate shape. Still, drivers appreciate tips, so they have long since learned not to be caught without clean champagne glasses and a bucket of ice.

9:25 A.M.

Inside Viva Las Vegas Anita McFarlin and Carol Baker are getting ready for the first wedding of the day. They both have the title wedding coordinator, a position that really resembles a jack-of-all-trades, doing whatever needs to be done to put the bride and groom at ease while keeping the wedding parties moving in and out of the chapel as quickly and smoothly as possible. They have both been in Las Vegas since the sixties, so they have observed, even taken part in, the city's many permutations. Yet they arrived at the Viva Las Vegas Wedding Chapel from different places.

Anita is from South Florida. She started her career at the wedding chapel at Circus Circus before being promoted into hotel management. Now retired, she works only part-time so as not to jeopardize her Social Security payments. Carol, who is English, came to Las Vegas via Paris, where she was a Blue Bell dancer with the Lido. She made the leap across the "pond" when she was signed as one of the original dancers at the legendary Casino de Paris show at the Dunes. This is her first foray into the wedding industry. She has been here only a few weeks. "I think I'm going to like this," she predicts. "A wedding is a happy occasion for all involved."

Despite the early hour the first bride of the day wears a sequin-patterned floor-length dress with spaghetti straps. The groom has on a suit. Having arrived fifteen minutes early, the soon-to-be newlyweds leisurely complete their marriage license, decide to go live on the chapel's Internet Web site, and sign a model release form with plenty of time to spare. In the roomy area near the bridal dressing room on the far side of the chapel, they now await their walk down the aisle.

Their guests in the lobby include parents, elementary-school-age children, and sisters. As they are led into the chapel, all are advised to sit in the pews on the left if they want to be seen in the Webcast and to sit on the right to be out of camera range. After everyone is seated, Anita closes the door between the lobby and chapel to ensure privacy and quiet during the service. The sounds of "Here Comes the Bride" come over the loudspeaker. The Reverend Ron Rogers stands at the altar. It's showtime.

"Who gives this woman to this man?" he solemnly intones.

Reverend Rogers has the posture of a soldier at roll call. His gray hair is cropped short and his white shirt is stiffly starched, so his pleasant demeanor is masked by a serious appearance. Only a stud earring suggests a glimmer of whimsy in an otherwise stern outlook. The reverend has two primary roles at Viva Las Vegas. For traditional services, such as this one, he performs the ceremony from start to finish. For themed weddings at which Elvis or some other character officiates, he confers a blessing during the service and says the magic words that make the couple husband and wife afterward. As Reverend Rogers tells those about to be joined, "All these other people make your wedding fun. I make it legal." So as not to hamper the festivities, this is done offstage away from the guests.

Reverend Rogers works here on Fridays and Saturdays. The rest of the week he attends to the needs of his congregation at the Salvation Army. "I'm a real preacher. On Sundays I have preacher responsibilities," he says earnestly.

An assortment of Elvis memorabilia and wedding souvenirs is for sale in the lobby.

According to Nevada law, officiants performing marriage ceremonies must lead an assembly of twenty people at least once a week.

The lobby is a long and narrow room, simply and comfortably decorated. A high ceiling keeps it from feeling claustrophobic, while a reddish brown tile floor suggests the American Southwest. The counter behind which the chapel staff meets and greets guests, answers the phone, confirms appointments, and coordinates with the drivers is stocked with wedding memorabilia for sale—everything from champagne flutes, garter belts, and other traditional offerings to Elvis sunglasses and aftershave, and "Married by the King" postcards. Elvis collectibles, such as early record albums and copies of *TV Guides* with covers bearing his image, are displayed in a cabinet at the far end of the room. A working telephone incorporates a foot-tall plastic figurine of a thin young Elvis wearing a tight gold suit, his guitar draped around his waist, singing in front of a microphone.

Lest anyone think that Elvis is the only theme at play here, the lengthy wall from the outside entrance to the door leading to the chapel is covered with framed photographs of themed weddings past. Brides and grooms, frequently accompanied by their wedding parties, are shown dressed head to toe in costumes appropriate to their chosen theme. In one frame there are grinning gangsters in spats, zoot suits, white ties, and black hats, their flapper girlfriends ready to Charleston. In another a Steve Tyler look-alike from the band Aerosmith leads a rock 'n' roll crowd ready to party.

At various points during the day the lobby is a beehive of activity. It is not only the place where the bride and groom sign in, but also where their guests gather before the ceremony and motel guests register. Couples shopping around for a wedding chapel pay a quick visit, check the place out, and review the various wedding packages while waiting for a peek into the chapel. The lobby is free of all but staff for just a moment or two before a tall, nice-looking older African

American walks in. He's wearing a tuxedo and appears nervous. He reveals the obvious: he is the groom at the next wedding.

"Any questions, sir?" Anita asks.

"I probably will have. Like why am I here?" he responds.

Anita has no answer to that question, so she resumes doing her paperwork. The groom paces back and forth. It is only 9:35, and there is little else to do to pass the time. While most couples arrive together and many choose to walk down the aisle hand in hand, the ten o'clock ceremony has been set up by the book. The groom, who drove himself to the chapel, will not see his beautiful bride, who will be arriving by limousine, in her long white wedding dress until she walks down the aisle. So at five minutes to the hour, after the current wedding party has left through the main doors at the back of the chapel, the groom is shown into the chapel and introduced to Reverend Rogers. With the groom out of the way, the bride and two women guests enter the lobby. Carol escorts them to the bridal dressing room on the other side of the chapel: It's time to do it again.

A few minutes after the hour, Marcello Dinicolantonio comes in. He is a fit and youthful 42-year-old, in much better shape than Elvis was when he died at the same age. Marcello has the type of build developed by working out that will allow him to wear a bejeweled white jumpsuit or turn heads in a black leather number for years to come. He wears his dark hair in a moderate pompadour and boasts long sideburns. His eyes are heavy-lidded, and his lips are full. Although he is wearing street clothes, one immediately knows that he is an Elvis impersonator.

In fact, Marcello does most of the Elvis impersonations at the Viva Las Vegas Wedding Chapel, freeing up Ron DeCar for "taking care of business," as Elvis might say. He found his calling a bit circuitously, although his admiration of Elvis dates back over thirty years, to when he saw a television advertisement for Elvis's greatest hits. The music and the singer's moves fascinated him. His father, a New York City police officer and an Elvis fan himself, bought his young son the double record album. Eleven years old at the time, Marcello played it religiously, learning the lyrics and picking up the sound. It was 1970, the second year of Elvis's contract playing the International Hotel in Vegas.

A serious musician, Marcello moved to Los Angeles to study and pursue a career. "My life took a turn when I showed up for a party wearing an Elvis costume and sang a couple of his songs," he recollects. "My friends thought I was great, and I started to do Elvis impersonations for extra cash. In the mid-1980s I took my act to Las Vegas, where I landed a variety of gigs. Then I got to do Elvis in *Legends in Concert* at the Imperial Palace. I also know lighting and sound systems, and I honed my audiovisual skills as director at New York New York." These skills come in handy when the chapel must be converted into a special setting for a themed wedding or converted back on short notice, something that happens several times a day. Everyone jumps in and helps out.

Marcello is planning on helping out in another way, too. He has embarked on a two-year study to become an ordained minister through his church, the Cornerstone Ministry Fellowship. Once ordained, he can conduct nuptials from start to finish. Despite the huge demand for this service, there is only one Elvis impersonator in Las Vegas who is also an ordained minister, Norm Jones at the Graceland Wedding Chapel. However, believing it detracts from the sanctity of the moment, he refuses to marry couples while he is in character. Marcello does not have any such concerns. "I get into the persona of Elvis and the other characters I do, but I am still myself," he says with the sincerity of Elvis. "I think I can merge the two roles without sacrificing meaning or giving up the good time."

Just as Marcello stops at the front counter to say good morning to his coworkers, a couple named Penny and Sean come in. They are staying at the Viva Las Vegas Villas, a short walk across the parking lot, and they arrive twenty-five minutes early in their wedding finery. Penny looks radiant in a long white dress with a scoop neckline that she brought with her from Charlotte, North Carolina, their hometown. Sean is wearing a long-sleeved black shirt and pants, and beige Western-style boots. A black cowboy hat Anita found for him in the chapel's wardrobe completes the outfit.

"We have an appointment with Elvis at ten-thirty," Penny excitedly announces.

"Well, I'm Elvis," Marcello says, introducing himself. There's a round of handshakes and big grins all around. "I think I took your call, too," he adds, looking at the schedule. Penny, beside herself, can only nod her head.

It is the second marriage for both Penny and Sean. They had picked the date back in May, but months went by without their making any definitive plans. When family demands concerning where the wedding should be held and who should be invited started to get out of hand, they decided that they had to do something to get out from under the well-intentioned, but nevertheless trying, requests from their relatives. Las Vegas gave them the perfect escape. They are here by themselves, Penny for the first time, and they will combine their wedding with a honeymoon. Not insensitive to the feelings of family and friends, they are including them by Webcasting the event over the Internet.

Penny and Sean have elected to have the Elvis Special, one of Viva Las Vegas's most popular wedding packages. "Elvis is like a member of our family," Penny explains, echoing the feeling of Elvis fans through the decades. The ceremony is a mix of the traditional with the novel. Most couples, like these newlyweds, dress up for the occasion, yet they walk down the aisle while a man who looks and sounds like Elvis sings "Can't Help Falling in Love." After promising "to love, honor, and cherish each other," the couple dances together for the first time as husband and wife while Elvis sings "Love Me Tender." And after rings are exchanged and blessed by the reverend,

Elvis sings the chapel's theme song, "Viva Las Vegas." The setting is churchlike, with light flooding through stained-glass windows and flowers decorating the pews. Yet it is Elvis standing at the altar.

Marcello excuses himself to change into costume, and yes, for the Elvis Special, he emulates the King's Vegas superstar image and wears a bejeweled white jumpsuit open to his navel. Anita takes over, checking the paperwork and reviewing the setup with the couple. She handles it like a brief rehearsal, showing the parties where they will stand, pointing out the cameras, and letting them know what will happen when. In turn, the couple settles its account. When Marcello returns, he spends a few more minutes with them, gathering some background information such as where they are from and making them feel comfortable. Finally, it is time. Penny and Sean take their places at the back of the room, from where they together will commence their wedding march. Marcello begins:

Wise men say only fools rush in
But I can't help falling in love with you.

"Good morning, ladies and gentlemen in Charlotte, North Carolina. My name is Elvis. As you can see, I am alive and well."

11:10 A.M.

Another Elvis Special is under way in the chapel. Marcello instructs the couple:

"I want you to repeat after me loud and clear: 'To have and to hold.'"

"To have and to hold," the couple promises.

"From this day forward."

"From this day forward."

"For joy and celebration." (He swivels his hips.)

"For joy and celebration." (They attempt to swivel their hips.)

"For love and understanding," he says in a deep, Elvis voice.

"For love and understanding," they repeat in a deep, Elvis voice.

"I pledge you my faith."

"I pledge you my faith."

And it is time for another song:

> *Love me tender, love me dear,*
> *Tell me you are mine.*

In the lobby the staff is in high gear, confirming appointments to make sure that the wedding is still on for the day, coordinating with the limousine drivers so they know when the next party will be arriving, and handling telephone requests and answering questions from new customers. Shannon Maloney, the assistant manager, sets up a reception for the forty guests of the eleven-thirty wedding. It will be in the motel's Disco Room; everything has a theme, complete with a rotating and reflective disco ball over the dance floor. So she keeps running back and forth between the chapel and the motel.

Shannon, an attractive brunette, is another of Ron's staff with a show business background. She is a dancer with the long legs to prove it, and she can sing and act if needed to fill a role in a themed wedding. Originally from Fresno, California, she has been in Las Vegas for over ten years. For much of that time, she kicked up her heels among the appearing and disappearing wildlife five nights a week in the Siegfried and Roy Show at the Mirage. Shannon has known and worked with Ron since the days when Ron was both onstage at the Tropicana and self-employed as an Elvis impersonator at wedding chapels around town. "Those were the good old days," she reminisces. "I would go over to his house in sweats to stuff envelopes with mailers describing his services. We would sit around, drink coffee, and tell stories. It's different now, dealing with the public."

Dealing with the public sometimes requires a unique set of skills, the importance of which becomes clear in the next few minutes. As guests of the eleven-thirty wedding gather outside, drinking and partying, the assigned limousine driver lets the staff know that the couple he is picking up is just getting into the car. Ten minutes later, when it is apparent that only the bride has come in the limousine, there is much consternation among the staff. They know that the large number of guests, some of whom are already under the influence, will eat into what is left of the allotted half hour just to enter and exit the chapel, let alone settle down. The staff is falling behind schedule and it is not even noon. There is little chance of catching up, and no one is quite sure where the groom is.

"We have a wedding booked at noon," Shannon says, attempting to explain the urgency of the situation to the mother of the bride, who is paying for the affair. The mother of the groom calls the Stardust Hotel, where the couple is staying, but there is no answer in the room. Wearing a long white dress with full skirt, perfectly lovely for the traditional service that has been planned, the bride seems oddly unaware that her big day could be in trouble. She cannot offer any insight as to where her fiancé is or when he might arrive. "I'd like a double-ring ceremony. Do you sell rings here?" she asks, startling Carol with the question. When told no, she initiates a search for a ring she can borrow for her betrothed.

What to do? What to do? Attempting to come up with a solution that is satisfactory to the chapel, to all the couples who have weddings planned for later that day, and to the party here now, Shannon assiduously studies the schedule. "Our first free opening is at eleven o'clock tonight," she notes, trying to put a positive spin on the situation. The mother of the bride rejects the idea out of hand. "That's not possible," she responds. "We fly out tonight."

Minutes tick by, and the lobby quickly fills up with relatives. The father of the bride, some flower girls, and a cousin or two arrive, but still no groom. The bride returns from the limousine with the marriage license in hand, so at least the paperwork will be taken care of. Then Shannon hits on another idea. "We can perform the wedding in the reception area. It is all set up, and you have it reserved for a couple of hours." "Is the price the same?" the mother of the bride asks, clearly unhappy with the way things are going. When told yes, she gets a bit huffy, even though the chapel is not responsible for the mishap. "What difference does it make?" a male relative says to her. "At the end of the day they are going to be just as married."

Who should arrive at five minutes before the hour but the man of the hour himself, unabashed and unapologetic. Rather than engaging in an argument about a change of venue, the staff briskly shepherds the entire group, from the bride and groom to the wedding party, and all the guests, into the chapel. Reverend Rogers stands at the altar. The music starts to play. Another wedding is under way.

The noon wedding is a no-show, and the chapel is soon back on track, running smoothly. It took time for the tension among the staff to ease, however. "I don't understand how someone can be late for his own wedding," Shannon wonders out loud. "We want every wedding to be special, but sometimes that's just not possible," Anita says sadly. "Sometimes people show an utter lack of consideration for others," Carol chimes in. "It puts a real damper on things."

1:45 P.M.

A Blue Hawaii wedding is one of the most popular themes at the Viva Las Vegas Wedding Chapel, just as the movie *Blue Hawaii* has always been one of the favorites of Elvis's adoring public. It is the first of three pictures Elvis would make in the fiftieth state of the Union, a locale he personally enjoyed. Designed as

Marcello Dinicolantonio as Elvis graciously poses for a wedding portrait with the couple of the half hour.

a star vehicle—Elvis played a guide at a tourist agency and had the opportunity to sing to many beautiful women around the picturesque islands—the movie was one of the top-grossing films of 1961. The LP of the sound track included the hits "Can't Help Falling in Love," which became Elvis's signature song and closing number at his 1970s concerts. It stayed at number one for twenty weeks, a record unbroken for sixteen years, and on the charts for seventy-nine weeks.

The people attending a Blue Hawaii wedding are almost always easy to spot. They are the ones wearing shirts, shorts, pants, and skirts with bright, boldly patterned flower designs. Sometimes the bride wears a long dress or muumuu in a pattern that matches the groom's clothing. Often the groom is indistinguishable from his best man because they are both wearing flip-flops and have hairy legs. Almost everyone has a lei.

This time the wedding party has found a way to meld the mood with a touch of casual sophistication. An older couple, Mary Kay and Richard, have both been married before. Mary Kay, her hair and makeup all done up, is wearing a pretty flowered dress with a bright shawl over her shoulders. Richard is wearing a light beige suit, no tie, and a flowered shirt. His brother and sister-in-law, son and daughter-in-law, and nephew accompany them. They are all dressed festively, but appropriately, for a wedding. And yes, they are all wearing leis. Even Marcello has replaced his red scarf with a pink one.

Marcello serenades the wedding party with the "Hawaiian Wedding Song," the song Elvis sings at his own wedding at the end of *Blue Hawaii*:

> *I can hear my heart singing,*
> *Soon bells will be ringing,*

The two hula dancers, who had preceded the couple down the aisle, are standing on the stage next to the singer, languorously swaying to the music. In their grass skirts, with layers of leis over their halter tops and with garlands in their hair, they appear to be enacting the words to the song, just as they would be doing if this were taking place on the big island. Richard and Mary Kay are obviously enjoying themselves. They are into the lush scene enhanced by theatrical fog and lighting effects and, of course, the music, slow-dancing together, rocking back and forth. They look happy. They are happy. Marcello finishes the song:

> *Blue skies of Hawaii will smile*
> *On this, our wedding day*

And now it is time for some very serious questions.

"Do you both promise and agree . . . to adopt each other's hound dogs?"

"We've already done that."

"To always be each other's teddy bear?"

"Absolutely."

"I do."

"To never wear your blue suede shoes out in the rain?"

"I do."

"Absolutely."

"To never have a blue Christmas without each other?"

"We wouldn't have it any other way."

"We selected the Blue Hawaii theme because we wanted to celebrate in joyful fun," Mary Kay explains. "This is perfect." To round out their weekend, the couple are staying in the Blue Hawaii Suite, one of thirty-two creatively imagined rooms in the motel. The mural on the wall behind the bed is a seascape bordered with palm trees. The island in the distance looks like a leisurely swim away, while the picture of the beach hut in the foreground actually surrounds the bathroom. "It's like sleeping on the beach, but without the sand," Richard declares admiringly. "I can almost hear the surf lapping the shore."

2:35 P.M.

"Feel free to take pictures during the ceremony, but please stay in your seats," Shannon instructs another group of guests before she shows them into the chapel. "You don't want to get in Fernando's way."

Fernando Alvarez is the photographer supreme. He has an impish grin and an easygoing, jocular manner, perfect for putting people at their ease and eliciting their best smiles. Yet he is also capable of controlling an unruly crowd, getting everyone to settle down before the service or stand up for a group portrait afterward. He works hard, putting in long hours, five days a week. If the couple have ordered one of the more extensive picture packages, Fernando makes sure that he has pictures of them at the altar by themselves, with Elvis, with their wedding party, with their wedding party with Elvis, and even one with all their guests. He then has just the two of them pose for several romantic shots, possibly gazing into each other's eyes, in the gazebo at the back of the chapel. The photo session can take as much time as the ceremony.

Fernando was born and raised in Guatemala. He immigrated to the United States twenty years ago, settling in San Jose, California, where he established himself as a professional photographer, specializing in sports and fashion. Three years ago he was in Las Vegas on business and started shopping for wedding chapels. When he went home, he told the future Mrs. Alvarez that they were getting married by Elvis. "It will be fun," he assured her.

It was so much fun that soon afterward the couple moved to Las Vegas. Fernando's first job in the city of neon lights was at Bally's Celebration Wedding Chapel, but that proved too slow for the energetic photographer. Shopping his portfolio around, he interviewed at the Viva Las Vegas Wedding Chapel. "'You look familiar,'" Fernando recalls telling Ron DeCar at their first meeting. "And Ron said that I looked familiar. But we couldn't figure out how we knew each other. It wasn't until I went home and looked at my wedding pictures that I realized that Ron was Elvis at my wedding before he had opened his own chapel. What a coincidence!"

Fernando enjoys working in the wedding industry, particularly the times when the humorous side of human nature shines through. "At this one wedding the maid of honor was given the rings to hold until the appropriate time of the ceremony," he says, telling one of his favorite stories. "When it was time for her to pass them to the officiant, she was flirting with one of the guests in the audience, you know, batting her eyes, throwing him kisses, and missed her cue. 'Who has the rings? Who has the rings?' was the buzz at the altar. When she finally realized that everyone was waiting on her, she jerked her hand and the rings went flying. There were close to a hundred people down on their hands and knees looking for those rings."

Like his colleagues, Fernando is multitalented and jumps in whenever he is needed. Marcello, Reverend Rogers, and he have just finished transforming the chapel into a Western setting. They set up a sawhorse complete with saddle and brought in a hitching post from which a lasso hangs at one end and a kerosene lantern hangs at the other. They scattered bales of hay across the stage and used water barrels to frame the scene. With preparations complete, red mood light bathes the chapel, while country music plays over the sound system. Fernando positions himself to take pictures of the bride as she walks down the aisle. She is dressed in white, from her Stetson hat with lace trailing down her back to her antique lace dress and cowboy boots. Marcello, dressed as a biker cowboy in black leather with lots of fringe from head to toe, greets the guests from the altar. "Everyone come on in and take your seats," he says. "Where you all from? Michigan? Well, wave to the camera for the Internet broadcast and say howdy to the Wolverine fans back home."

Twenty minutes later, as the Western theme wedding comes to a close, the country-and-western song "American Honky-Tonk Bar Association" filters into the lobby, where the guests of the next ceremony, a renewal, gather. Renewals are very popular at the Viva Las Vegas Wedding Chapel, constituting up to half of all ceremonies performed here.

"I like renewals. They can be quite inspiring," Shannon comments. "If I know a groom is going to say something or do something special, I will try and take the time to go into the chapel and listen. We had a couple in here recently celebrating their ten-year anniversary with their young son. At the opening of the ceremony, Elvis sang 'Can't Help Falling in Love,' as usual. Then at the end of the ceremony a busty Marilyn Monroe look-alike in a low-cut, clingy dress sang in a raspy, throaty voice 'Happy Anniversary to You' and surprised the wife by presenting her with the largest diamond ring I have ever seen."

Some renewals are quite traditional and use the services of a minister, although one is not required. "This is my favorite thing to do: renewals," the Reverend Rogers expounds from the altar to a Florida couple married for fifteen years. "People come in here all the time and haven't a clue what they're in for. You guys know what it's all about." Usually a traditional renewal service is spiritual, the vows familiar. "Repeat after me," the reverend decrees. "I take you to be my beloved and to live in the holy state of matrimony, to cherish and care for you, to trust you and respect you, to love you and to comfort you, as long as we both shall live." Many, like the one coming up, are Elvis Specials.

When the last straw from the previous wedding has been picked up from the chapel floor, the guests of Holly and Pat Emerick from Carlsbad, California, are shown in. They are a lively group, bopping to the Elvis music now playing over the sound system in keeping with the selected theme. The group of seventeen is festooned for a party. The women, in particular, are colorfully attired. One is wearing a pink wig, halter top, miniskirt, and knee-high boots. Another has a long white feather boa draped across her shoulders. A couple of the men take pictures, hoping to capture the spirit of the occasion. Holly, quite dressed up in a floor-length red and gold brocade dress with a mandarin collar, waits in the wings. Pat at the altar chats with Marcello, who has changed back into his white bejeweled Elvis jumpsuit. When everyone is seated, Marcello once again sings:

> *Take my hand, take my whole life, too,*
> *For I can't help falling in love with you.*

And Holly, with a bounce and a spring to her step, takes her walk down the aisle.

In comparison to traditional renewal ceremonies, which tend to be sedate, Elvis renewal ceremonies, while no less heartfelt, are often rowdy. The guests feel free to express themselves loudly and frequently with little or no prompting, and this one is no exception. "Marriage is a beautiful and holy state instituted in the time of man's beginnings," Marcello recites. "Marriage is also a marvelous adventure, a journey Holly and Pat embarked on ten years ago." "Yeah. Yeah," the crowd shouts. When Marcello curls his lips or swivels his hips, he is greeted with wild applause and laughter. When Holly reaches over to give Pat a kiss, there is more clapping. "By the power invested in me, the King," Marcello asserts at the end of the ceremony, "I now repronounce you husband and wife." And everyone cheers. By the time Marcello launches into "Viva Las Vegas," the group is primed to hit the dance floor.

Bright light city gonna set my soul
Gonna set my soul on fire,

A conga line led by the bride and groom forms spontaneously. They go around the dance floor passing the camera, everyone waves, and around the dance floor they go once again.

Viva Las Vegas, Viva Las Vegas,
Viva, Viva Las Vegas.

Elvis sings the song "Viva Las Vegas" several times in the movie of the same title: over the opening credits, at a talent contest, and after his character, Lucky Jackson, has married Ann-Margret's character, Rusty Martin, at the very end. The song itself, however, has nothing do with either love or marriage and everything to do with having a good time, particularly when the dice are hot and Lady Luck is on a roll. Still, it is the chapel's theme song, and with everyone clearly enjoying themselves, deservedly so.

4:45 P.M.

"Do you both have rings you want to exchange?" Ron DeCar as Elvis asks the newlyweds at the altar. "May I have them, please." The best man hands him a ring. "Thank ya," Ron says. The bridesmaid hands him the other ring. "Thank ya very much."

Ron DeCar has come in, and he has sent Marcello home. Marcello has put in several twelve-hour days recently, often without eating lunch or dinner, and he has earned the time off. Ron will work the remainder of the day and night and the next day, impersonating Elvis or enacting any other character needed for a theme wedding.

Other personnel have also turned over. Darlene Christensen is the wedding coordinator on duty this Saturday evening. She followed her grown children to Vegas from California eight years ago, and she has never regretted the move. She got involved in the wedding chapel business, learning how to interface calmly between staff and patrons in the potentially emotionally charged situation that any wedding can be. She works weekends, when the chapel is busiest and her unique skills are most likely to be put to use.

At Ron's request, Vivian Rickhoff—whose presence subsequently surprises everyone, since she retired two weeks ago—is working the hotel desk for the evening. Vivian is very fond of Ron and only too happy to help out. She has known him since she and her husband moved west to escape windy Chicago winters over six years ago. She met him when he sang at the wedding chapel at which she worked. When he opened his own chapel, Vivian jumped ship and was there at Viva Las Vegas's opening. "That first day we opened at eight. I put on the coffee, and then we waited," she recalls. "When a couple walked in at ten a.m. and wanted to get married, you had to pick me up off the floor. I had to scramble to get the minister, but we pulled it off. It was a great moment."

Jamie Richards, the chapel's manager, relieves both Fernando, who has been working side by side with Marcello, and Shannon, who goes off to her dancing gig at the Mirage. With his show business background, Jamie handles everything, from the video camera to the sound system to the telephones, with aplomb. In fact, if he dyed his wavy dirty-blond hair black, he could even pass as a tall, good-looking Elvis impersonator.

The son of dancers, Jamie grew up in Las Vegas, never expecting that he would ever call the town home or that he would be part of its wedding industry. A dancer himself, he tried doing the starving-artist bit in Los Angeles and New York, and he had some success in productions in Paris and Tokyo. He finally realized, however, that he could have steady work and lead a regular life in Las Vegas. Five knee operations before he was 34 years old ended his career onstage.

Jamie has a cool, calm, and collected persona, perfect for his current calling. "If you think of each wedding as a little production, it goes smoother," he says, explaining his role at the chapel. "That's what I do, that's my background. I put it all together, working with choreographers, producers, and musicians. The trick is to keep it moving without the couples feeling rushed. You know you have prevailed when the mother of the bride, who walked in horrified, absolutely horrified, at the situation, walks out saying, 'Oh, my goodness, it was beautiful.'"

Meanwhile in the chapel, Reverend Rogers participates in his last wedding of the day. "Bless these rings. Bless these two wonderful people," he exuberantly proclaims. "Cause their love for each other and their lives together to explode with all the joy and happiness." The Reverend Daphne Mendeloff will subsequently assume his responsibilities for the remainder of the day, adding the requested spiritual touch or saying the required legal words.

Reverend Daphne enters the lobby in a billowing cape and a swirl of good humor. Her short, spiked red hair suits her chirpy manner, and she speaks with a slight English accent. When not doing outreach and hospice work with her small congregation, the nondenominational Eternal Hope Ministry, the ordained minister marries eighty to ninety couples each month. In fact, she is Viva Las Vegas's primary minister, working during the week plus being on call on the weekends and performing most of the chapel's gay and lesbian commitment ceremonies. Most independent, as well as hotel-run, chapels recoil at the suggestion of same-sex services; managements justify their policy by the law, which doesn't recognize homosexual unions, or by their ministers, who don't believe in it. Here same-sex couples are accepted and welcomed. "My personal opinion doesn't matter," Reverend Daphne explains. "If two people feel it is the right thing for them to do, it is not for me to sit in judgment. 'He who believe in me, I won't turn asunder.'"

Reverend Daphne loves what she does, and she imbues her services with much feeling. "In Las Vegas there is never any time to do marriage counseling," she posits. "So I try to make the ceremony as meaningful as possible." She throws in a bit of advice, too. "Remember that you came here today because you love each other," she instructs newlyweds standing before her. "It will help you through the difficult times."

6:20 P.M.

"Do you want to walk down the aisle together?" Jamie asks the couple scheduled for the 6:30 p.m. service, coordinating the last-minute details. "Or do you want to meet at the altar?" As the couple talk it over, Jamie hands the bride her bouquet of red roses, and Darlene pins the groom's matching boutonniere on his suit jacket lapel. As soon as the chapel has been cleared—of smoke, props, and guests from the previous wedding—Jamie escorts the couple to the waiting area off the chapel. Some of their dozen guests wait outside; others congregate in the lobby.

"I feel like I'm getting married," one of the women guests says. "I'm so nervous for her."

"It's happening. It's so exciting," says another as the guests are shown into the chapel.

With the lobby temporarily free of visitors and the commotion that accompanies them, Jamie and Darlene review the evening's calendar.

"I'm not sure the seven-thirty wedding is on," Darlene advises. "We have been ringing their room, but we haven't gotten through."

225

"At least it is not a theme wedding that requires elaborate staging, but let's keep trying to reach them anyway," Jamie responds. "It's nice to know what is going on."

"There is also a question about the ten-thirty wedding. I have been given two different credit cards, and neither works, but the bride tells me that they really want to do this."

"Well, it should be all right as long as they pay cash. I just hope they don't have a large, rowdy wedding party with them. A Blue Hawaii at that hour, you never know. Hello, Viva Las Vegas Wedding Chapel," Jamie says, picking up the telephone without missing a beat. "Yes, we have thirty-two rooms here. If you go to our Web site, you can see pictures of them. No, we recommend making a reservation. Sometimes one or two wedding parties will book all the rooms for a weekend. Let us know if we can help. Thank you for calling." Turning back to Darlene, he asks, "Did we get the nine-thirty taken care of?"

"Yes, I asked Scottie if he could pick them up. He wasn't happy about it, but he said he would. His first stop was at nine o'clock this morning, so he has had a long day. I don't know how we missed making arrangements for them."

Scottie Robb is one of the limousine drivers for Viva Las Vegas, and it is difficult to imagine the chapel finding a better spokesman to represent them. His is the first face from the chapel that a couple sees on their wedding day. It is not a pretty face—he was a professional boxer until 1958—but it is a friendly face, and he has a personable demeanor to go with it.

Like most of his colleagues, Scottie is from someplace else. "I first came here thirty-four years ago on my honeymoon. We really liked it, and we vacationed here over the years. It's so different from New Jersey," he expounds. "One time we went to London, and my wife said, 'Let's go back to Vegas.'" They moved to Vegas twelve years ago, and they are glad they did. "From my days as a fighter and then as a manager, I know people from all over the world. And sooner or later, they find their way to Vegas. So I'm always running into people I know or who know of me. It's a small world, and I like that," Scottie

explains. "And then there's the climate. I'm 70 years old, and I work out five days a week. I can swim outdoors nine months out of the year here and run year-round."

White stretch limousines taking brides and grooms to the chapel of their choice can be seen on the Strip from early morning to late at night.

Scottie is conscientious, too. "I often get the newlyweds here early, too early to suit the ladies, you know, the wedding coordinators, and they get put out with me. But if I have a pickup at the Luxor, clear at the other end of the Strip, I don't want to worry about getting stuck in traffic." True to form, Scottie drops off the couple scheduled for the seven o'clock Elvis Special fifteen minutes early.

8:10 P.M.

"The bride and groom aren't here yet," Darlene informs the guests of the eight-thirty ceremony. "If you wait outside, you can see them arrive."

With that suggestion, Darlene politely clears the lobby as the party of eight moves to the outside waiting area, actually

227

more comfortable for anyone wanting to drink, smoke, or just carry on. Everyone in the group is wearing black, many clad head to toe in leather. Looking like bikers just off their Harleys, these 30-somethings are here for a Gothic-themed wedding.

With Halloween less than two weeks away, otherworldly themes are popular, and the ghouls and goblins are creeping out of the woodwork. To oblige the mischievous spirits running rampant around the premises, the stage in the chapel for a Gothic wedding is transformed into a cemetery. If there is any doubt, there is a sign that says CEMETERY sitting atop the tall, broken metal gate decorated with cobwebs that frames the scene. Dilapidated tombstones marked with R.I.P. and pithy epitaphs have been placed, crookedly of course, around the landscape. It feels like the clock is about to strike midnight and bats are ready to sweep down from the rafters. The only thing missing from the picture is a black cat archly strutting its stuff around the graveyard, hissing and clawing at anything that invades its territory.

Just before the wedding begins, the lights are dimmed and the fog machine is turned on. From the small mezzanine overlooking the stage, an actor dressed as Dracula plays eerie organ music, accompanied by the sound of howling wind. The bride and groom, both wearing black leather jackets and pants similar to their guests' outfits, march down the aisle. As they wait for the officiant in front of an upright casket center stage, a ghostly glow envelops them. If they felt at all uneasy before they entered the chapel about what they were about to undertake, their discomfort must surely be heightened by the special effects.

When the music stops, the Grim Reaper, enacted by Ron DeCar, emerges from the casket. He wears a flowing black robe, suggesting the amorphous shape of a phantom soul. A hood completely covers his presumably ugly and terrifying face. In his hands, fitted with skeletal gloves at the end of which are long, long nails, he holds a scythe, the symbol of his profession. "Do you solemnly agree to adopt each other's frightening personalities?" he asks at one point. "To only walk through the cemetery gates . . . together?"

But it is not all fun and games. As part of the service, there is a traditional, deeply felt candle-lighting ceremony. "Use the outer candles to light the center flame," the Grim Reaper instructs. "The center flame, you'll notice, burns bright, and so shall your love for each other." After he pronounces the couple "husband and wife by the power vested in me by the state of Transylvania," they are escorted to the waiting room off the chapel. There Reverend Daphne pronounces the couple "husband and wife by the power vested in me by the state of Nevada," making it official. After the photography session, which includes pictures with both Dracula and the Grim Reaper, the couple, just like all the other couples who came before them, are introduced to their friends for the first time as Mr. and Mrs., and they are warmly greeted with applause and cheers, hugs and kisses.

Dracula is the officiant at the next wedding, another themed fantasy called "The Tomb." The stage decorations are the same as for the Gothic wedding, so the staff doesn't have to tear down the elaborate props and put up different ones, saving precious time. Knowing that the guests and wedding party had left through chapel doors at the back of the room, Darlene looks in to ask if the staff is ready for the nine o'clock wedding party. "Bring them in," Jamie tells her.

Jamie introduces himself to the couple and then walks them through the ceremony, showing them where to stand and explaining the candle-lighting ritual to them. The young couple, Dan and Morgan, are somewhat nervous, but sure about their commitment to each other. They flew into Vegas from Connecticut on Friday by themselves and will return home on Sunday. "No one knows that we're here to get married," Dan confides. "Well, they probably do now," Morgan counters. "My 3-year-old daughter went to a family party, and I know she told everyone."

Why fly across the country with so little free time to spend on the city's pleasures? "We were just looking for something fun and different," Dan relates. "Really different," Morgan adds. Dan continues, "I've never been to Vegas, but I always thought I would get married here. The no-fuss aspect of a Vegas wedding really appealed to me." He also appreciates the cost. "We spent in total what some people spend on a wedding dress!" he brags.

Morgan and Dan are both wearing outfits acquired from a costume store. Looking like a Romanian count, Dan has on a black fitted jacket with a high rose-colored collar and oversize lapels. The material appears to be satin, but it probably isn't. Morgan has donned a floor-length organza dress in white with black trim. Given the setting, it has a surprisingly romantic appearance, and it flounces when she moves. The matching black and white streamers in her hair attractively frame her face. Despite the black lipstick and heavy eyeliner, she looks comely but fragile. The kicker is, she wears hiking boots.

Waiting onstage listening to the organ music, Dan and Morgan hold hands. Dracula emerges from the casket and begins, "My dear people of the night."

9:35 P.M.

"Who gives this woman to this man?" Reverend Daphne asks.

Not all weddings after eight o'clock are wacky or weird, and the nuptials under way are about as traditional as they can be. The bride wears white; the groom, a dark suit. Her father walked her down the aisle, and her best friend is her bridesmaid, just as the groom's brother stands up for him. Additional family and friends bear witness to the event.

"This is a very special occasion, as you are here to exchange your vows of marriage," Reverend Daphne continues, "and to publicly proclaim your love, your devotion, and your commitment to each other. It is a happy event, and I am glad to see you're both smiling."

When the ceremony is over, two guests reenter the lobby to arrange for taxi service to take them to their hotel. "It's so different from the way it's shown in movies. Not at all what I expected," one is overheard saying. "It was so nice."

Reverend Daphne also conducts the lesbian commitment ceremony that follows. The two participants and their five guests are subdued, not quite sure what to expect. The women are dressed similarly, distinguished by the color of their blouses, one white and one blue, which they are wearing with black pants. They both carry red roses that they set on the floor in front of them when they recite their personally composed vows. "Worry about being the best partner you can be," Reverend Daphne enjoins, "rather than whether you picked the best partner." At the end, everyone laughs and cries.

The couple for the ten-thirty Blue Hawaii wedding chose not to use the chapel limousine, and they arrive early. Jamie's concerns were for naught: the couple is alone, no entourage into heavy partying or causing trouble. As soon as the previous wedding is over and the guests have left the chapel, Jamie and Ron move quickly to transform the stage into paradise. When everything is under control, Ron goes to change, once again, into his Elvis costume, and the next newlyweds are brought into the chapel.

> *... Like a river flows surely to the sea,*
> *Darling, so it goes, some things are meant to be. ...*

As Ron sings "Can't Help Falling in Love," the lovebirds hold hands.

> *Love sweet Aloha*
> *I will love you longer than forever. ...*

When he sings "Hawaiian Wedding Song," the lovebirds slow-dance.

> *. . . Oh, there's black jack*
> *And poker and the roulette wheel,*

And when he launches into "Viva Las Vegas," the couple takes a quick turn or two around the dance floor, and then slow-dances. It was just that type of wedding.

At ten minutes before eleven, a very handsome but very young couple walk into the lobby. Almost as if they are trying to appear more mature than they really are, they have dressed up. The woman is wearing a black cocktail dress with spaghetti straps and backless high heels. The man is wearing a dark suit with a white dress shirt. "We want to get married," he says. And so, on that Saturday night at the Viva Las Vegas Wedding Chapel, another couple in love, one more than expected, says, "I do."

11:35 P.M.

The last ceremony, a one-song Elvis Special, is relatively quick. Once the couple leaves the building, the doors are locked, and cleanup begins. Jamie puts away the props from the chapel, Ron changes into his street clothes, and Darlene closes out the cash register. Reflecting on the day, Darlene notes, "It was a pretty easy Saturday. Not every wedding was a large wedding. We can get bogged down with large parties. Just getting them into and out of the chapel can take time. We kept pretty much on schedule today. Yes, all in all, it was a good day."

After they've finished their chores, Ron turns out the lights and relocks the door as he, Jamie, and Darlene head home for the night.

Elvis has left the building.

Candlelight
WEDDING
CHAPEL
MARRIAGE INFORMATIO
MARRIAGE INFO
OPEN 24 HRS

part

4

" I T ' S   N O W

O R   N E V E R "

In Las Vegas, wedding chapels and neon go together like love and marriage.

THERE ARE ALMOST AS many reasons to get married in Las Vegas as there are chapels on the Strip. Some couples choose Vegas because weddings here are quick and convenient. Other couples believe that romance flowers in the glow of the neon lights. Whatever reasons people have, they are in good company. Couples arrive from all fifty states and around the world. Almost a third of the newlyweds are from California, while about 12 percent come from abroad. Whatever the betrothed are looking for, they will almost certainly find it in the town with the anything-goes attitude.

Even though Las Vegas has changed, most of the freestanding wedding chapels with the little white steeples and the big neon signs are still located on the northern stretch of Las Vegas Boulevard approaching downtown. While there might be one too many chubby cherubs peering over a bright red heart to suit uptown sensibilities, many of these small chapels offer a heartfelt ceremony in pleasant surroundings. Those in love can feel free to drive through or walk in, dress up or dress down, or come alone or with friends and family. Is the bride looking for Elvis? He's here; so are Garth Brooks and Bruce Springsteen, and Marilyn and Cher. Does the groom want something more novel? Nuptials on horseback in the Red Rock Canyon area or a ceremony in a helicopter in a night flight over the Strip can be arranged.

For those who feel that bigger is better, the large resort hotels now have wedding chapels that either incorporate the theme of the resort or have no theme at all. And they will permit ceremonies to be performed poolside or around the premises. In keeping with a three-, four-, or even five-star resort, there is a high level of customer service, a welcome feature when meltdowns or blowups are just a hair trigger away. Yet the traditional setting found in most hotels means sacrificing spontaneity for artificiality, festivity for formality. On the other hand, Mom will approve.

While free spirits might opt for a funky freestanding wedding chapel and first-timers might want a more formal atmosphere, everyone wanting to get married must go to the marriage license bureau at the Clark County Courthouse at 200 South Third Street downtown before the big moment arrives. In exchange for $55 cash and proper identification that proves that both participants are at least 18 years old (or notarized parental consent if they are underage), the couple, unless they are obviously inebriated, will be issued a license good for one year. The license bureau is open from 8:00 a.m. to midnight Monday through Thursday and around the clock on Friday, Saturday, and holidays.

Couples in a hurry can walk from the marriage license bureau to the Office of the Commissioner of Civil Marriage at 309 South Third Street for a $50, no-frills civil ceremony performed by a county official. The hours are 8:00 a.m. to 10:00 p.m. daily, including weekends and holidays. No appointment is necessary, and there is usually no wait.

ALL THINGS CONSIDERED

Contrary to popular belief, most chapels are not open twenty-four hours a day, seven days a week. Even on weekends, most of the freestanding chapels lock their doors at midnight, if not earlier. The hotel chapels close up earlier still. It is also unlikely that walk-ins will be waited on immediately. Almost all chapels need at least two hours to collect the required personnel, including the minister to perform the service, a photographer, and a florist. So even elopers need to do more than just show up.

If getting married on a specific date or at a specific time is important, then a reservation should be made as early as possible. Saturdays are the busiest day of the week. Many chapels won't have a moment to spare except in the early morning or late evening. Valentine's Day is the most popular day of the year for Las Vegas weddings, with a four-hour wait at the Marriage License Bureau not uncommon. Women like Valentine's Day because it is

238

romantic. Men like it because it makes it easier to remember anniversaries. Halloween brings out the ghouls and vampires, while New Year's Eve, the second most popular holiday, is preferred by those who want to begin a new year as husband and wife, whatever the tax consequences.

And then there are lucky numbers. Many of those moved to marry in Las Vegas reason that when gambling on love, why not increase the odds of success by tying the knot on a lucky day at a lucky time? The superstitious were out in force on September 9, 1999. People started to book the second day of the second month in the year 2002 the previous summer, and two o'clock only happens twice a day. Many had to settle for the $222 wedding package to commemorate the day.

Aside from the obvious, such as location and appearance, chapels vary in numerous ways. The time allocated to each party in the chapel can vary from fifteen minutes to an hour, more for a fee. Sometimes the minister's fee is included in the price of the wedding package and sometimes it isn't. If it isn't, the charge is usually $50. Limousine drivers should always be tipped. In some facilities, shooting pictures is strictly verboten, except by the chapel's professional photographer. Sometimes this policy is posted clearly and implemented diplomatically. Other times it isn't. Attitude can never be hidden, certainly not for long. A word over the phone or a gesture in person can be a giveaway as to whether a chapel is committed to making each and every wedding special, regardless of how many weddings came before or how many will follow.

A word to anyone who wants a Las Vegas wedding might be in order here. If in doubt about the chapel, the ceremony, or anything at all, wait. If you don't want to wait, at least be sure you can get your deposit back if you change your mind. If you want to try another chapel, one more compatible with your personality and conducive to fulfilling your dreams, go ahead. There are enough of them.

The list of chapels here is not all-inclusive. All prices and packages are subject to change.

Funky and Fanciful

Candlelight Wedding Chapel
2855 Las Vegas Boulevard South
800-962-1818 or 702-735-4179
candlelightchapel.com

The Candlelight Wedding Chapel sits across Las Vegas Boulevard from Circus Circus and on the other side of Riviera Boulevard from the Riviera Hotel and Casino. A Las Vegas block to the north is the Sahara, while the Stardust is an equal distance away in the opposite direction. This small, freestanding building with its New England–style spire and roof was built in 1967 in the heart of the Strip, albeit the old Strip, as much of the glitz and glamour have moved farther away from downtown. Yet there is still a buzz surrounding the place.

Candlelight is one of the few chapels, independent or not, that is open seven days a week until midnight. Saturdays, particularly in the summer, are very busy, so be prepared to wait, even if you have a reservation. If you find yourself at the last minute wanting a wedding cake for the celebration afterward, the chapel has a small selection, as well as fresh flowers, in the cooler in the entryway.

The chapel seats up to fifty people. But as chapel time is kept to fifteen minutes, larger wedding parties might feel rushed getting in and out. Packages begin at $189, not including the minister's donation or the gratuity to the limousine driver. A professional organist is available as an option.

Chapel of the Bells

2233 Las Vegas Boulevard South
800-233-2391 or 702-735-6803
chapelofthebellslasvegas.com

Of all the independent wedding chapels, the Chapel of the Bells has the best neon on the Strip. The façade of the roof, shaped like a large peaked gable, is strung with lights, giving off a reddish glow. The three chimes, outlined in neon, appear to be not only merrily ringing, but loudly proclaiming that the chapel's "Weddings" are "World Famous." These neon symbols are then repeated on a stand-alone structure in the middle of the parking lot the chapel shares with the adjacent Fun City Motel, whose own sign helps light up the sky. For visual excitement alone, it is easy to see why movies such as *Vegas Vacation*, *Indecent Proposal*, and *Honeymoon in Vegas* used the Chapel of the Bells for their Las Vegas weddings.

Inside, the chapel has a pleasant waiting room with couches and chairs for those whose nerves are calmed by sitting rather than pacing. For brides wanting to look like brides in the pictures of the big event, there is a small selection of formal wedding gowns. The facility allocates fifteen minutes for the ceremony but lets couples linger a few extra moments in the chapel for pictures.

The chapel seats twenty-five. The altar is dressed in white drapery trimmed with gold braid. The are several candelabra, a pair of gold birdcages, and lots of silk flowers creating a halo effect around the pulpit. At the back of the room an organ can provide live music.

For a $40 deposit, time can be reserved. Packages begin at $155, although quick, simple weddings can be arranged for $115 inclusive. Couples wanting to take their own pictures or video are welcome to do so.

A Chapel by the Courthouse

201 East Bridger Avenue
800-545-8111 or 702-384-9099
achapelbythecourthouse.com

If you are looking for convenience above all else, A Chapel by the Courthouse, as its name suggests, is located downtown around the corner from the marriage license bureau in the county courthouse. But be warned: impersonal government buildings dwarf the tiny facility at this desolate intersection, masking any charm it might once have had. Then again, if you are in a hurry, you probably won't notice the buses from the municipal jail sometimes parked across the street or mind that a fresh coat of paint has not been applied to the chapel's façade in quite a while.

Inside, it is standing room only because there is so little room. Once you have walked through the front door and entered the waiting area, the chapel is two feet right in front of you. The room is pure kitsch, crowded with knickknacks and fraying about the edges. The receptionist is friendly, if somewhat eager to make a sale. With luck the minister is there, and you will soon be on your way, happily married.

The chapel fee is $40. Wedding packages begin at $159.

Chapel of Love

1430 Las Vegas Boulevard South
800-922-5683 or 702-387-0155
vegaschapeloflove.com

One would never know that the Chapel of Love was a Bob's Big Boy restaurant in the 1960s. Today it houses several chapels, each with its own theme. There's the Short & Sweet, a small room for no more than twelve guests, for couples eager to begin married life. The Lovers' Pathway, with seating for fifty, provides a more traditional setting. Its wide white tile aisle lined with white benches is the perfect canvas for a bride to add her choice of colors and decorations.

The third chapel, relocated from the Las Vegas Wedding Gardens, brings air-conditioned tranquillity to a garden party. Heavy wrought-iron benches are set on plush green carpet. The fountain at the front of the room has running water. Statues of angels and silk flower arrangements complete the decor.

At the Chapel of Love comfort and convenience are available with every wedding ceremony. There is a large waiting room for guests to gather before the ceremony while the bride retires to one of the dressing rooms for last-minute primping. Digital photography has made it possible for the couple to leave hand in hand with pictures in hand. And the large parking lot will accommodate just about any size crowd.

The Chapel of Love also has a drive-through window, where for $25 lovebirds can say "I do" without leaving their car. A ceremony in the chapel's convertible or a Camaro is an option for $95. Family and friends can park around the wedding party in their own cars. Anyone asking for burgers and fries with the wedding is directed to the Burger King across the street.

Wedding packages range from $139 to $399, plus minister's fee. The cordial staff, pleased to be assisting on this momentous occasion, is on the house.

Cupid's Wedding Chapel

> 827 Las Vegas Boulevard South
> 800-543-2933 or 702-598-4444
> cupidswedding.com

The large neon heart rising over Las Vegas Boulevard is an emblem of the care and concern given to each and every couple at Cupid's Wedding Chapel. Nuptials are scheduled an hour apart so that no one feels hurried or crowded. The service lasts a long and meaningful twenty minutes. "If the ceremony doesn't touch someone," Linda James, the chapel's manager, rhetorically queries, "how long can the marriage be expected to last?"

Cupid's has one chapel that comfortably accommodates parties

Cupid's has the biggest heart on Las Vegas Boulevard, hands down.

of up to fifty people. It is a light and airy room, decorated simply. The modern stained glass with doves and roses, situated behind the altar, is the perfect background for photos. Three video cameras situated around the room provide different angles of the goings-on.

A variety of traditional and nontraditional ceremonies is available. The family unity ceremony includes children from previous marriages. A child is handed a ring or a pendant and asked, "Do you accept this token of our love?" Another version has a role for the parents of the bride and groom. As a pioneer in catering to same-sex couples, Cupid's also has a commitment ceremony.

If you want Elvis at your ceremony, "ours is the best," asserts Linda. "He not only looks and sounds like Elvis, he is a real nice guy, too." For weddings, Elvis can escort the bride down the aisle or serenade the newlyweds. For marriage renewals, he can conduct the ceremony.

Packages are priced from $89 to $799, exclusive of tax, the minister, and limousine service. For an additional $149, live doves will be released to circle overhead. This romantic gesture takes place outdoors, of course, following the ceremony.

Gay Wedding Chapel of Las Vegas

See Viva Las Vegas Wedding Chapel

Graceland Wedding Chapel
619 Las Vegas Boulevard South
800-824-5732 or 702-474-6655
gracelandchapel.com or elvisweddings.com

The Graceland Wedding Chapel rocks.

If you want to pay homage to Elvis, as many musicians do, this is the place to come. The walls of the tiny reception area are covered with autographed photographs of the melodious and harmonious who have said "I do" or renewed their vows here. There are two members of the British pop group the Thompson Twins (who married each other and are not really twins), and the Neville Brothers (who really are brothers, as well as bandmates). Members of Deep Purple, Def Leppard, and Kiss have also done it here. Jon Bon Jovi of the rock band that bears his name has a personal connection to the chapel. He married his childhood sweetheart at Graceland Las Vegas in 1989 and keeps returning for the weddings of family, friends, and fans.

Yet initially the chapel had little to do with the King beyond its name. One of the previous owners, a friend of Elvis's from Memphis, asked him if he could use the name. Permission was granted, and the place has been hopping ever since. Today, of course, it helps that some of the best Elvis impersonators in town are on call here. "Norm Jones, an older Elvis, puts a lot of heart into his performance," Peggy Johnson, one of the current owners, says with pride. "For renewal of vows, he walks the couple down memory lane. They really appreciate it."

The chapel is small. It has a cozy, homey feel, a reflection of its inception over sixty years ago as part of a family residence. The stained glass behind the altar pictures a dove. Silk flowers abound, and pew markers line the aisle. Couples wear everything from T-shirts to tuxes, shorts to gowns.

Wedding packages range from $55 to $495, not including the minister's fee. Elvis is available for $145.

The Hartland Mansion
525 Park Paseo Drive
702-387-6700 or 702-387-0222
vegasweddings.com/hartland

Dr. Toni Hart, owner of the Hartland Mansion, makes no claims that Elvis slept here and diligently points out that a couple of fires destroyed the original property, requiring it be rebuilt from the ground up. However, local lore has it that Elvis was friends with the previous owner, and neighbors report that his bus was often parked on the street in front of the house after his performances at the International Hilton in the seventies. In this Elvis-infatuated town, stories have been kept alive on a lot less.

Wedding ceremonies are held in the mansion's elegant foyer, decorated with a touch of the Old South. The grand staircase sweeps down from the second floor on both sides of the room so the bride can make an entrance like Scarlett O'Hara if she wants. The black-and-white checkerboard-patterned floor is bold and dramatic. A baby grand piano sits in a corner of the room.

For simple nuptials, packages are priced at $150 and $395. For a reception or dinner with dancing for one hundred to three hundred guests in the party room, call for details.

A Hollywood Wedding Chapel

2207B Las Vegas Boulevard South
800-704-0478 or 702-731-0678
ahollywoodweddingchapel.com

For a small piece of Las Vegas history, A Hollywood Wedding Chapel is worth checking out. It was once the home of the Red Fez, a popular nightclub frequented by the Rat Pack of the sixties, the Blues Brothers of the eighties, and musicians like Count Basie and Louis Armstrong throughout the decades. However, this portion of the Las Vegas Strip bears no resemblance to the Sunset Strip, and the Hollywood connection ends with the celebrity pictures on the wall behind the reception counter.

The facility has one chapel seating up to fifty, but parking, apparently shared with the motel next door, is limited.

Packages begin at $40 for the use of the chapel and wedding music. The minister's fee is extra.

Las Vegas Villa

Sistine Wedding Chapel
4982 Shirley Street
877-588-4552 or 702-795-8119
lasvegasvilla.com

The Las Vegas Villa, the former home of Liberace, is available for weddings celebrated in true Las Vegas style. It is located on a quiet residential street where Liberace had bought two adjacent houses, razed them, and then built a mansion and decorated it in the grand, flamboyant manner for which he was known. The number of etched mirrors, the amount of gilt and gold trim, the variety of pianos, and the extravagance of the crystal chandeliers and marble statues will amaze and amuse all who set foot on the premises.

The chapel is in Liberace's former bedroom. For weddings the bedroom furniture is removed and an altar, flowers, and guest chairs are brought in. There is plenty of room for fifty guests. The crowning touch is the ceiling, a reproduction of the Vatican's Sistine Chapel in Rome. It took over a year to paint, reportedly by one of Michelangelo's direct descendants, and cost $1.5 million.

The bride is invited to come over a half an hour early to dress in one of the large guest rooms with private bath. Impressionist paintings by Mary Cassatt and others adorn the walls. The groom can gather his thoughts before the ceremony in the English library elsewhere in the house.

The villa has the facilities for a buffet for 30 in the salon or a sit-down dinner for 1,200 in the ballroom. For something simpler, perhaps just for two, the Grand Piano Wedding Package, available only Monday through Friday, includes photos, flowers, and wedding cake, and costs $550.

Little Chapel of the Flowers

1717 Las Vegas Boulevard South
800-843-2410 or 702-735-4331
littlechapel.com

The Little Chapel of the Flowers takes weddings seriously. Before the big day a staff planner will make any arrangements requested, from limousine pickup to dinner afterward. Arriving at the chapel, the couple will be met by a wedding coordinator, whose job it is to make sure everything comes off as planned. And before they walk down the aisle, they will have had the opportunity to ask the minister to incorporate any special requests into the ceremony.

The facility is very self-contained. On the grounds there are three pleasantly decorated chapels for different-size wedding parties, the largest seating up to seventy, and two indoor waiting areas, so guests can escape the summer heat. The small garden, with waterfalls, bridge, and gazebo, is perfect for pictures. The chapel has its own photography department, so pictures are always ready the day after, as well as a flower shop. As an option, the nuptials can be broadcast over the Internet so that faraway family and friends can join in the special moment.

All wedding packages incorporate a candle-lighting ceremony into the service and begin at $195, not including the minister's fee. For something different, couples can add a limousine tour of the Las Vegas Strip to their wedding package for $495 or a helicopter trip over Hoover Dam to Lake Las Vegas Resort for dinner for $1,195.

Little Church of the West
   4617 Las Vegas Boulevard South
   800-821-2452 or 702-739-7971
   littlechurchlv.com

Roy Rogers would still feel comfortable at the Little Church of the West over sixty years after he ushered at the first wedding held there. Although the buckskins draping the windows have been replaced with lace and brocade curtains, the small chapel still exudes a rustic charm reminiscent of pioneer days on the range.

The historic chapel was originally part of the Western theme park of the Last Frontier Hotel. It is an exact, half-size replica of a church built in a California mining town in 1849, right down to its shingled roof, redwood interior walls, and nineteenth-century hanging lamps, long since converted from gas to electricity. To the right of the entrance, there is an antique davenport desk circa 1860, atop of which a desk lamp with a green glass shade emits a nostalgic golden glow. Across the aisle, as modern needs dictate, there is video recording equipment. The hardwood benches look just as uncomfortable as they have always been, but Las Vegas wedding ceremonies rarely last long enough for that to make a difference.

The Little Church of the West refers to itself as "Chapel to the Stars," and the roster of celebrities tying the knot at this facility over the decades is indeed impressive. They range from Betty Grable and Harry James, who were besieged by fans in the forties, to Angelina Jolie and Billy Bob Thornton, who snuck into town so recently that gossip magazines still wonder what went wrong. Fortunately, there are no signs of ghosts of marriages past or present to upstage you on your wedding day. In fact, the kitsch factor is kept to a minimum here.

As Las Vegas casinos and hotels have gotten bigger and bigger, the Little Church of the West has been forced to move three times. Today it is located past Mandalay Bay, so far south it is almost off the Strip. Yet this location affords it an attractive setting surrounded by green grass and trees, enough land for an outdoor gazebo, and plenty of guest parking. Presumably, the traffic on Las Vegas Boulevard fifty feet away cannot be heard when the chapel doors are closed.

Wedding packages range in price from $199 to $525, plus a $40 donation to the minister.

A Little White Wedding Chapel
1301 Las Vegas Boulevard South
800-545-8111 or 702-382-5943
alittlewhitechapel.com

If you are driving down Las Vegas Boulevard trying to decide where to tie the knot, you might be tempted to stop at A Little White Wedding Chapel. Don't. At first glance, it appears more charming than tacky. It's not. While the white wrought-iron fence surrounding the property suggests old-fashioned friendliness, it's a front. But if you end up here, hopefully it is off-hours during the off-season, when the wedding bell blues can barely be heard.

Enter into the reception area cum retail site, and it is readily apparent that the commercial reigns over the spiritual. There are few seats for the weary but plenty of salesgirls for the willing. The staff, presumably paid by commission, squabble over customers, but they have no qualms about keeping anyone waiting. Their top priority is locking in a date and collecting the deposit for the reservation.

Enforcing the rules is another concern. If you get caught violating the NO PICTURES OR VIDEO ALLOWED IN THE CHAPEL sign, expect to be chastised. There is no guideline, however, on how long the ceremony might last or the length of time a wedding party can spend in the chapel. Don't be surprised if you are hurried along to make room for the parties that follow, especially on crowded Saturdays.

There are two chapels right off the reception area. The smaller of the two is decorated with a mural of a waterfall. The larger chapel, with several stained-glass windows along the sides of the room, has white wood pews for up to thirty guests. Fake white roses on toile are strung around the room. Ornamental candelabra are squeezed in wherever there is an inch of space. For simplicity, go with one of the wedding packages, rather than trying to customize a service. Packages range from $179 to $799.

If you are looking for something different, A Little White Wedding Chapel also offers nuptials in its drive-through Tunnel of Vows. If you keep the pedal to the metal and your eye on the sky portrayed overhead, it will be over before you know it. Best of all, you don't have to venture outside your car. Packages for tunnel weddings range from $40 to $100.

Mon Bel Ami Wedding Chapel

607 Las Vegas Boulevard South
866-503-4400 or 702-388-4445
monbelami.com

Mon Bel Ami Wedding Chapel is the newest addition to the Las Vegas Strip. Located a few blocks from the Fremont Street Experience, it has no resemblance to the downtown chapels of old, or even to the Silver Bell Wedding Chapel, which it replaced. Except for a three-dimensional wall decoration of some cheery cherubs hanging in the hallway opposite the chapel, gone are the cupids, angels, and other symbols of matches made in heaven. Vanquished, too, are the red hearts, pink flowers, and yards of white satin, more appropriate for a sweet sixteen party than a sophisticated wedding ceremony. Instead, the modern facility is tastefully decorated and color coordinated. What a find!

The chapel itself can be gussied up, although there really isn't a lot to do. A rose-strewn aisle runner can be added for a romantic gesture, or the candelabra at the front of the room and at the ends of the pews can be lit to enhance the atmosphere. Weddings are booked an hour apart, so the nuptials are not rushed. Afterward, champagne can be served to guests in the garden while the newly-weds have their picture taken.

Wedding packages range from $229 to $1,599. For weddings on Tuesday, Wednesday, or Thursday, the chapel will pay the $55 for the marriage license. The chapel is pleased to offer renewal of vows and commitment ceremonies as well.

San Francisco Sally's Victorian Chapel
1394 Las Vegas Boulevard South
800-658-8677 or 702-385-7777

San Francisco Sally's rents every type of fashion wear imaginable for a romantic, traditional wedding with a hint of the past. Victorian costumes are popular, but so are southern belles and beaux and Western wear. For those wanting to emphasize the traditional, black tuxedos start at $50. Shoes, hats, canes, gloves, scarves, ties, and cummerbunds can be added to complete the look. Brides have their choice of short, midlength, or floor-length wedding gowns for $60 to $140, including veil and slip. Hats, parasols, earrings, and necklaces can augment the bride's ensemble. Customers can keep their outfits for twenty-four hours if they have selected another locale for their ceremony.

But there's no reason to leave. At the back of the establishment is the Victorian Chapel, a small room decorated to the hilt, as its name implies, with Victorian touches, flourishes, and embellishments. The rose-colored carpet sets off the deep pink love seats, velvet draperies, flowered wallpaper, and crystal chandeliers. The props throughout the place are perfect for pictures. There's the cardboard three-tier wedding cake that looks good enough to eat. The JUST MARRIED sign posted on the carriage in the store will forever

remind you of why you were so dressed up. With limited space, nuptials are usually an intimate affair, kept to the couple, the witnesses, and the minister.

One of the best deals here is one-hour chapel time, soft background music, candlelight service, the minister, photos, and choice of any gown and tuxedo in the shop for $305.

A Special Memory Wedding Chapel
800 South Fourth Street (at Gass Avenue)
800-962-7798 or 702-384-2211
aspecialmemory.com

A Special Memory Wedding Chapel was constructed from the ground up as a wedding chapel. What a novel idea! Fashioned after a New England church, the facility opened in 1996 on a quiet street, a block away from Las Vegas Boulevard. It still has a new and fresh feeling about it, inside and out.

The two chapels are simply, but pleasantly, decorated. The main, larger chapel has a high gabled ceiling, white walls, stained-glass

The many boutiques in town make it possible to rent all sorts of wedding paraphernalia for brides, grooms, and their attendants—at the last minute, too.

windows all around, and an extra-wide aisle for the bridal processional. In other words, it is nice and airy. The smaller of the two rooms also feels like a house of worship, but on a more intimate scale. However, it is named the Royal Chapel, and its predominant theme is the color purple. There is purple carpet, purple cushioned pews, and purple drapery used as a backdrop behind the pulpit.

Wedding packages range from $199 to $799, or the personable staff can help customize the flowers, photos, and extras.

Despite its traditional veneer, A Special Memory Wedding Chapel still retains a sense of whimsy. In a hurry? There's a drive-up window at the corner of Lovers Lane and A Special Memory where vows are administered for $25. Stuck on Elvis? For $589, Elvis will chauffeur the newlyweds from hotel to chapel and back. The mode of transportation? A 1955 pink Cadillac, what else? Want to get away from it all? The chapel can arrange weddings in the air in hot-air balloons or on the ground on horseback. Prices vary.

Sweethearts Wedding Chapel
1155 Las Vegas Boulevard South
800-444-2932 or 702-385-7785

Sweethearts is part boutique and part chapel. The retail side of the store is crammed full of formal wedding accoutrements. Beautiful bridal gowns for sale and for rent in sizes 3 to 30 come in a wide variety of styles—from fitted, beaded bodices to full and flowing skirts in every shade of white, ivory, and beige. Attire for the groom from head to toe, that's hats to shoes, is available as well. Boutonnieres in a rainbow of colors are displayed near the cash register at the entry.

The spiritual side of the store simulates a garden setting. The walls of the chapel are strung with silk flowers resembling ivy growing on a gazebo. Any empty wall space has been covered with cutout red felt hearts.

The bars on the window indicate that the facility is not on the best part of Las Vegas Boulevard, and it shares the block with an adult bookstore and a Cuban restaurant. Service, however, is friendly, and there is a parking lot behind the building.

Wedding packages range from $65 to $375, including the minister.

Viva Las Vegas Wedding Chapel
1205 Las Vegas Boulevard South
800-574-4450 or 702-384-0771
vivalasvegasweddings.com

If you don't walk into this chapel singing "Viva Las Vegas," there's something wrong with your 'tude, dude. But nothing that the friendly staff, including some guys who look and sound like Elvis and a couple of bathing beauties dressed for *Blue Hawaii*, can't fix. This is the home of the themed wedding, and the staff at Viva Las Vegas Wedding Chapel knows how to combine fantasy with fun for a marriage ceremony made to client specifications.

The chapel is light and airy with a high beamed ceiling and modern-design stained-glass windows overhead. The pulpit at the front of the room is professionally lit and perfect for staging nuptials with a wide variety of different motifs, from the traditional and romantic to the weird and wacky. Does the bride fondly remember twisting the night away? If so, a sixties ceremony can be set up. Or if the groom comes down with an attack of Saturday-night fever, the knot can be tied to a disco beat. If the couple dream of space travel, an intergalactic ceremony can easily be arranged. But if time travel is their thing, the setting can easily be shifted to Chicago of the 1920s or the Old West of the 1880s. As many as a hundred guests can be comfortably seated for the production.

Themed wedding packages begin at $600, and they include the use of the chapel decorated with props and backdrops and populated with characters appropriate to the theme. Additional characters, such as muscle men for a beach party or showgirls for a casino scene, are available at $150 each. Suitable music is always used to set the tone, ranging from an electric guitarist playing the "Wedding March" at a rock 'n' roll wedding to heavy organ music for lovers of the gothic.

The Viva Las Vegas Villas located on the property provides additional services such as a place for wedding receptions following the ceremony. The Villas is a motel that is run as a bed-and-breakfast. Breakfast is served in a diner furnished with fifties memorabilia. The guest rooms, priced from $75 per night for a standard room to $225 for the honeymoon suites, much less during the week, are imaginatively decorated to correspond to the themed weddings. Couples who just can't get enough of Elvis can stay in the Elvis and Priscilla Suite. The bedroom is painted to look like Graceland, and there is the front half of a custom-made pink Cadillac enclosing the foot of the bed.

The Viva Las Vegas Wedding Chapel has a nondiscrimination policy. Same-sex couples are welcome, and commitment ceremonies are conducted with the same care as traditional ceremonies and renewals of vows.

Wee Kirk o' the Heather

231 Las Vegas Boulevard South
800-843-5266 or 702-382-9830
weekirk.com

Anyone standing on the courthouse steps, marriage license in hand, wondering where to go next should try the Wee Kirk o' the Heather. It lies a short two-block walk away. If the minister is available, vows could be said soon after walking in the door.

Take away the steeple, lavender trim, and neon sign, and the chapel looks like a small house. That is exactly what it was when it was built in 1925 in a residential neighborhood two blocks south of Fremont Street downtown. Ever since a minister began conducting nuptials in his living room in 1940, it has been a wedding chapel, one of the oldest continually operating chapels in Las Vegas. Its memorable name, which means Little Chapel of the Lucky Flowers, came from a six-hundred-year-old Scottish church.

This modest, well-maintained structure has a fresh feeling about it. The anteroom is decorated with statues of angels and pictures of cupids. The cozy chapel seats twenty guests comfortably, thirty if absolutely necessary. The wood pews are painted white and decorated with bows and tulle. Large floor-standing candelabra are at the back of the room. Despite its size, there is a dressing room for the bride.

Wedding packages range in price from $129 to $479, not including the minister's fee. All options, including photography, flowers, and first dance, are also available à la carte so that a bride can create her wedding and decide how she wants to preserve its memories. While the emphasis here is on the traditional, same-sex commitment ceremonies will be conducted upon request. The chapel is open 9:00 a.m. until midnight, seven days a week.

Because the chapel has been in the marriage business such a long time, couples who married at the Wee Kirk thirty, forty, fifty, even sixty years ago now return to renew their vows. It was a wonderful experience then, and it would be a wonderful experience now.

Aladdin Resort and Casino
Aladdin Wedding Chapel

3667 Las Vegas Boulevard South
866-945-5933
aladdinweddingchapel.com

The Aladdin Wedding Chapel is located on the second-floor mezzanine and overlooks the casino. All the tumult below reaches up and envelops waiting guests. Coins clang, bells tinkle, and whistles blow whenever the genies grant a wish or gamblers cash in their gold and silver pieces for real money. It is an exciting scene, if not a spiritual one. However, once you're inside, the facility is a nice place to get married.

Of the two chapels, one can accommodate a crowd of sixty; the other is more intimate, for fifteen to twenty. Both are decorated in soft desert colors, beiges, pinks, and purples. Both have a mural with a faux balcony that creates the illusion that the ceremony takes place on a terrace overlooking a tranquil sea surrounded by cypress trees. It provides a backdrop for photos and videos. Neither Ali Baba nor any of his forty thieves are anywhere in sight.

Elvis, however, makes a modest appearance, as the Love Me Tender wedding package commemorates his 1967 wedding to Priscilla Beaulieu in room 246, the private suite of owner Milton Prell, of the old Aladdin Hotel. The ceremony can take place in your suite or in the chapel. In addition to chapel time, flowers, and souvenirs, $999 buys the presence of an Elvis impersonator who sings two songs and will walk the bride down the aisle, if desired. As an add-on, a one-hour tour around town with the Elvis impersonator in his pink Cadillac can be arranged.

Traditional wedding packages begin at $379, plus $50 minister's fee.

At Bally's Las Vegas
Celebration Wedding Chapel

3645 Las Vegas Boulevard South
800-872-1211 or 702-892-2222
ballyschapel.com

"We just want to get married," a young groom-to-be with his soon-to-be bride on his arm moaned to a wedding coordinator while shopping around for an appropriate place for their upcoming nuptials. "We don't want anything fancy."

The couple might have found just what they were looking for at the Celebration Wedding Chapel. An independent operation inside Bally's, the chapel is conveniently located for guests of mid-Strip hotels. At the far end of the underground pedestrian mall, near the stop for the monorail that connects casinos, the facility is pleasant, but rather nondescript. The larger of the two chapels seats up to fifty guests. The carpet and cushioned pews are done in burgundy, while the patterned wallpaper is predominantly beige. As expected, candelabra and silk flower arrangements are displayed on either side of the decorative stained glass at the front of the room. At least the mauve-colored ceiling with recessed lighting, as well as a large chandelier, emits a rosy glow.

The chapel has complete access to Bally's hotel services, such as room reservations and catering. The staff will also assist with tuxedo and gown rentals, as well as setting up a limousine for the mandatory trip to the courthouse for a marriage license.

A renewal-of-vows ceremony costs $195. Wedding packages range from $275 to $1,345, plus minister's fee, for thirty, forty-five, or sixty minutes of chapel time and other amenities.

Bellagio
The Wedding Chapel at Bellagio

3600 Las Vegas Boulevard South
888-987-3344 or 702-693-7700
bellagiolasvegas.com

A large arrangement of fresh flowers from Bellagio's botanical gardens sits on a table in the lobby of the Wedding Chapel. The smell is sensuous. Pachelbel's *Canon* plays in the background. The sound is soothing. In fact, everything about the luxurious setting is designed to calm the nerves while the staff caters to the needs of the prospective bride and groom.

Although there are two chapels on the premises, the Bellagio adheres to a strict policy of only one wedding at a time, lest anything distract from a couple's big day. The smaller, more intimate chapel seats 30 guests. The larger one is able to hold a wedding party of 130.

The least expensive wedding, available only Sunday through Thursday, is $1,800. It covers the use of the chapel for an hour plus a combination of florals,

The Bellagio fountains are amazing for their use of water in the desert and mesmerizing for the artistry with which they dance.

photography, and other amenities. Roses, hydrangeas, calla lilies, and other exotic blooms can be fashioned into cascade-, nosegay-, or handheld-style bouquets, and put into boutonnieres, baskets, or corsages. Photography sessions around the resort—in front of the dancing fountains, perhaps—or in the glass-domed conservatory, as well as in the chapel, are popular.

The deluxe Cosa Bella Wedding Package costs $15,000 plus tax. Among its many features are two hours of chapel time, floral pew markers, and a walkway of white petals for the bride's processional. To prepare for the occasion, there are spa passes, side-by-side massages, and, for the bride, a manicure, pedicure, and makeup session. For the newlyweds to celebrate in style, the package also includes a bottle of Cristal Champagne, a box of Belgian chocolates, dinner at the exclusive Picasso Restaurant, tickets to Cirque du Soleil's "O" Show, two nights in a penthouse suite, and breakfast in bed.

The Bellagio does not offer theme packages, unless the $1,800 upgrade to the Terrazza di Sogno can be considered a theme. And why not? The terrace where the ceremony takes place overlooks Bellagio's Lago di Como. Its views of a Tuscan landscape, although make-believe, bear a striking resemblance to Italy's Lago di Como. And if not a theme, it is certainly a dream. At the moment of the kiss, the fountains dance.

Caesars Palace
Caesars Palace Wedding Services
3570 Las Vegas Boulevard South
877-279-3334 or 702-731-7422
caesars.com

The wedding chapel at Caesars Palace is a beautiful room. The Roman motif is subtle, but present, depicted in the columns in the stained glass and in pictures of urns and flowers on the wall. If an outdoor setting is preferred, that, too, can be arranged with a touch of class. After all, the grounds around the pool favor an imperial forum. A blushing bride in a traditional white wedding gown and her handsome tuxedoed groom would not be the least bit embarrassed to have their faraway family and friends join them here for a Las Vegas wedding. Besides, who doesn't like Italian love songs?

But for a setting with more pizzazz than Corinthian colonnades arranged around a piazza, no matter how majestic the milieu might be, invite Caesar and Cleopatra to the party. Hire handmaidens to serve grapes to the guests, centurions in full regalia to carry the bride down the aisle in a litter, or buff gladiators to stand around looking good. It is all in good fun.

A simple weekday wedding costs $500 in the chapel or $800 in the garden. This includes thirty minutes of location time for a group of twenty people or fewer. Wedding packages range from $3,500 to $15,000 for up to ninety minutes at the location, accommodations, meals, entertainment, and numerous other service and treats.

Circus Circus
Chapel of the Fountain

2880 Las Vegas Boulevard South
800-634-6717 or 702-794-3777
circuscircus.com

At family-friendly Circus Circus, the Chapel of the Fountain goes out of its way to make everyone in the wedding party comfortable, and that means children, too. As part of a traditional nondenominational or civil ceremony, the chapel performs at no charge a Medallion Service, whereby a soon-to-be stepparent presents a piece of jewelry, a ring, necklace, or bracelet, to his or her spouse's children. It's an inclusive gesture, one that reinforces the family feeling. Besides, where else would balloons be considered a wedding accessory?

The Chapel of the Fountain opened in 1969. It was the first indoor casino wedding chapel in the first theme resort. To this day it is a popular and busy place, particularly on Saturdays. The chapel is located on the second floor above a relatively quiet part of the casino. It is in its own world far away from the midway games and free circus acts.

The amiable, professional staff wants every wedding to be a happy occasion, and the facility has many nice features that help ensure that it is as stress-free as possible. While the bride completes her preparations in the dressing room, the minister preps the groom and the bride's escort, organizing the processional and arranging the parties at the altar. Meanwhile, as guests enter the chapel from the anteroom through the original stained-glass doors and get seated, the video rolls.

The pretty chapel itself is decorated in shades of peach, cream, and beige and fashioned after an English garden. The fountain, from which the chapel derives its name, shows two cherubs cavorting merrily in the water. It sits at the front of the room amid large displays of silk flowers. The cushioned pews comfortably seat up to fifty guests.

Vow renewals are very popular here and cost $100. Wedding packages range from $235 to $450, including the minister. Packages that include one or two nights in the hotel range from $375 to $875.

Excalibur Hotel-Casino
Canterbury Wedding Chapels

3850 Las Vegas Boulevard South
800-811-4320 or 702-597-7278
excalibur-casino.com

The Canterbury Wedding Chapels at the Excalibur are on the second floor above the casino, in the Medieval Village section of the hotel. The entry is wedged between two retail establishments, not too far from the busy food court. Children are playing. Pandemonium abounds. Yet at the far end of the hundred-foot corridor, it is quiet and peaceful. The noisy marketplace has been left far behind, and the quiet sanctuary of a Gothic church prevails.

Of course, the setting is much more luxurious than it would have been in the days of King Arthur and Lady Guinevere. The reception area is large. The high ceilings give the chapel an airy feeling, while the plush carpet mutes the sounds. The smaller of the two chapels, seating twenty guests, is elegant; but it is the larger chapel for sixty-five guests with its vaulted ceiling, stained glass, and arched entrance that most resembles a cathedral in Merry Olde England. The crown-shaped chandeliers and the extra-wide aisle for the bride's processional are memorable features.

True fanciers of the 2001 film *A Knight's Tale*, and followers of Robin Hood, can add to the fun and festivities by dressing in medieval garb. The chapel has a small selection of authentically designed one-size-fits-all costumes in brocades and satins and touches of lace. The bride and her ladies-in-waiting can choose among gowns with hoop skirts and layers of petticoats in deep, rich reds, golds, and other colors. The groom and his entourage can bedeck themselves in capes, waistcoats, and pantaloons in Sherwood Forest greens, true blues, and royal purples. But, men, be advised: if you have your heart set on wearing tights, you must bring your own. Each costume rents for $75.

Wedding packages, some of which include a one- or two-night stay, range from $365 to $1,275 plus minister's fee. Renewal-of-vows ceremonies are available for $100 less than the comparable wedding package.

Flamingo Las Vegas
The Garden Chapel

> 3555 Las Vegas Boulevard South
> 800-933-7993 or 702-733-3232
> flamingogardenchapel.com

The Flamingo's Garden Chapel is the perfect setting for anyone who has his or her heart set on a garden wedding in Las Vegas. Located in the midst of the resort's fifteen-acre backyard, the freestanding facility and adjacent gazebo are replete with pink Chilean flamingos and African penguins and overflowing with streams, lagoons, and waterfalls. Photo opportunities abound. The Bugsy Siegel Rose Garden, a memorial to the gangster founder of not only the resort, but modern Las Vegas as well, is situated near the chapel's front door.

Inside in the pleasant anteroom, vases of fresh white and yellow daisies provide a nice touch of color. There are comfortable sofas for planning your nuptials or waiting for them to start. The chapel itself has a high domed ceiling, creating a feeling of spaciousness. The carpet is pink. The pews are cushioned and covered in a floral pattern, and an abundance of silk flowers is displayed at the front of the room. The room holds up to sixty guests comfortably.

The gazebo chapel is perfect for up to a hundred family members and friends. It is decorated with ivy, ribbons, and tropical silk flowers. The sound of falling water from the many fountains surrounding the gazebo blocks out noises from the nearby swimming pool and creates a relaxing and pleasant environment.

The staff functions as wedding coordinators and can manage all the before, during, and after ceremony details—everything from the bride's bouquet to arrangements for a sit-down dinner.

Wedding packages, including hotel accommodations, start at $549 plus tax and the minister's fee.

The Golden Nugget

See TI.

Hard Rock Hotel and Casino
4455 Paradise Road
800-473-7625 or 702-693-5000
hardrockhotel.com

The Hard Rock does not have a wedding chapel, but the hotel has facilities for receptions. Ask for Catering.

At the Imperial Palace
We've Only Just Begun Wedding Chapel

3535 Las Vegas Boulevard South
800-346-3373 or 702-733-0011
alittlewhitechapel.com

We've Only Just Begun is an independently owned chapel on the fourth floor of the Imperial Palace. Located far above the casino, down a long, nondescript corridor, and past first the hair salon and then an upper-level entrance to the race and sports book, it is not easy to find. The wedding coordinator suggests going to the chapel fifteen to twenty minutes early to avoid that panicky feeling that comes from feeling lost or getting married—whatever makes you sweat.

The chapel is large enough to accommodate easily seventy-five guests. The seating consists of a mixture of Victorian love seats covered in a plush burgundy material to match the carpet and chairs. The bride with her processional can make an entrance through the doors at the back of the room. At the front of the room there has been an attempt to turn a plain room into something special with an abundance of green silk trees and a profusion of white silk flowers. As an added touch, silver organza is draped from the ceiling.

Hardworking personnel do their best under restrictive policies. The professional photographer as part of a wedding package is the only person allowed to take pictures in the chapel. The newlyweds can remain in the chapel as long as the ceremony and photography are going on.

Wedding packages, which increase in price with the amount of flowers, the number of photographs, and other assorted extras, range from $189 to $569.

At the Las Vegas Hilton
Star Trek: The Experience

> 3000 Paradise Road
> 888-GO-BOLDLY or 702-697-8750
> startrekexp.com

"Will you both continue to make life interesting for each other by taking occasional recreation in the holodeck? And will you both continue supporting and loving each other even when your warp drives are running low?"

And so go the vows on the bridge of the USS *Enterprise* at Star Trek: The Experience. The officiant is dressed as a Starfleet officer, as are the bride and groom, unless they have decided to go in formal wedding wear or twenty-first-century casual wear. They are surrounded by Klingons and Ferengi, as well as up to thirty invited guests who have been beamed aboard. Afterward, a journey through space on the shuttlecraft can deliver the wedding party to the Deep Space Nine Promenade for shopping or to Quark's Bar and Restaurant for some reception refreshments.

For true Trekkies who think of marriage as an intergalactic adventure, wedding packages begin at $500 for twenty minutes on the bridge, time enough for the ceremony and some pictures. Tickets to the History of the Future Museum cost extra.

Luxor Las Vegas
The Chapels at Luxor

> 3900 Las Vegas Boulevard South
> 866-I-Luv-You or 702-730-Love

The Chapels at Luxor is located on the "Attractions" level of the resort, one floor up from the casino. It is near the Games of the Gods Arcade and around the corner from Pharaoh's Theater, the home of the topless dance revue known as Midnight Fantasy. But there are no mummies, sphinxes, or hieroglyphics adorning the wedding facility itself. For better or worse, all remnants of ancient Egypt have

been relegated to public spaces of the hotel. Even the art deco flourishes have been consigned to the lobby.

While not as awesome as its Egyptian counterpart, the sphinx at Luxor can be seen from the plane when landing at McCarran International Airport.

Instead, the two chapels, almost identical except that one seats sixty and the other more, are very formal rooms with a European sensibility. But they can hardly be called overdone. Although heavy gold curtains frame the windows, a pretty patterned rug leads down the aisle. A mural of a floral arrangement is painted on the wall behind the altar. It matches the silk floral arrangements at the sides of the room.

The emphasis here is on service. A wedding coordinator works with each couple to help select the music, florals, photography, and videography, as well as schedule any of the extras that might be desired, from the spa and beauty shop to dining and entertainment. Wedding packages range from $625 for thirty minutes of chapel time to $1,400 for an hour of chapel time plus a one-night stay in a suite with a Jacuzzi. King Tut never had it so easy.

Mandalay Bay Resort and Casino
Chapel by the Bay

> 3950 Las Vegas Boulevard South
> 877-632-7701 or 702-632-7490
> mandalaybay.com

Palm trees and other lush foliage surround the Chapel by the Bay, located behind the hotel-casino complex near its eleven-acre tropical sand beach and swimming pools. While the sun might not come up like thunder out of China across the bay, it is an exotic setting, usually accompanied by dry heat and blue skies, and made to order for a picture-perfect ceremony.

The wedding facility comprises two identical chapels, each seating fifty guests, separated by a folding door. To accommodate groups of up to a hundred, the two chapels can be combined for a $500 fee. The decor is simple but elegant, and Mandalay's elephant imagery has been left to other locales around the resort. White silk orchids, birds of paradise, and lilies are arranged in urns placed around the rooms. Matching *Fantasia*-style murals, each with a young woman walking or sitting amid a profusion of flora and fauna, decorate the outside wall of each chapel. The carpet has a stylized Oriental design in beige, orange, and brown. The nearly floor-to-ceiling windows behind the pulpit look out on a courtyard and visually bring the outside greenery inside.

The wedding facility is spacious, with plenty of room for nervous brides, grooms, or parents of the same to pace. His and her dressing rooms, another nice feature, are available a half hour before the service.

Full floral, photography, and videography services are offered. The three wedding packages include a pianist and the minister's fee. They range from $675 to $1,955. The latter includes champagne dinner for two, the honeymoon suite for one night, and breakfast in bed the following morning.

MGM Grand
Forever Grand Wedding Chapel

3799 Las Vegas Boulevard South
800-646-5530
mgmgrand.com

Walking through the main door of the Forever Grand Wedding Chapel, one is immediately transported back to a period reminiscent of Hollywood's golden age. Oversize black-and-white photographs of both movie wedding scenes and actual celebrity weddings adorn the walls of the lobby and hallways. There is Spencer Tracy walking his movie daughter Elizabeth Taylor down the aisle in *Father of the Bride,* and Bing Crosby and Grace Kelly at the altar in *High Society*. And so the city of entertainment, as the MGM Grand describes itself, confers movie magic on the state of matrimony.

For traditional weddings there are two chapels, the larger accommodating up to sixty guests, on the Forever Grand premises. Each chapel has been equipped with three video cameras to provide different views of the ceremony and a baby grand piano for live music during the service. There is a separate dressing room for the groom, who enters the chapel by the altar, and for the bride, who walks down the aisle. Packages generally range from $549 to $1,199, plus $200 on Fridays and Saturdays.

The staff handles requests from guests at New York New York Hotel and Casino.

Mirage

See TI.

Monte Carlo Resort and Casino

3770 Las Vegas Boulevard South
800-822-8651 or 702-730-7575
monte-carlo.com

The European-style Monte Carlo has a lovely wedding chapel with a garden theme. French doors in the corners of the large room look out at a mural of a flowered landscape. When it is time for pictures, the doors open for the perfect backdrop in the climate-controlled environment. There is no muss and no fuss, and certainly no heat and dust. There are also the prerequisite large silk flower displays on either side of the pulpit.

The chapel is conveniently located on the second floor in the hotel tower. The brides and grooms, most of whom are dressed in formal wedding clothes, do not have to go through the casino to reach their destination, so getting misplaced or distracted on the way is unlikely.

The chapel is so well laid out that the large number of guests attending a large number of weddings on busy Saturdays can easily be managed. Guests are asked to stay outside the chapel so as not to disturb the wedding in progress. When the ceremony is over, guests exit the chapel through doors leading to the hotel corridor while those waiting for the next wedding enter the chapel lobby. Unless someone decides to go against the crowd, confusion is kept to a minimum. The bride-to-be, meanwhile, can do last-minute makeup and hair touch-ups in the chapel's dressing room.

Despite the formal setting, the staff is happy to recruit Elvis to participate in the event. "All I need to know is whether the couple prefers a young Elvis or a bigger Elvis," Nancy Kissel, the accommodating wedding chapel manager, diplomatically says. "Then it's a matter of *Blue Hawaii* or *Viva Las Vegas,* so that the backup singers know how to dress."

Wedding packages range from $375 for a simple weekday ceremony to $1,350, the latter including a two-night weekend stay and dinner for two. The minister's fee is an additional $50.

New York New York

See the MGM Grand.

The Palms Casino Resort

    4321 Flamingo Road
    866-942-777 or 702-942-777
    palms.com

The Palms does not have a wedding chapel, but the hotel can accommodate receptions and other celebrations.

Paris Las Vegas

    3655 Las Vegas Boulevard South
    877-650-5021 or 702-946-4060
    parislasvegas.com

For formal French chic, there's the Paris Las Vegas.

This spacious wedding facility is tucked away on the second floor in the guest-room tower, far away from the noise and confusion of the casino. Entering the beautifully appointed, if not comfortable, anteroom, one is struck by the boldly patterned gray-and-white fleur-de-lis wallpaper. It should clash with the ornamental purple carpet, but wondrously, it does not. Souvenir wedding memorabilia sit in a glass case, tastefully placed in a corridor out of immediate view. However, the limited seating is for couples waiting to see a wedding coordinator rather than families waiting to watch a wedding.

The Chapelle du Jardin, the smaller of the two chapels, for up to twenty-five guests, is light and airy, pretty enough to be a scene from an impressionist painting. It is decorated with floor-to-ceiling garden murals behind cathedral-style windows. The ceiling boasts florals, too.

The Chapelle du Paradis, with seating for up to a hundred guests, has enough gold leaf adorning the walls to fill the coffers of a king or possibly an emperor. Ornate crystal chandeliers light up the bridal path, while puffy-cheeked cherubs cavort across the blue sky painted on the ceiling. Even Marie Antoinette would feel comfortable giving up her hand, if not her head, here.

If you think a trip to the City of Lights is incomplete without a trip to the top of the Eiffel Tower, one can be arranged, either as part of a one-hour photography session around the Paris property or as a wedding package. Ceremonies on the observation deck of the Eiffel Tower are offered at 9:30 a.m. daily for $3,100 for up to twelve people.

Traditional ceremonies in one of Paris's wedding chapels range from $675 to $8,000, the latter including a four-night stay in the honeymoon suite. Generally expect to pay the minister's fee of $50 and a premium for weekends and holidays.

At the Plaza Hotel and Casino
Heritage Wedding Chapel

1 Main Street
888-241-5000 or 702-731-2400
heritagechapel.com

If you are taking in the sights at the Fremont Street Experience and impulsively decide to cover up your naked ring finger, check out the Heritage Wedding Chapel in Jackie Gaughan's Plaza Hotel and Casino. It is the only chapel in a downtown hotel.

The chapel is simply decorated in green, white, and yellow. Calla lilies are the predominant theme. The large stained-glass picture at the front of the room incorporates calla lilies into its design, and calla lilies are displayed in the large silk flower arrangements on either side of the stained glass and in a small vase on the piano.

Like its fancier brethren on the Strip, the chapel can make reception arrangements and hotel reservations with its wedding services. Wedding packages range from $189 to $899, the latter including two nights in the hotel plus dinner for two with cake and champagne.

The Rio All-Suite Hotel and Casino
Wedding Chapels at the Rio
3700 Flamingo Road
888-746-5625 or 702-777-7986
playrio.com

It is difficult to find the wedding facility in the sprawling Rio casino resort because it is situated in the Masquerade Tower, and there are no signs. However, if a crowd is coming, this place is worth considering. There is an ample waiting area with cushy sofas and easy chairs, dressing rooms galore for both brides and grooms, and long corridors separating the three chapels, the largest of which has seating for up to 160 people.

The chapels are some of the most hotel-like, least churchlike of any in Las Vegas, and that is not at all bad. Throughout the upscale, contemporary wedding facility, modern works of art hang on the walls, as they do all over the resort. Since the walls, carpet, and padded chairs are all beige, nothing jars the senses. At the front of each chapel, a platform in front of formally draped windows has been set up. Aside from some ample floral arrangements, that's about it for decorations. The rest is up to the wedding party.

Traditional services, vow renewals, and commitment ceremonies are available. Wedding packages include the minister's fee and a pianist for the ceremony, and they range from $350 to $4,600. The latter includes a two-night stay in the Honeymoon Suite with lots of amenities. A premium is charged for Fridays, Saturdays, and holiday weekends. Be sure to ask for carnival beads for all revelers and partygoers.

At the Riviera Hotel and Casino
Royale Wedding Chapel

2901 Las Vegas Boulevard South
800-242-7322 or 702-794-9494
rivierahotel.com

"Call if you're nervous about anything or if you've forgotten anything," Lynda Rae Price, the wedding coordinator at the Royale Wedding Chapel, is overheard saying in a soft, soothing voice to a bride-to-be over the telephone. "Because that's what we're here for." One gets the feeling that she will knock herself out to accommodate the needs of her clients and do a grand job in the process.

Independently owned and operated, the Royale has a relaxed, informal atmosphere. Yet its location in the Riviera Hotel means it has many of the advantages of hotel-casino chapels. In the summertime, when Saturday weddings are booked back-to-back, being able to wait in an air-conditioned environment tops the list. If the bride wants to remain hidden before her march down the aisle, she has a dressing room for last-minute preparations. The wedding chapel offers hotel rooms for the newlyweds with some of its wedding packages and is able to make hotel reservations for the wedding party.

The chapel has a pink and burgundy color scheme. Large silk flower arrangements stand on either side of the altar. Floor-to-ceiling windows display a desert scene at night in which twinkling lights emulate the stars. A piano for live music sits at the back of the room. About half the couples take advantage of the traditional setting and wear formal wedding clothes. During the week, dress is more casual.

The staff suggests that weddings be reserved at least two weeks in advance, so that there is adequate time to coordinate all the components of the event without stressing any of the parties involved. Walk-ins, however, are welcome, and a ceremony can be pulled together in about two hours.

Packages begin at $179, not including the minister's fee.

TI, formerly known as Treasure Island at the Mirage
The Weddings Chapels at TI

    3300 Las Vegas Boulevard South
    888-818-0999 or 702-894-7700
    treasureisland.com

There is always a nice hustle and bustle in the pretty lobby of Treasure Island's Wedding Chapels, even in the middle of the day in the middle of the week. There might be a couple planning their big event, a wedding party beginning to gather, or people getting married. It is easy to tell the latter from all others because the bride and groom are usually dressed for the occasion. Formal wedding attire just feels right here.

Treasure Island was the first of the large hotel-casino resorts built in the 1990s to have a wedding chapel. There are two chapels in the facility. The chapel in which the ceremony is held can accommodate sixty-five people. The smaller one is usually reserved for photo sessions. Wedding packages range from $499 to $999 during the week. Saturdays and holidays incur a premium.

For those wanting to combine adventure with romance, nuptials aboard the HMS *Britannia* can be arranged. The frigate, attacked by pirates several times daily in the man-made bay in front of the hotel for the amusement of passersby, is cleaned up and decorated with flowers. As a special touch, fresh rose petals are strewn along the walkway for the bride's processional. The minister, dressed as the ship's captain, administers the vows, and a pirate swoops down from the crow's nest to deliver the rings. The package costs $1,999, more on Saturdays and holidays.

The staff also handles wedding preparations for guests of the Mirage and the Golden Nugget.

At the Tropicana Resort and Casino
Island Wedding Chapel

3801 Las Vegas Boulevard South
800-325-5839 or 702-798-3778
tropicanachapel.com

The Island Wedding Chapel, an independent enterprise at the Tropicana Resort and Casino, has the lock on location. It is situated on the grounds of the lushly landscaped hotel, where blossoming trees and flowering foliage abound. There are pools and palm trees, waterfalls and exotic fish. The desert feels far away, as does the big city, any big city, although the skyline of New York New York looms on the horizon.

With its thatched roof and rough-hewn timber supporting beams, the chapel is a replica of a South Pacific church. The bamboo altar, hardwood pew benches, and ceiling fans, which rotate despite the air-conditioning, add to the effect. The chapel can easily accommodate fifty guests.

The Island Chapel also has a garden gazebo for those relishing an outdoor setting. There is room for thirty guests, although only eight can be given seats under the gazebo roof. The remainder are seated along the path leading to the structure. The gazebo is decorated with silk flowers and provides a nice background for photos. Another option is a chapel wedding, saving the gazebo for a reception afterward.

The staff is eager to please and has references for gown and tuxedo rentals, restaurants, and other requested services. Wedding-package prices begin at $399, not including the minister's fee. The deluxe Blue Hawaii package combines the wedding with the honeymoon. It costs $3,500 and includes a five-night stay in the Tropicana's Island Tower.

At the Venetian
Madame Tussaud's Las Vegas

3377 Las Vegas Boulevard South
702-862-7805 or 702-367-1847
madame-tussauds.com

Las Vegas weddings are commemorated in a quiet corner of Madame Tussaud's, the London-imported museum renowned for its wax portraits of the famous and infamous. The area is festively decorated. A three-dimensional plaster-of-paris version of Elvis and Priscilla's six-tier wedding cake takes up a good portion of a wall. Pink and white cupids peek out from bows, hide behind rosebuds, and climb from one layer to the next. A svelte-looking Elvis in a black leather outfit poses nearby. Elizabeth Taylor, looking serene as well as svelte in a purple gown, stands underneath a photograph of her and Eddie Fisher cutting their wedding cake and smiling for the camera. Lifelike figures of Paul Newman and Joanne Woodward are positioned under a picture of the genuine articles, again cutting their wedding cake. While statues

The wedding chapels at the Strip resorts do not yet have drive-up service, but offer every other conceivable amenity.

of Frank Sinatra and Sammy Davis Jr. are located with the Rat Pack in another part of the museum, they are noted here in photographs: Frank with his bride, the youthful Mia Farrow; Sammy with his bride and wedding party. Even though most of these marriages did not last, everyone looks happy.

A banquet room in the museum can be rented for weddings, receptions, and other events. The affair can be as simple as cake and canapés washed down with champagne or as elaborate as a formal sit-down dinner. Regardless, it is sure to be a star-studded party and most memorable occasion.

The Venetian
Venetian Weddings

3355 Las Vegas Boulevard South
866-548-1807 or 702-414-4280
venetianweddings.com

The Venetian offers the sights and sounds of the Italian city of canals and cathedrals as a backdrop for nuptials. Very small weddings consisting of the bride, groom, witness, and officiant can be held in a gondola. A singing gondolier, serenading the party with songs of romance while guiding the group down the man-made waterways, completes the occasion. Larger groups can be accommodated on one of the many bridges connecting the shops and restaurants along the Grande Canal. Legend has it that kissing the one you love under the Rialto Bridge in St. Mark's Square ensures everlasting love. It's worth a try.

For something more traditional, the Venetian has three chapels, each seating about 50 guests, or when combined, a group of 150. A wedding coordinator works with each couple to ensure that all the details are attended to. Photography, flowers, wedding albums, and video services can be customized. Wedding packages, starting at $2,500, include a thirty-minute rehearsal and sixty minutes in the chapel.

Selected Bibliography

History and General-Interest Books

Denton, Sally, and Roger Morris. *The Money and the Power: The Making of Las Vegas and Its Hold on America.* New York: Vintage Books, 2001.

Early, Pete. *Super Casino: Inside the "New" Las Vegas.* New York: Bantam Books, 2000.

Land, Barbara, and Myrick Land. *A Short History of Las Vegas.* Reno: University of Nevada Press, 1999.

Moehring, Eugene P. *Resort City in the Sunbelt: Las Vegas, 1930–1970.* Reno: University of Nevada Press, 1989.

Pileggi, Nicholas. *Casino: Love and Honor in Las Vegas.* New York: Simon & Schuster, 1995.

Rothman, Hal K. *Devil's Bargains: Tourism in the Twentieth-Century West.* Lawrence: University Press of Kansas, 1998.

Thomson, David. *In Nevada: The Land, the People, God, and Chance.* New York: Alfred A. Knopf, 1999.

Tronnes, Mike, ed. *Literary Las Vegas: The Best Writing About America's Most Fabulous City.* New York: Henry Holt, 1995.

Weatherford, Mike. *Cult Vegas: The Weirdest! The Wildest! The Swingin'est Town on Earth!* Las Vegas: Huntington Press, 2001.

Biographies and Autobiographies

Amburn, Ellis. *The Most Beautiful Woman in the World: The Obsessions, Passions, and Courage of Elizabeth Taylor.* New York: Cliff Street/HarperCollins, 2000.

Anderson, Christopher. *Citizen Jane: The Turbulent Life of Jane Fonda*. New York: Henry Holt, 1990.

Ann-Margret with Todd Gold. *Ann-Margret: My Story*. New York: G. P. Putnam's Sons, 1994.

Basinger, Jeanine. *Silent Stars*. New York: Alfred A. Knopf, 1999.

Bragg, Melvyn. *Richard Burton*. Boston: Little, Brown, 1988.

Brown, Peter Harry, and Pat H. Broeske. *Down at the End of Lonely Street: The Life and Death of Elvis Presley*. New York: Dutton, 1997.

Caine, Michael. *What's It All About?* New York: Turtle Bay/Random House, 1992.

Cassiday, Bruce. *Dinah! A Biography*. New York: Franklin Watts, 1979.

Cassidy, David, with Chip Deffaa. *C'mon Get Happy*. New York: Warner Books, 1994.

Cher, as told to Jeff Coplon. *The First Time*. New York: Simon & Schuster, 1998.

Collins, Joan. *Past Imperfect*. New York: Simon & Schuster, 1984.

Collins, Tom. *Jane Fonda: An American Original*. New York: Franklin Watts, 1990.

Crawford, Joan, with Jane Kesner. *A Portrait of Joan*. New York: Doubleday, 1962.

Cremer, Robert. *Lugosi: The Man Behind the Cape*. Chicago: Henry Regnery, 1976.

Crosby, Kathryn. *My Life with Bing*. Wheeling, Ill.: Collage, 1983.

Curtis, Tony, and Barry Paris. *Tony Curtis*. New York: William Morrow, 1993.

Davis, Ronald L. *Linda Darnell and the American Dream*. Norman: University of Oklahoma Press, 1991.

Davis, Sammy, Jr., and Jane and Burt Boyar. *Why Me?* New York: Farrar, Straus & Giroux, 1989.

Doss, Erika. *Elvis Culture: Fans, Faith, and Image*. Lawrence: University Press of Kansas, 1999.

Douglas, Kirk. *The Ragman's Son*. New York: Simon & Schuster, 1988.

Falkner, David. *The Turbulent Life of Billy Martin*. New York: Simon & Schuster, 1992.

Farrow, Mia. *What Falls Away: A Memoir*. New York: Nan A. Talese/
Doubleday, 1997.

Francisco, Charles. *Gentleman: The William Powell Story*. New York:
St. Martin's Press, 1985.

Fricke, John. *Judy Garland, World's Greatest Entertainer*. New York:
Henry Holt, 1992.

Gabor, Zsa Zsa, with Wendy Leigh. *One Lifetime Is Not Enough*. New
York: Delacorte Press, 1991.

Goldman, Albert. *Elvis*. New York: McGraw-Hill, 1981.

Gregory, Neal, and Janice Gregory. *When Elvis Died*. Washington,
D.C.: Communications Press, 1980.

Hall, William. *Raising Caine*. Englewood Cliffs, NJ: Prentice-Hall,
1981.

Harris, Warren G. *Cary Grant: A Touch of Elegance*. New York: Doubleday, 1987.

Heymann, C. David. *Liz: An Intimate Biography of Elizabeth Taylor*.
New York: Carol Publishing Group, 1995.

Huston, John. *An Open Book*. New York: Alfred A. Knopf, 1980.

Jordan, Michael. *For the Love of the Game*. New York: Crown Publishers, 1998.

Kelley, Kitty. *His Way: The Unauthorized Biography of Frank Sinatra*.
New York: Bantam Books, 1986.

Krugel, Mitchell. *Jordan: The Man, His Words, His Life*. New York: St.
Martin's Press, 1994.

Leaming, Barbara. *If This Was Happiness: A Biography of Rita Hayworth*. New York: Viking, 1989.

Levy, Shawn. *Rat Pack Confidential: Frank, Dean, Sammy, Peter, Joey,
and the Last Great Showbiz Party*. New York: Doubleday, 1998.

Mair, George. *Bette: An Intimate Biography of Bette Midler*. Secaucus,
N.J.: Carol Publishing Group, 1995.

McGee, Tom. *Betty Grable: The Girl with the Million: Dollar Legs*.
Vestal, N.Y.: Vestal Press, 1995.

Moore, Mary Tyler. *After All*. New York: G. P. Putnam's Sons, 1995.

Morella, Joe, and Edward Z. Epstein. *Paul and Joanne: A Biography
of Paul Newman and Joanne Woodward*. New York: Delacorte
Press, 1988.

Newton, Wayne, with Dick Maurice. *Once Before I Go*. New York: William Morrow, 1989.

Pastos, Spero. *Pin-Up: The Tragedy of Betty Grable*. New York: G. P. Putnam's Sons, 1986.

Presley, Priscilla Beaulieu, with Sandra Harmon. *Elvis and Me*. New York: G. P. Putnam's Sons, 1985.

Quirk, Lawrence J. *Totally Uninhibited: The Life and Wild Times of Cher*. New York: William Morrow, 1991.

Rich, Sharon. *Sweethearts: The Timeless Love Affair—On-Screen and Off—Between Jeanette MacDonald and Nelson Eddy*. New York: Donald I. Fine, 1994.

Riese, Randall. *Her Name Is Barbra: An Intimate Portrait of the Real Barbra Streisand*. Secaucus, N.J.: Carol Publishing Group, 1993.

Rodman, Gilbert B. *Elvis After Elvis: The Posthumous Career of a Living Legend*. London: Routledge, 1996.

Rooney, Mickey. *Life Is Too Short*. New York: Villard Books, 1991.

Ross, Diana. *Secrets of a Sparrow*. New York: Villard Books, 1993.

Schickel, Richard. *Clint Eastwood*. New York: Alfred A. Knopf, 1996.

Shipman, David. *Judy Garland: The Secret Life of an American Legend*. New York: Hyperion, 1992.

Spada, James. *Streisand: Her Life*. New York: Crown Publishers, 1995.

Taraborrelli, J. Randy. *Call Her Miss Ross: The Unauthorized Biography of Diana Ross*. New York: Birch Lane Press, 1989.

Thomas, Bob. *Joan Crawford*. New York: Simon & Schuster, 1978.

Tormé, Mel. *Mel Tormé*. New York: Viking, 1988.

Tornabene, Lyn. *Long Live the King: A Biography of Clark Gable*. New York: G. P. Putnam's Sons, 1976.

Underwood, Peter. *Karloff*. New York: Drake Publishers, 1972.

Vadim, Roger. *Bardot Deneuve Fonda*. New York: Simon & Schuster, 1986.

White, Betty. *Betty White in Person*. New York: Doubleday, 1987.

Selected Newspapers and Periodicals

In addition to numerous news stories in the *Las Vegas Evening Review-Journal* (and its successor, the *Las Vegas Review-*

Journal), Las Vegas Sun, National Enquirer, and *People,* the following articles were consulted:

Allen, Stephen. "Going to the Chapel." *Nevada,* March–April 1990.

Alvarez, A. "Learning from Las Vegas." *New York Review of Books,* January 11, 1996.

Andersen, Kurt. "Las Vegas, U.S.A." *Time,* January 10, 1994.

Aurthur, Robert Alan. "Hanging Out." *Esquire,* February 1974.

Beebe, Lucius. "Las Vegas." *Holiday,* December 1952.

Daly, Steven. "The Perils of Paula." *Vanity Fair,* February 2001.

Didion, Joan. "Marrying Absurd." *Saturday Evening Post,* December 16, 1967.

Gabriel, Trip. "From Vice to Nice." *New York Times Magazine,* December 1, 1991.

Hill, Gladwin. "Atomic Boom Town in the Desert." *New York Times Magazine,* February 11, 1951.

Horton, Susan. "The Six-Week Cure." *Nevada,* November–December 1981.

Lang, Daniel. "Blackjack and Flashes." *New Yorker,* March 20, 1952.

"Las Vegas Strikes it Rich." *Life,* May 26, 1947.

Liebling, A. J. "Dressed in Dynamite." *New Yorker,* January 12, 1963.

Marshall, Jim. "To 'Vegas, Darling." *Collier's,* October 25, 1941.

Moreno, Richard. "Wed and Wild." *Nevada,* January–February 1994.

Munk, Nina. "Easy Nuptials." *Fortune,* April 25, 1994.

Newcott, William R. "Believing in Las Vegas." *National Geographic,* December 1996.

Peretz, Evgenia. "The 'It' Parade." *Vanity Fair,* September 2000.

Polaneczky, Ronnie. "Kelly Ripa Has a Secret." *Redbook,* November 2001.

Richman, Alan. "Lost Vegas." *Gentlemen's Quarterly,* November 1992.

Rocha, Guy Louis. "Gable vs. Gable." *Nevada*, November–
December 1981.

Schaap, Dick. "Las Vegas: The Greatest Show-off on Earth."
Holiday, December 1968.

Scott, Walter. "Personality Parade." *Parade Magazine*, June 3,
2001.

Stout, Wesley. "Nevada's New Reno." *Saturday Evening Post*,
October 31, 1942.

Wolcott, James. "King of Kings." *Vanity Fair*, November 2001.

Wolfe, Thomas K. "Las Vegas!!!!" *Esquire*, February 1964.

Wolkomin, Richard. "Las Vegas Meets La-La Land." *Smithson-
ian*, October 1995.

Wyden, Peter. "How Wicked Is Vegas?" *Saturday Evening Post*,
November 11, 1961.

Photograph Credits

Part One: Once Upon a Time

Wee Kirk, © Bettmann/CORBIS, page 4.

Burros in Bar, Special Collections, UNLV Libraries, page 10.

Night Scene, Special Collections, UNLV Libraries, page 18.

The Hitching Post, © Hulton-Deutsch Collection/CORBIS, page 25.

Dancing girls, Special Collections, UNLV Libraries, page 30.

At the slots, Special Collections, UNLV Libraries, page 37.

Frank et al., Special Collections, UNLV Libraries, page 43.

Janet Leigh, Special Collections, UNLV Libraries, page 46.

Swimming Pool, Special Collections, UNLV Libraries, page 49.

Roulette Wheel, Special Collections, UNLV Libraries, page 58.

The Mirage, © Bob Krist/CORBIS, page 64.

Fountain/Eiffel, © Stuart Westmorland/CORBIS, page 67.

Caesars Statue, © Ross Pictures/CORBIS, page 73.

Sign at Chapel, © Susan Marg, page 78.

Part Two: Star Light, Star Bright

Little Church, Special Collections, UNLV Libraries, page 82.

Sinatra and Daughter, Special Collections, UNLV Libraries, page 98.

Curtis and Bride, © AFP/CORBIS, page 113.

Elvis and Cake, © Bettmann/CORBIS, page 125.

Little White Chapel, © Joseph Sohm; ChromoSohm Inc./ CORBIS, page 143.

About the Author

SUSAN MARG has a B.A. in English and an M.Sc. in market research. She knows how to ask questions, spot trends, and anticipate fads. Her interest in pop culture comes from her days in advertising, when knowing what was hot and who was in was part of the job. She first visited Las Vegas in 1977 out of curiosity. Finding the place unique, and not losing too badly at the tables, she has been back often over the years, experiencing firsthand the town's many permutations and enjoying its diversions. On one trip a bride in a long white wedding gown emerging from a stretch limousine caught her eye, and she began wondering what tales of the altar could be found in the many old-fashioned wedding chapels lining Las Vegas Boulevard. After more trips to Las Vegas and lots of research, she wrote *Las Vegas Weddings*.

Ms. Marg lives with her husband, James C. Simmons, a published author with sixteen books on travel, history, and biography to his credit. They did not marry in Las Vegas, but they had a renewal-of-vows ceremony with an Elvis impersonator there to celebrate their most recent anniversary. They reside in San Diego, California.